All About Weaving

Books by Clara Creager:

WEAVING: A Creative Approach for Beginners

ALL ABOUT WEAVING

All About Weaving

A Comprehensive Guide to the Craft

CLARA CREAGER

DOUBLEDAY & COMPANY, INC.
Garden City, New York, 1984

All weaving by Clara Creager unless otherwise noted.
All line art by Robert L. Creager.
All photography by Tom Maloy of the Ohio State
University Department of Photography and Cinema, unless
otherwise noted.
Title page photograph by Julie Linden
Book design by Elfriede Hueber

Library of Congress Cataloging in Publication Data

Creager, Clara.
  All about weaving.

  Bibliography: p. 281
  Includes index.
  1. Hand weaving.   I. Title.
TT848.C636   1983   746.1'4
ISBN: 0-385-13164-X
Library of Congress Catalog Card Number 78-22311

This book is dedicated with love to my husband Bob, daughter Valerie, and sons Robert, Duncan, and Malcolm

Acknowledgments

I gratefully acknowledge and thank the individuals who have contributed in so many ways to this book, and I am appreciative of the encouragement and support my family, friends, and students have given me.

The Ohio Historical Society and Shelburne Museum, Shelburne, Vermont, graciously shared their coverlet collection.

It has been my good fortune to have worked with a superb editor, Karen Van Westering. Having also edited my first book, she has become a friend as well.

And thanks, too, to Elaine Chubb for a fine copy editing job.

Finally, my appreciation is extended to all who have been a motivating force through my many years of weaving. It is their influence that has made this book possible.

Contents

3

4

5

6

Introduction

Weaving can be described in infinite ways, and there are endless methods of weaving to explore. This is what makes handweaving so appealing and satisfying to the many individuals who are personally involved.

I would like to feel that this book is a complete manual of handweaving. That accomplishment, however, would be almost impossible. Nevertheless, I present here a comprehensive study of the tools, techniques, and weaves related to handweaving. This book is intended to be a resource for use by anyone who is interested in beginning or continuing a study of weaving. I have tried to keep descriptive information basic, and the techniques are generously illustrated. My prime thought as I have compiled this information is the individual artist-craftsperson involved.

One person could not weave all the possible weaves in a lifetime, for they are never-ending. But I hope you will get from this book a clear understanding of basic weaves and techniques and the differences between them. You will find essential information about looms—you must know your tools and what they will do. Of uppermost importance is to understand the reasoning behind each process or technique. Then, when you have mastered a technique, you can incorporate your personal choices of color, texture, and combinations of weaves and techniques. In that way you will have expressed your individual thoughts and feelings through your weaving. Do not be afraid to try something that has not been done before.

Many weaves and techniques in handloom weaving have no certain history—they exist, but details about their origin are not completely known. Some people hold adamant views about the historical context, but such views are quite often opinions, personal feelings, and insight. Nevertheless, these views are interesting, so I have included a few stories that are interesting and pertinent to some processes. Use all the information presented here, enjoy it, add to it, but above all adapt it to your personal circumstances. What is convenient for one weaver is not necessarily so for another. The terms of the past hold a certain charm; I hope you will look for them throughout this book and continue to use them if you like them.

We have evidence from prehistoric times of technical inventiveness in making looms for weaving. The industrial revolution of the nineteenth century enabled the weaver to produce in quantity. More recently, chemists and engineers have produced a whole new range of materials for the weaver. Weaving continues to develop, even today; a new and distinct weaving culture is emerging. The underlying principle, however, remains the same: the weaver hopes, by interlacing yarn, to achieve strength and surface interest in a product that is pleasing to the eye and to the touch.

A student of weaving has basically three areas of research: history, technique, and design. Through the study of what has gone before, we can build a foundation on which to develop individual ideas and to experiment with knowledge others have gained. By studying early works, we get insight into skill, ingenuity, and always the weaver's love of beauty. And by being aware of current trends, we can execute a visually pleasing composition.

Weaving, then, is a multifaceted activity.

Its popularity can be attributed to not one but many reasons. With its strong ties to the past and the ability to adapt to modern technology, weaving can be interpreted in any number of ways.

There is room for all who are interested— you can weave part time or full time. You can easily adapt your way of weaving to your way of life. Your tools for weaving can be as simple or as complicated as you wish. The amount of investment in equipment is also your choice. Working with fibers of all kinds is easy for everyone because fabric is so integral a part of our everyday life.

In most art forms you are concerned with line, shape, space, and color. This is true in weaving as well, but in addition there is one other element: texture. The type of yarns used, the weave, and the finishing are the elements involved in texture.

So that you may understand the delicate manipulation of fibers into yarns, I have described the process of spinning raw fibers into yarn and putting color in this yarn with vegetable dyes. It is all, historically, part of the craft. For a more detailed, in-depth study of these processes you should consult books that deal solely with them.

My task has been to organize the information that I feel is essential to handweaving. My experiences enable me also to present some findings and conclusions of my own.

The study of handloom weaving has its own fascination; this ancient art has been pursued by generations in more ways than any one volume could explain. I present here a way of weaving that has worked for myself and my students.

1

Looms and What Each Type Can Do

The weaver's primary tool is the loom. Indeed, the word loom comes from the Old English *geloma,* which means "tool" or "utensil."

There are many looms available to the handweaver. They are made of various kinds of wood and metal, have several different mechanical motions, come in a range of sizes and styles, and perform the weaving methods with varying degrees of efficiency. To sum it up, there is not one universal, ideal loom.

But to do quality work a weaver must have a proper loom. This means, not a highly refined one, but instead a loom that will best do the techniques the individual wishes to pursue.

Form and function are one: what you wish to accomplish through weaving will determine whether you choose a tapestry loom *(left),* this jack-type floor loom *(right),* or something either simpler or more complex. *Photos courtesy Nilus Leclerc Inc. and Harrisville Designs.*

 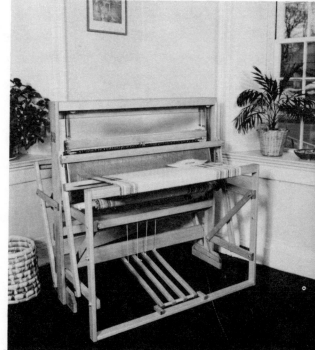

Acquiring a loom involves a major decision, especially for the beginner. There are many looms on the market to consider, and friends and colleagues may try to convince you that their loom is best. It may be right for them, but your requirements for loom performance may be very different. Nevertheless, there are several basic decisions to make before choosing a specific kind of loom.

A Floor Loom and Its Parts

Before you read further, acquaint yourself with the names of the parts of the loom shown in the illustration. You must become familiar with the function of each part. All looms work essentially the same way. One set of warp yarns must be raised while another set is lowered. The wedge-shaped space thus created is called the *shed*.

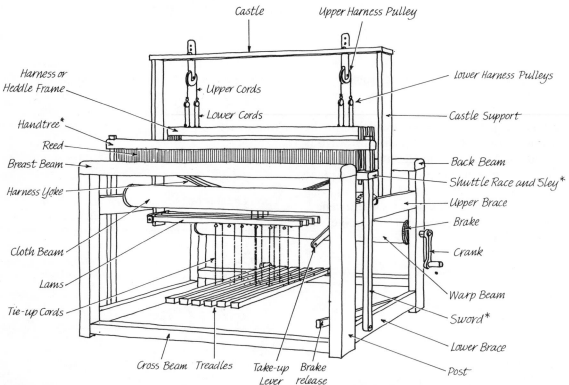

Castle

Upper Harness Pulley

Harness or Heddle Frame

Upper Cords

Lower Cords

Lower Harness Pulleys

Castle Support

Handtree*

Reed

Breast Beam

Harness Yoke

Back Beam

Shuttle Race and Sley*

Upper Brace

Brake

Crank

Cloth Beam

Lams

Tie-up Cords

Warp Beam

Sword*

Lower Brace

Cross Beam   Treadles   Take-up   Brake
                         Lever   release

Post

*The sword, handtree, shuttle race, and sley
 are collectively called the Beater or Batten.

Basic Principles of a Loom

A loom's main function is to (1) hold the *warp yarns* or *warp ends*—the lengthwise or vertical threads—under tension, through the brake system; (2) provide a means of separating selected warp yarns, with heddles and harness frames, to make a shed for *weft yarns*—the crosswise or horizontal threads—to pass through; and (3) provide a way to beat the weft yarns into place, with

the *beater*, or *batten*. Most looms have a method of storing the warp yarn (*warp beam*) and the finished cloth (*cloth beam*).

The *brake system* on a loom is crucial. It is mounted on the cloth and warp beams, generally on the right-hand side of the loom. It enables you to keep the warp yarns under tension. Many looms are equipped with a friction brake on the warp beam, which is convenient because of the infinite adjustment it allows. The warp can be moved forward without the weaver leaving the weav-

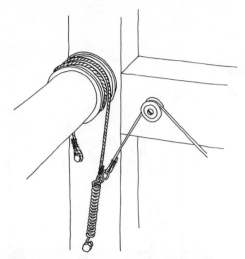

Friction brake on warp beam. Steel cable, chain, or flat steel wire (sometimes rope) wraps around the brake drum on the warp beam and is held tight by a heavy spring. Attached to the spring is a release cord that extends to the front of the loom.

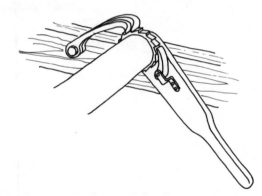

A pawl (or dog) and ratchet wheel with large teeth for take-up on a cloth beam. Double pawls allow for a finer adjustment.

ing position. A *pawl* (or *dog) and ratchet wheel* with large teeth is also sufficient for the warp beam, but the cloth beam should have a ratchet wheel with smaller teeth for finer adjustment.

Each warp yarn or end passes through a *heddle*, which is held in place by a *harness frame*. These frames are connected to the *treadles* on a floor loom or to *levers* on a table loom. The relationship of harness to treadle—how one is attached to the other—

is called the *tie-up*. Moving the treadle or lever raises or lowers the harness frame with the heddles, thus separating the warp ends. The simplest loom has two harness frames; the most common loom has four harness frames. Additional harness frames enable more complicated patterns and techniques to be woven.

It is most important that a loom have front-to-rear strength and stability and be heavy enough for the designed use. A wobbly loom that is out of line will not allow you to weave efficiently or produce quality work.

A strong frame and rigid bracing that won't give under tension make a good loom. Other favorable attributes are having the greatest possible length from the front to the back of the loom and at least 20 inches (50 cm), on floor looms, from breast beam to harness frames to allow sufficient weaving space. A high, or "good," shed is also a requisite of a well-designed loom.

Side view of a basic loom with necessary front-to-rear strength and stability.

Criteria for Loom Selection

First—consider the space available for weaving. You must be aware not only of the dimensions of the loom but of the space needed around a loom to allow certain

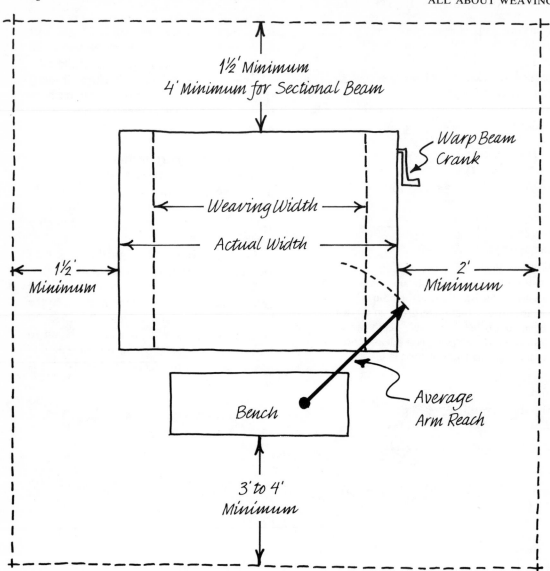

Minimum space needed for ease in setting up a floor loom and for weaving movements.

movements while working. The loom should be accessible from all sides. Allow enough room in the back so you can sit down while dressing the loom (putting the warp on it), and as much space in front as possible. Study the diagram. Many loom manufacturers list the weaving width only. The floor space is generally a foot more than the weaving width. Looms vary in depth dimension from slightly less than the width to about square. Be sure to allow about 2 feet (0.6 m) on the side of the loom where the warp beam crank is located.

Second—consider your own physical build and what type of loom and size you relate to best. A very large loom used to capacity requires strenuous labor. Maybe this is the way you want to work, but if it isn't, don't be burdened with a large loom that would seldom be used to capacity. A 36-inch (90 cm) is wide enough for most pieces of any garment. There are many ways of joining pieces of weaving to achieve a larger size (this is frequently needed with rugs, blankets, and wall hangings). Manufacturers generally make each model in several weaving widths. The wider ones are generally the best dollar value. The end or side frames are the same whether the loom is narrow or wide. The crosspieces for a narrow loom, although shorter, cost almost as much to make as the longer pieces for a wider loom.

Third—consider the type of weaving you wish to do. This is perhaps the hardest decision for the person just starting out. If you feel your work will be light and delicate, then perhaps a lightweight loom that folds would be adequate. It is possible to do a fair range of weaving on a table loom, so a floor loom is not a necessity. If, however, you prefer heavier fabrics, such as rugs, it is necessary to have a very sturdy, solid loom. On this point there is no compromise.

All looms make a little noise, some more than others. If noise is annoying to you or those around you, then get a loom made mostly of wood—some looms use chains and metal for moving parts. The loom frame should be strong and bulky. A heavy frame allows less vibration, and therefore there is less noise.

Or if you prefer tapestry weaving, you will need an upright loom that allows you to see a large design area at once. All the alternatives will be explored in the pages to come.

Fourth—consider how much you can afford to spend. This will influence your choice of loom and the type of weaving you embark on.

Ways of Acquiring a Loom

The ways one comes by a loom are almost as numerous as the looms themselves. Looms are readily available, and my advice is not to order a loom and wait months for delivery. If you have made the decision to get involved in weaving, then that is what you should do right now, not wait up to a year to get your most basic tool. Do what is best in *your* set of circumstances:

1. You can buy a new loom made by a reputable manufacturer from a dealer who can demonstrate it to you and also provide service and parts if needed. Resale value is always good on this type of loom.

2. You might wish to import a loom from a country that is known for its beautiful weaving. One pitfall here is that you cannot know if the loom you pick will function well. You should not have to immediately make modifications to a new loom's working parts in order to have it perform efficiently; part of the price of a loom is the manufacturer's cost for research and engineering. When an individual imports a loom there are also shipping, tax, and duty charges that cannot be accurately estimated.

3. A custom-built loom is another possibility. This can be expensive, and the designer and builder should have a thorough knowledge of how a loom works. This is, however, the way to get the exact loom you desire. Only after you have woven for a while do you know what operations you wish to perform, so a custom-built loom should not be the first you own.

4. You can build your own loom. Plans for construction are offered in Chapter 13. This can be economical, but only if you already have the tools and access to the right materials. Again, you should also have a good working knowledge of a loom, as well as some experience in woodworking, before you attempt to build one.

5. You can purchase a kit loom. This will provide you with the opportunity of feeling a total part of your craft. Before attempting a kit you should know how to work with basic carpenter's tools. Kits do not always include basic equipment that is part of what a manufactured loom offers. Finding the correct size of equipment can present a problem as well as additional cost. Uncured wood, which could warp, is also a consideration. A kit is not that inexpensive, and the resale value is not the highest on this type of loom. It is for people who value personal involvement.

6. A secondhand loom made by an estab-

A VARIETY OF CONVENTIONAL FLOOR LOOMS YOU MIGHT ACQUIRE SECONDHAND.

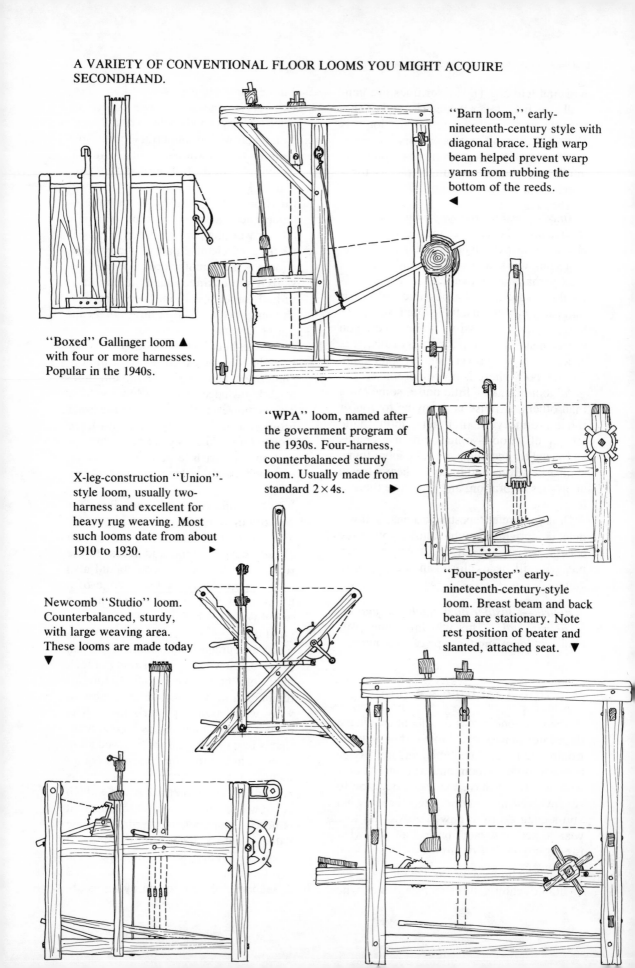

"Barn loom," early-nineteenth-century style with diagonal brace. High warp beam helped prevent warp yarns from rubbing the bottom of the reeds. ◀

"Boxed" Gallinger loom ▲ with four or more harnesses. Popular in the 1940s.

"WPA" loom, named after the government program of the 1930s. Four-harness, counterbalanced sturdy loom. Usually made from standard 2×4s. ▶

X-leg-construction "Union"-style loom, usually two-harness and excellent for heavy rug weaving. Most such looms date from about 1910 to 1930. ▶

Newcomb "Studio" loom. Counterbalanced, sturdy, with large weaving area. These looms are made today ▼

"Four-poster" early-nineteenth-century-style loom. Breast beam and back beam are stationary. Note rest position of beater and slanted, attached seat. ▼

lished manufacturer can be a wise purchase. If there are any damaged or lost parts they can be easily replaced. Secondhand looms can be located in classified sections of local newspapers and in weaving publications (see the "Periodicals" list in the back of this book). They may also be found through the local Weavers Guild. The Handweavers Guild of America can give you the address of a guild near you. Bulletin boards in local weaving schools and shops may also lead you to exactly what you are seeking, and the present loom owner may be helpful with explanations. You will find that weavers, like antique collectors, enjoy "trading up"—selling one of their looms because they are ready for something better or different.

7. A variation on this is a secondhand loom of unknown origin (including homemade). This is a wise investment only if you have the opportunity to weave on it first and thus can be sure it functions well. Consider it if it is inexpensive and if you are in a position to make major repairs and adjustments yourself if necessary.

8. Some people also acquire looms that are passed on in families or as gifts. If you have such a loom and do not know much about it, consult a friend who weaves or a professional to get information about your specific piece of equipment. Antique looms should also be considered here. They are interesting in appearance, quite often conversation pieces, but very few perform as efficiently as a new loom.

A loom becomes a very personal tool to the serious weaver. Make every effort, therefore, to find the one that best fits your needs. No loom does all kinds of weaving equally well. This is why professional weavers—and many hobbyists—possess several looms.

A loom should have good design: in other words, be pleasing to look at as well as functional. Yet its performance as a tool must never take second place to visual appeal or to the ease with which it can be knocked down. The loom's prime function is as a tool to be used in the weaving process of interlacing warp and weft.

Maintenance

There will always be maintenance on a loom. If you have acquired a used loom, first run through the following reminders to make sure your loom is ready to perform.

Keep the screws and bolts reasonably tight. Thumb-tighten wing nuts on the batten and be sure the swords do not rub on the frame or bind. Cords need to be replaced from time to time. If you must replace one, then replace them all.

Moving parts need lubrication with light oil or petroleum jelly. Use light household oil sparingly on the jack shafts, rollers, pulleys, batten and treadle support bolts, and cloth and warp beam bearings. Never oil a friction brake. Use a fine spray rust preventive or mist kerosene on heddles and steel parts to prevent corrosion.

Wooden looms and parts should be dusted (a feather duster works well) and rubbed with lemon oil or tung oil and occasionally waxed. Rarely should varnish or paint be used. Every year or so a wooden loom may be washed with mild soap suds and dried thoroughly. A complete overhaul, including disassembly, is rarely needed.

Always remove any tape or string you may have used for marking as soon as its use is past.

A properly cared for and maintained loom will last forever.

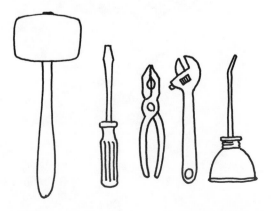

Tools used to keep a loom in good working order.

Frame Looms

The simplest loom is a *frame loom*. It is little more than a device to keep the warp yarns under tension. When first trying weaving, you can use almost anything for a loom. Use any object that is readily available to you—picture frame, window screen, found object, tree branch, cardboard box,

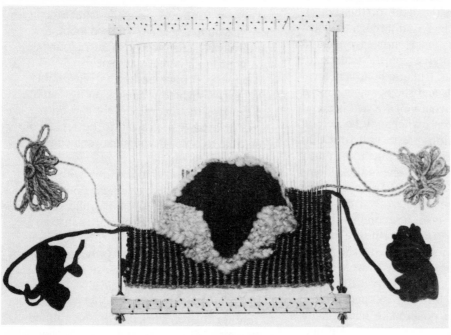

▲ Simple frame loom. *Photo courtesy Nilus Leclerc, Inc.*

Controlled weaving done on a frame loom using many textures of spun and unspun fiber. ▼

A weaving on a found object. ▶

A weathered window frame as a loom. *Photo by Charles Vorhees.*

Weaving on a round box top, in many textures of white yarn, by Mary Nice.

Ideas for simple frame looms. ▶

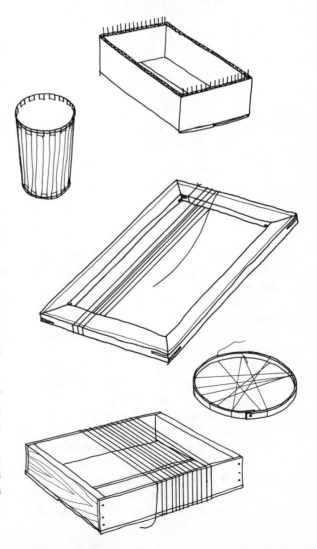

paper plate, four pieces of wood joined at the corners, an artist's canvas stretcher, and on and on—there is no limit.

For your first project you could use a door as the frame to weave on. It is something that everyone has at hand. It can be a regular door or a closet door. This does not take any additional space, it is easy to work on, and actually two pieces of weaving can be made, one on each side. You need a ball of yarn; then you simply open the door, make an overhand knot in the end of the yarn, and fasten it to the top of the door with a pushpin. Now wind the yarn around the door: down the front, under the bottom, up the back, over the top; and then start around again. The yarn ends should be placed about ½ inch (1.3 cm) apart. Continue in this manner until you have the width you want. Fasten the end just as you did the beginning, or tie it to the doorknob. Fold a towel or piece of cloth over the top near the hinge side to prevent accidental closing of the door.

Now you have the warp, or lengthwise, yarn under tension and are ready to put in the weft, or crosswise, yarn. You are, in

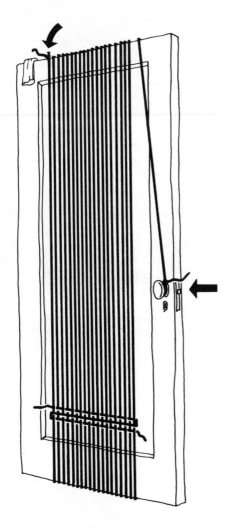

ready to go on to more structured, technical weaves, then move to a loom that is mechanically designed to accomplish your goal.

Combined Reed and Heddle Loom or Rigid Heddle Loom

One step beyond the simple frame is the loom that has a device for separating the warp ends to let the weft pass through the shed that has been created. This, too, is a loom for basic weaving. Exciting pieces using any basic weave or technique that requires no more than two sheds can be done on this loom.

The device used on a loom of this type is known as a *rigid heddle*. Within a frame there are flat narrow strips, placed with

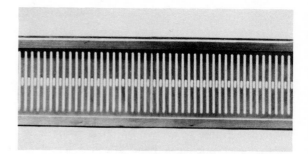

A rigid heddle. *Photo courtesy Nilus Leclerc, Inc.*

A door becomes a frame loom.

other words, ready to weave. Weaving on a frame loom is a very free form of the craft, but it is slow because the weaver must with the fingers separate the warp yarns —raising alternate or some other grouping of threads—so the weft yarns may pass through.

The frame looms just talked about are very basic, uncomplicated tools for the beginning weaver. You can use many of the weaving techniques described later in this book, but you are weaving an object that stems from creative free expression. A frame loom is not intended to produce well-controlled objects or complicated weaves. Enjoy your frame loom for its simplicity and direct method of weaving. When you are

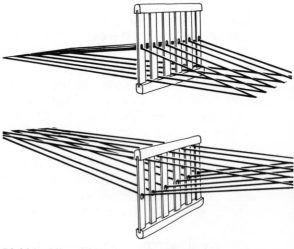

Rigid heddle with warp yarns. *Top:* Position of warp yarns when rigid heddle is raised.
Bottom: Position of warp yarns when rigid heddle is lowered.

Weaving on a backstrap loom, traditionally
used by certain American Indian tribes. *Photo
courtesy Nilus Leclerc, Inc.*

spaces between them, serving to separate
the warp ends horizontally. On other looms
this function is performed by the reed. But
this loom has the reed and the frame or harness containing the heddles combined: each
strip has a hole in the center, to serve as a
heddle. The warp ends are threaded one
through the space, the next through the hole.
The drawing shows that raising or lowering
the rigid heddle separates alternating warp
ends vertically. This is the principle behind
all *two-harness looms.*

The rigid heddle is generally used in two
kinds of loom. One is mounted in a usual
loom frame; the other is known as a *backstrap loom.* In the latter, the warp yarns are
securely fastened to a stationary point at one
end, the other end being fastened to the
weaver's waist. By leaning back, the weaver
creates the tension on the warp yarn necessary for weaving.

The backstrap loom as such has been used
for centuries, and the application of its basic

principle remains the same today. This is an
excellent loom for use outdoors and for
traveling because it can be rolled up into a
very compact unit even while the weaving
is in progress.

Upright Tapestry Looms

You can build a large frame loom and
weave tapestries and rugs. Unless you make
a special device for separating the warp
yarns, the work is very slow but nonetheless
satisfying.

There are also table- and floor-model upright tapestry looms that have harness
frames and treadles to make the weaving
process easier. These looms are a simple,
direct way of weaving, especially of pictorial
tapestries. Since the weaving progresses
vertically, you can see it as you would view
the work on an artist's easel.

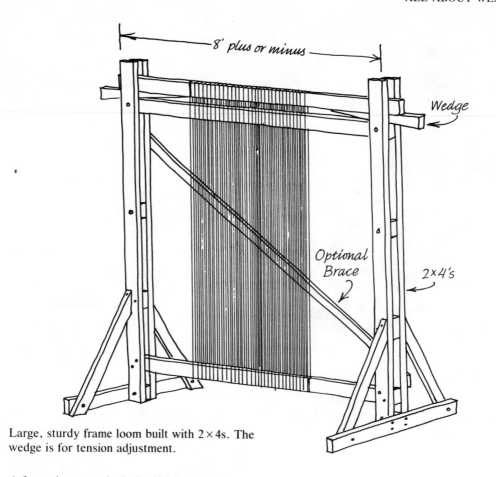

Large, sturdy frame loom built with 2 × 4s. The wedge is for tension adjustment.

A frame loom can be built with heavy logs suspended from a tree branch or any stationary point. Native Americans often worked with a warp similarly weighted, sometimes with stones.

Weaving in progress
on a large frame loom;
work is by student
Linda Fowler.

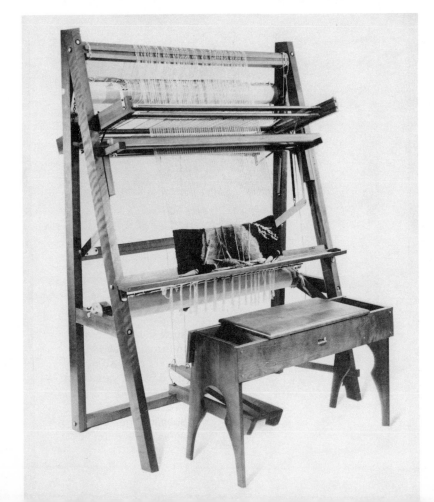

Widely manufactured
upright tapestry loom
with two harnesses and
foot treadles. Such
looms are also
available in small table
models, without the
foot treadles; in this
case the weaver
creates the shed
manually. *Photo
courtesy Nilus Leclerc,
Inc.*

The Inkle Loom

Another basic two-harness loom is the *inkle loom,* which weaves narrow bands or belts in a warp-faced weave, that is, when the warp covers the weft. By using color stripes in the warp, many interesting designs and patterns can be woven on this type loom, as illustrated in color elsewhere in this book. Color, as opposed to texture, is the important element involved when designing inkle patterns.

This loom is built in several styles, but all are portable and quiet in operation. The warp is wound around pegs in a taut circle.

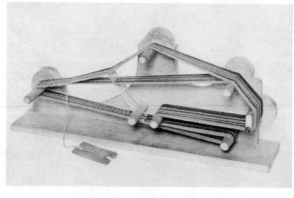

Table-model inkle loom built by Robert L. Creager, Jr. Note the string heddles. The principle of the shed is akin to that in any frame loom. The way the warp is directed around the pegs determines the length of the woven band.

Floor-model inkle loom, also called an English inkle. The pegs here are movable, and obviously longer strips are possible. A small stick shuttle is shown in the shed. The weaver can also use a small ball of yarn, yarn worked into a "butterfly," or a bobbin. *Photo courtesy Nilus Leclerc, Inc.*

Table Looms

So far we have discussed two-harness looms. These looms make only two sheds; that is, half the warp ends are up while the other half are down, and then these reverse. Now we will discuss table looms, which can have two harnesses but most often have four harnesses. The term *table loom* generally refers to the looms that rest on a table while being used and have levers, usually on the side, that you operate with your hands to lift or lower the harness frames to make a shed (see the photograph).

A table loom offers more control and ease in weaving than do simpler looms. While still being able to weave patterns and use techniques you would employ with a large loom, you have the advantage of convenient size. A table loom doesn't use much space and is portable: it is available with its own stand as well. The disadvantage or limit of a table loom is the weaving width; generally 24 inches (61 cm) is the maximum. If the loom is much wider, it ceases to be easily portable.

The working principles of the table and floor looms are similar; the main difference is in operation. Table looms require the use only of the hands, but a floor loom requires the use of hands and feet.

The cost is lower, so a table loom is an excellent investment for the beginner. If you start with a table loom you will probably keep it for a second loom when you move on to a larger one. The table model is excellent for small projects, for taking to workshops and on vacations, and certainly for making samples before attempting a large project.

Four-harness table loom. The number of harnesses determines the way groups of warp ends can be raised or lowered—and thus the woven pattern. In this case, two shuttles are needed for the contrasting weft yarns. *Photo courtesy Nilus Leclerc, Inc.*

Floor Looms

A loom that stands on the floor is referred to as a *floor loom*, a *foot-power loom*, or sometimes a *handloom*. Usually such looms are four-harness or more (some two-harness "rug looms" are made). Floor looms are usually sturdier and will weave wider pieces than will table looms.

The harness frames on a table loom are set in motion by hand levers, which are directly attached to the frames. On most floor

◀
Four-harness
floor loom.
*Photo courtesy
Nilus Leclerc, Inc.*

looms the harness frames are attached to
lams, then to the treadles (see the accompanying illustration). When the treadles are
depressed, the harness frames are raised or
lowered.

When a loom has more than two treadles,
it is necessary to have *lams*. These are
straight pieces, one for each harness, generally fastened to the inside of the castle
supports. Each lam is fastened to the bottom
of the harness frame with a yoke. The lams
are then tied to the treadles. The advantage
of the lams is that the treadles can be attached in a straight line. Each lam should
have a hole or screw eye for each treadle,
and each treadle has a place to be attached,
one for each harness. The lams are parallel
to and just underneath the harness frames.
The lams serve to equalize and balance
the harness frames as they are pulled by the
treadles, which are perpendicular to the
lams and harness frames.

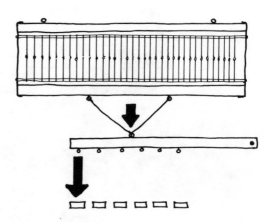

The manner of fastening harness frames to
lams and lams to treadles on a
counterbalanced loom.

Weaving on a floor loom is a rhythmical
procedure: the weaver uses hands and feet
alternately.

Floor looms for the handweaver can be
classified according to the manner in which

Four-harness counterbalanced floor loom with ▲ rollers. *Photo courtesy Nilus Leclerc, Inc.*

Four-harness counterbalanced floor loom with pulleys and horses. *Photo courtesy Nilus Leclerc, Inc.*
◀

Four-harness jack-type floor loom. *Photo courtesy Nilus Leclerc, Inc.*

Countermarche loom. *Photo courtesy Bexell & Son, manufacturers of the Cranbrook weaving loom.*

they work. They will do substantially the same type of weaving, with each having a specific advantage. The three types are counterbalanced, jack-type, and counter-marche.

Counterbalanced Looms are mechanically the least complicated. The harness frames are hung from either pulleys, rollers, or pieces of wood called *horses*, or a combi-

nation of these, at the center uppermost portion of the loom—the castle. The harness frames are attached directly to the lams, and the lams to the treadles. When a treadle is pushed down, the harness frames attached to that treadle go down, and so the counterbalanced loom is known as giving a *sinking shed*.

When the counterbalanced loom is prop-

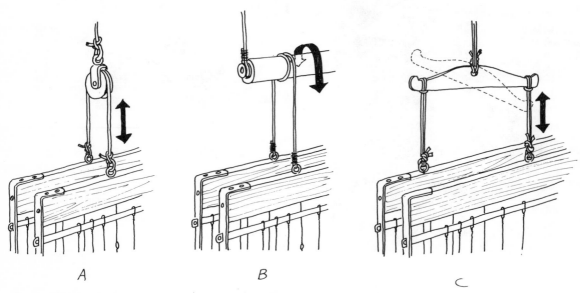

A   *B*   *C*

Different methods of hanging the harness ▲ frames on a counterbalanced loom: *A,* pulleys; *B,* rollers; *C,* horses.

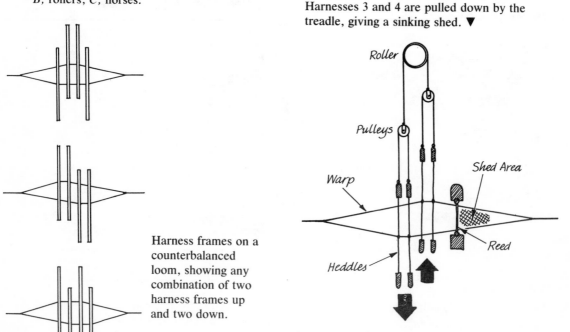

Warp yarn on a counterbalanced loom. Harnesses 3 and 4 are pulled down by the treadle, giving a sinking shed. ▼

Harness frames on a counterbalanced loom, showing any combination of two harness frames up and two down.

erly tied up and in balance, it is the easiest to operate and most often the quietest. It also produces the best shed because of the pulley system. Friction is all that is working against you. The harness frames that are not pulled down by the treadles automatically go up like a counterbalance. This allows the warp ends to be pulled apart, making a wide, clean shed.

The disadvantage of this type of loom is that it generally produces the best shed when any two harness frames are lowered and the other two rise. However, many of the counterbalanced looms that are currently being manufactured are so well engineered that it is possible to get a reasonably good shed when three harnesses are used against one.

If you are planning to build a loom, then the counterbalanced type is the ideal model to attempt, at least for the first project. It

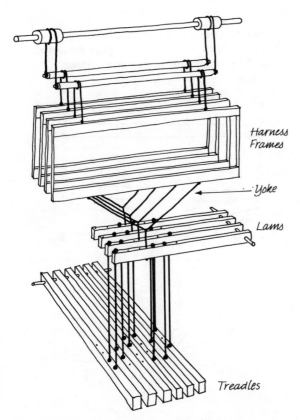

Counterbalanced loom with rollers, showing complete tie-up of harness frames to lams and to treadles.

has a simple, direct action, and major adjustments can easily be made. A counterbalanced loom cannot be surpassed for performance when weaving traditional weaves and especially when weaving long lengths of fabric. The best counterbalanced looms have four harness frames. With more frames they tend to be clumsy, complicated, inefficient, and difficult to adjust. A four-harness counterbalanced loom should have six treadles or possibly more hinged at the front or rear of the loom.

Jack-Type Looms have become popular. There are two kinds of jack-type model; on one the harnesses are pulled up by overhead jacks, and on the other (which is more common) the harnesses are pushed up by jacks beneath the harness frames. On the latter the frames rest on jacks that are attached to the lams, then to the treadles. When a treadle is pushed down, the jack rises and pushes one or more harness frames up. These looms then produce a *rising shed* because the harnesses attached to the treadles go up—as opposed to the counterbalanced loom, which makes a sinking shed because the harnesses attached to the treadles move down when pushed. Working against you here are both friction and weight.

The advantage of jack-type looms is that they always work well when the independent action (one against three) of each harness is required. These looms take more effort to operate on the part of the weaver and therefore reduce the weaving speed. If the warp yarns are close set and tend to stick together, it is sometimes difficult to open the shed because there is nothing to hold down the harness frames that are not being used. They tend to move up with the frames that are being pushed up by the jacks.

The warp line (from back beam to breast beam) on a jack-type loom should dip down in the center because the part of the warp that is raised by the harnesses is very stretched compared to the part that is not moved. The warp tension, then, should not be as tight as on a loom where the shed moves up and down. A very tight tension on a jack-type loom reduces the size of the shed. Some kinds of weaving are therefore

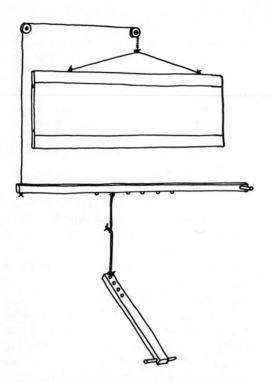

Jack-type loom using pulleys instead of jacks. These looms were popular in the forties and several are made today.

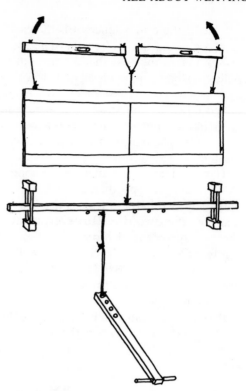

Jack-type loom using overhead jacks and "floating lams," which will pivot at the farther side from the treadle tie-up for maximum leverage.

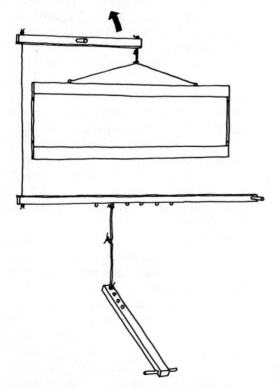

Jack-type loom using an overhead jack. As the lam is moved down, the jack is raised. Note long lam for better leverage of a jack.

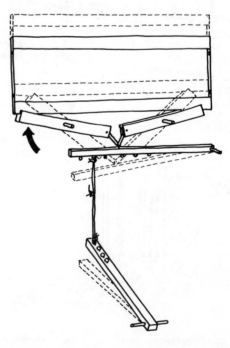

Jack-type loom with the more common positioning of jacks, underneath the harness frames. As the treadle and lam are moved down, the jacks (arrow) push up the harness frame.

COMPARISON OF WARP LEVELS ON
JACK-TYPE, COUNTERBALANCED, AND
COUNTERMARCHE LOOMS.

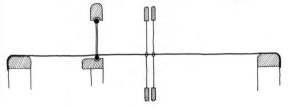

Warp line on a jack-type loom.

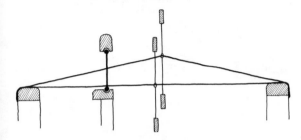

Warp yarns on a jack-type loom. Harness 2 is
pushed up by jacks, which are attached to the
treadle. This is a rising shed. Note excess
tension on raised warp yarn.

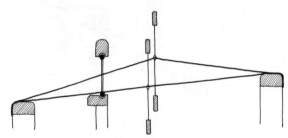

On a rising shed, the excess tension on warp
yarns can be slightly relieved by raising the
back beam.

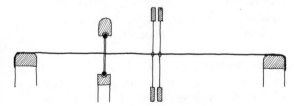

Warp line on a counterbalanced or
countermarche loom.

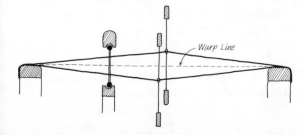

less easily done on this loom. Rug weaving,
for instance, requires a very tight tension.
It is also easier to weave an even selvage
on a tight warp.

The jack-type loom is for the individual
who is interested in experimental and free-
expression weaving. There is no restriction
on weaves or design possibilities. Up to sixteen harnesses are practical on some jack-
type looms.

Almost all table looms are jack-type: the
harness frames are attached to levers, and
when the lever is depressed the individual
frame rises.

All jack-type floor looms should have at
least two more treadles than harness frames,
since the advantage of a jack-type loom is
being able to use any combination of harness
frames. Therefore on a four-harness loom
with only four treadles it would be difficult
and time-consuming to have to use three
treadles at once when weaving an unbalanced weave.

The *Countermarche Loom* is the all-pur-
pose loom, but in principle only. It has all
the advantages of a counterbalanced loom
and of a jack-type. It can have any number
of harnesses and any tie-up, balanced or not.
(On a four-harness loom, a tie-up is called
balanced if two harnesses are attached to
one treadle.) The shed opens from a neutral
position, going both up and down, and
therefore a clean shed is made even when
the warp yarns are close and tend to stick
together. These looms usually have from
four to sixteen harnesses.

The disadvantage is that a basic tie-up
cannot be used because only one treadle can
be used at once, restricting the number of
sheds to the number of treadles. (A basic
tie-up is when each harness is tied to one

Warp yarns on a counterbalanced or
countermarche loom. Yarns rise and sink or
fall to make a shed. On a counterbalanced
loom the warp yarns that are not pulled down
by the treadle automatically move up because
of the pulley or roller system. On the
countermarche loom the warp yarns are pulled
up and pulled down to make a shed, as a result
of the double tie-up system.

◄

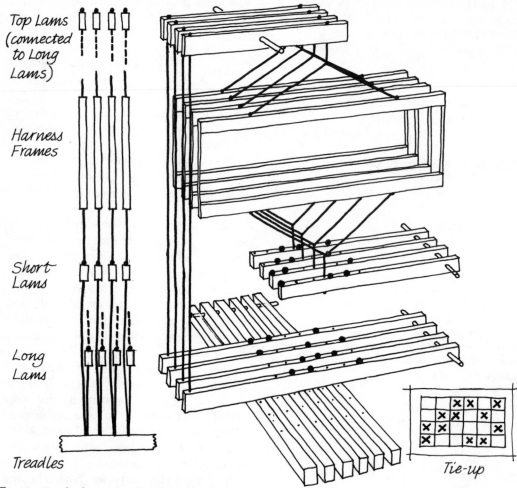

Top Lams
(connected
to Long
Lams)

Harness
Frames

Short
Lams

Long
Lams

Treadles

Tie-up

Countermarche loom showing the three types of lam *(left)*. Each harness is connected to the top lam's inner end. Each long lam is connected to the top lam's outer end with long cords. Each short lam is connected to the bottom of a harness frame. The long lams and short lams are connected to the treadles. For each harness frame there is one lam of each kind. In a tie-up, every mark represents the tying of the short lams to the treadles and every unmarked space represents the tying of the long lams to the treadles. The cords from the short lams go between the long lams and straight to the treadles.

treadle.) To raise or lower the required number of harnesses, one or more treadles must be used.

The countermarche loom is also known as a *double tie-up loom* because there is a double set of lams. Each treadle is tied to all harness frames. One set of lams is for the rising shed; the other set, for the sinking shed. This doubles the number of tie-ups necessary on the counterbalanced and jack-type looms. The double tie-up is so time-consuming that it is impractical to change it easily.

The countermarche loom, then, is good for production, that is, weaving long lengths without changing the tie-up. However, production must depend upon speed, and not all countermarche looms are so well designed that the weaver does not have to make frequent adjustments. It is difficult to maintain in balance all parts of the countermarche loom, especially those where cords stretch and knots slip. Some countermarche looms have preset cable or chain that will not stretch or break; this is a definite advantage. Also, some countermarche looms are built with all the lams on one level, in which case part of the balance problem is eliminated.

A well-balanced and -adjusted countermarche loom is a pleasure to weave on. For the most part, these looms have superior beauty and styling.

Looms with Fly Shuttles

The *fly shuttle* equipment can be attached to most looms. It is for production weaving and for weaving widths of fabric wider than that produced when the shuttle is thrown from hand to hand. It consists of boxes or traps attached at each end of the batten. Each box is equipped with a free-sliding hammer block. The hammers are joined by a cord which, when jerked in either direction, gives a blow to the shuttle, sending it across the shuttle race to the opposite box. The flying shuttle takes more getting used to than an ordinary shuttle and is useless if the weaving requires the use of two shuttles (each carrying different yarn) alternately.

There is also an *automatic fly shuttle rug loom*. Among the looms that a handweaver uses, this comes closest to being a power loom. By the movement of the beater back-

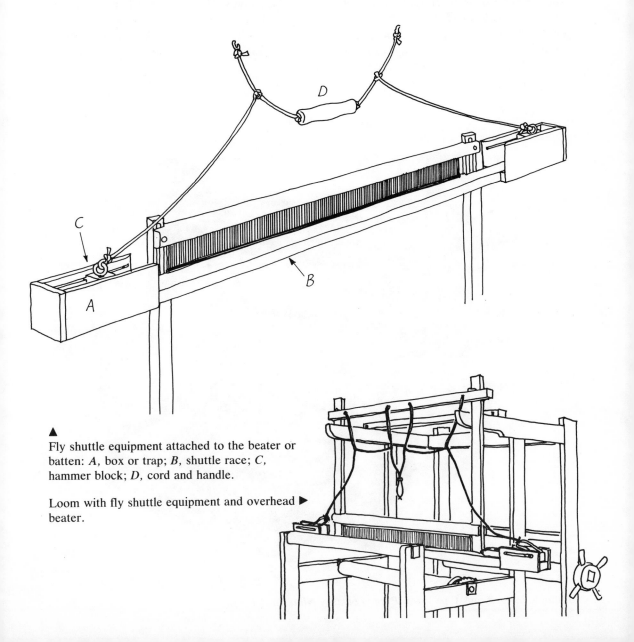

▲
Fly shuttle equipment attached to the beater or batten: *A,* box or trap; *B,* shuttle race; *C,* hammer block; *D,* cord and handle.

Loom with fly shuttle equipment and overhead ▶ beater.

ward and forward, all the other operating parts of the loom are automatically set in motion—the warp is released from the warp beam; the harness frames are shifted; the shuttle is thrown; and the woven fabric is moved forward and automatically wound onto the cloth beam. This loom is mostly used by people who are interested in production-type weaving of rag rugs.

Multiple-Harness Looms

A loom that has more than four harnesses is referred to as a *multiple-harness loom* or *multiharness loom*. Such a loom is very specialized. A basic understanding of the theory of weaves and *drafts* (graphed charts of the loom action needed to produce particular weaves) for four harnesses is a must

before you advance to a multiple-harness loom if you are to make the best use of this type.

More involved patterns can be woven on a multiple-harness loom, but even if this is not the weaver's main interest, better results in the woven fabric can be attained, especially with fine yarns, because there is less friction on the warp yarns when they are distributed among a greater number of harnesses. In addition, multiple-harness looms greatly expand the possibilities of double weaves and layered weaves.

Even though its greater capabilities are tempting, it is important to consider the disadvantages of a multiple-harness loom. These looms are very heavy and cumbersome. They do not work as efficiently as four-harness looms. The weaver must ex-

Multiple-harness jack-type loom. *Photo courtesy Nilus Leclerc, Inc.*

A type of pulley ▲
system for a
counterbalanced
multiple-harness
loom.

Multiple-harness ▲
jack-type loom with
overhead jacks and
floating lams. This
loom is also
equipped with a fly
shuttle. *Photo
courtesy Nilus
Leclerc, Inc.*

Counterbalanced
multiple-harness loom
showing use of
pulleys and horses. ▶

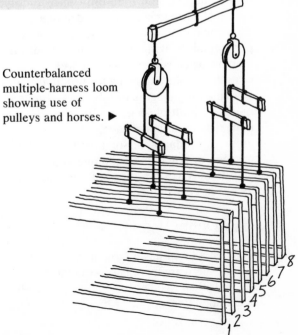

pend much more energy in weaving. (These
points do not apply to the lightweight looms
intended only for exercises and samples.)

The most versatile multiple-harness loom
is the jack-type. It is easy to set up and adjust, and any number of harness combinations can be used at the same time. The
countermarche loom takes a long time to set

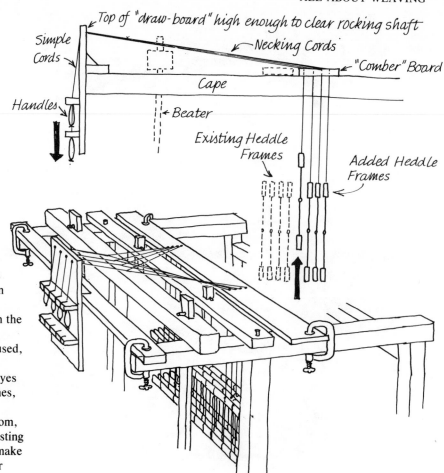

A method of adding any number of extra harness frames to a loom with an overhead cape. Harness frames rise by pulling on the simple cords. Complete harness frames are not used, just the heddle bars and string heddles. Heddle eyes on the new harness frames, whether on a counter-balanced or jack-type loom, are lined up with the existing heddles. The C-clamps make the unit easy to install or remove.

up and adjust, and then only one combination of harnesses can be used at one time. This one factor virtually eliminates any experimental weaving, as the time in setting up must be considered. Yet the weaving operation is easier, allowing for production or weaving long lengths of fabric. A counterbalanced multiple-harness loom is almost nonexistent, although some Scandinavian looms are adaptable for up to eight harnesses—or you could build one yourself. It will do only certain types of weaving, and its use is very limited.

The Dobby Loom

When a loom has a large number of harnesses, there are more harness combinations or sheds than treadles that can be physically accommodated on an ordinary loom. The following formula gives an idea of the possible shed combinations: $S = 2^H - 2$ (S = number of sheds; H = number of harnesses). To figure out the number of shed combinations, take 2 as a factor the same number of times that there are harnesses, then subtract 2. A four-harness loom, then, offers 14 different shed combinations ($2 \times 2 \times 2 \times 2 = 16 - 2 = 14$), while a twelve-harness loom offers 4,094 sheds. To permit full use of all harness combinations, the *dobby mechanism,* which is an automatic shedding device, or variations of it are used.

The dobby can take up to thirty-two harnesses. The warp is threaded through the heddles of the loom as usual. Each harness is hung from a hook. A treadle is tied to a horizontal lever that is connected to a cam and interacts with the hooks. The lever sets in motion the cylinder holding the pegs, or lags, which are set according to a specific pattern or weave. When the treadle is pushed down, a knife rises and pulls up all hooks (or harnesses) required for that shed. When the treadle is released, the knife and harnesses or hooks return to their original position.

The dobby loom permits simple weaves and special designs to be woven mechanically. Its limitation is that the shed order is set and design variations require a change in peg order.

Individual handweavers can use the dobby loom. New ones are being made, and older models are available.

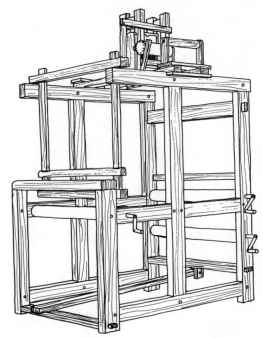

Frame of small dobby loom with mechanism on top. Note double warp beam and single treadle.

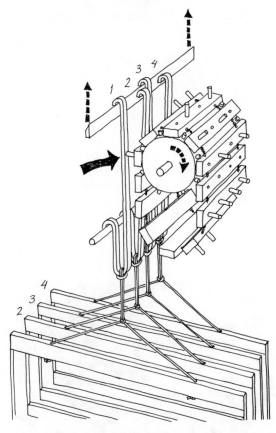

The dobby mechanism, which sits on top of the loom, is composed of pegged boards that revolve around a cylinder. There is a peg, or a space for a peg, and a hook for each harness frame. In the drawing, pegs 1 and 3 have pushed hooks 1 and 3 forward and the knife is ready to lift harness frames 1 and 3. Only four harness frames are shown here; most dobby looms have many more.

The Jacquard Loom

The *jacquard loom*, sometimes called a machine, was invented in the early nineteenth century by Joseph-Marie Jacquard. A selector mechanism works on the punched-card principle. Very elaborate patterns can be woven. These looms are not for individual use, but they can be observed in working order in museums.

Drawlooms

Drawlooms do not need the space that the dobby and jacquard looms do. They are used by designers because they do not require the pegboards or punched cards of those looms. The drawloom uses up to thirty-six harnesses. Since most of the harnesses are raised or lowered by hand, much freedom of design is allowed. These looms may be floor- or table-size.

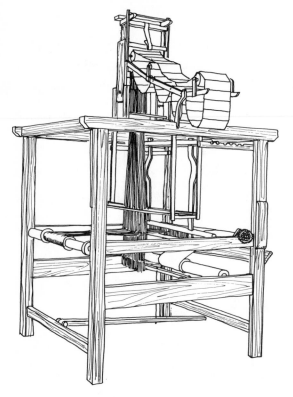

Jacquard loom dressed, ready to weave. The number of punched pattern cards draped from the rollers on the top determines the complexity of the weave. A fly shuttle was used on most of these looms. This is the type of loom used to make many of the nineteenth-century "Signature" coverlets. *After a drawing from Bettman Archives, Inc.*

A close-up view of a jacquard mechanism, which has been removed from the loom. It is attached to the top of the loom, as shown in the drawing. The punched pattern cards can be seen in the lower right-hand area of the photo. *Photo courtesy Bettman Archives, Inc.*

Portion of a coverlet woven on a jacquard loom. "Eagles and Stars" was woven in 1838 in blue and white. *Collection of the Ohio Historical Society.*

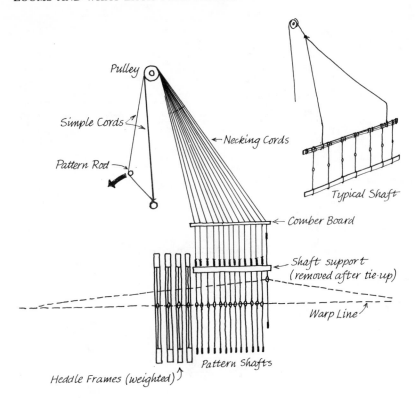

Pulley

Simple Cords

Necking Cords

Pattern Rod

Typical Shaft

← Comber Board

Shaft support
(removed after tie-up)

Warp Line

Pattern Shafts

Heddle Frames (weighted)

Fourteen-harness drawloom. Note that its mechanism is the same as that used when extra harness frames are added to a loom: you raise harness frames by pulling on the simple cords. The last shaft is raised ready for weaving. In the inset drawing of a typical shaft or harness, notice the heddles laced to the shaft.

A designer's drawloom adapted from a four-harness table loom. The original harness frames are for ground weave, and there is space for twenty pattern shafts.

Loom Equipment Options

The many looms available offer a still-wider range of options through variations in style and mechanical operation. There are choices of equipment, some of which can be added or attached to allow for more complex or experimental weaving. Some of these loom accessories are necessary for specific weaving techniques, while in other instances additional equipment simplifies or facilitates the weaving process. Not to be overlooked is each weaver's personal preference for equipment that best suits his or her way of working.

BATTEN OR BEATER

Looms can have a beater that is hung from the cape of the loom (called an *overhead beater*), or the beater can be pivoted from the lower brace. Looms have either one or the other, but on a few looms the beater can be changed and used in either position. By understanding the movement of the beater,

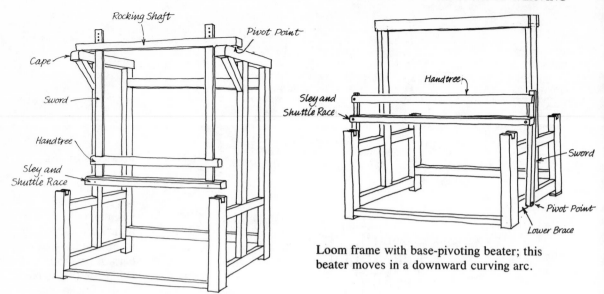

Loom frame with base-pivoting beater; this
beater moves in a downward curving arc.

Loom frame with overhead beater; this beater
produces an upward curving arc as it moves.

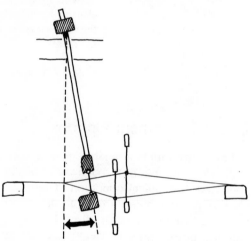

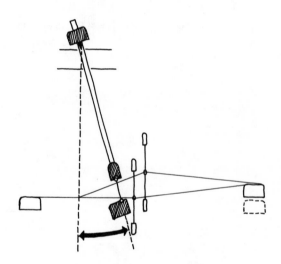

Left: Overhead beater as it swings to strike the
fell. Note bottom part of shed rubbing in base
of reed, limiting height of shed and wearing
warp yarns.
Right: Overhead beater pushed back for
insertion of shuttle. Note raised back beam,
which makes warp ends higher, eliminating
wear on warp and interference with shed.

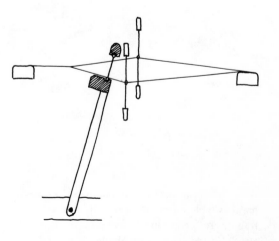

Base-pivoting beater in rest position. Shuttle ▶
race is parallel to warp ends on bottom part of
shed.

the weaver can decide which pivoting point is better for the types of weaving preferred and the style of loom.

In the weaving process the beater moves back and forth in an arc of up to 10 inches (25 cm)—this arc can move up or down depending on the adjustment of the beater swords.

The pivot point, whether at the top or the bottom, is directly above or below and in line with the point where the beater strikes the weaving (the *fell*). This allows the greatest possible weaving space.

The beater strikes the weaving or fell of the cloth at a different angle depending on where it is pivoted—top or bottom. If the fell is in front of the overhead beater, this strikes with the top of the reed slanting away from the weaver, giving an unobstructed view of how the weft is beaten into place. The base-pivoting beater slants forward as it strikes the weaving, slightly covering the fell from view if the fell is in front of the beater pivot point.

When the beater is hung from overhead, the weaver must push it back and hold it there to allow space in the shed to insert the shuttle. On some old looms ("barn" type) the overhead beater pivot point is off center, allowing the batten to hang at an angle away from the fell.

The overhead beater moves up in an upward arc and can (if not properly adjusted) interfere with the warp yarns on the bottom shed. Rubbing warp yarns in the bottom of the reed subjects them to unnecessary wear and limits the height of the shed. This problem can be alleviated by raising the back beam so the warp yarns are higher in the back. Looms with a rising shed—such as the jack-type—are best for the overhead beater because when the shed is opened the warp yarns that form the bottom of the shed remain horizontal.

The overhead beater allows fast weaving with one shuttle because the beater moves back by its own weight. The position of the beater can be moved forward or backward, allowing for additional harness frames or adjustment. A finer adjustment can also be made in height. The supports, or capes, for the overhead beater can be used for other loom mountings, such as the drawloom or dobby mechanism. The construction of the overhead beater is very strong because the swords and sley of the whole beater are fixed.

The bottom-pivoting batten remains at rest in the back position without being held there. This leaves both hands free for using shuttles. The warp yarns of the bottom shed remain parallel with the shuttle race, and this permits the shuttle to move across the warp on the race without falling.

The choice of type of beater is a matter of preference; either one, when properly used, will give beautiful results.

Rocking Shaft
Pivot (off center)
Cape
Sword
Handtree
Reed
Sley
Shuttle Race

Off-center pivot point on overhead beater typical of old "barn"-style or "four-poster" looms. Note that shuttle race is attached to sley of beater.

SHUTTLE RACE

The *shuttle race* is a smooth, flat piece of wood that is standard equipment on many looms. It is a necessary part of a fly shuttle loom. The shuttle race performs most effectively on jack-type looms or on sinking-shed looms with a base-pivoting beater. It is attached to the front of or is part of the sley, which is below the reed in the beater. When the shed is opened the shuttle moves along this race. If the warp yarns are soft and set far apart in the reed, the shuttle race supports the shuttle as it moves through the shed.

This piece of equipment will add weight to the beater, which can be an advantage. It should be wide enough for the shuttles used, and designed so the beater doesn't rub the warp yarns when the shed is fully opened. On the other hand, it is useless if the shed is too high and warp yarns do not touch it. Use of the shuttle race requires proper adjustment of the beater and may also necessitate adjustment of the height of the harness frames.

DOUBLE WARP BEAM AND BACK BEAM

Adding a second warp beam and back beam to a loom is relatively easy. Many loom manufacturers offer this option, but if they don't, just add brackets for the beams to the rear corner posts below the original warp beam. The second warp beam must have its own brake. There are also many do-it-yourself methods for constructing a second warp beam.

Reasons for using two warp beams are numerous. The basic principle, however, is to be able to keep all the warp ends under even tension while weaving. Situations when a second warp beam would be convenient are:

◇ when using varying weights of yarn in one warp;

◇ on certain pile weaves when part of the warp becomes the pile;

◇ on many layered weaves where all the layers are not the full width of the weaving, when uneven buildup in certain areas on one warp beam will affect the tension;

◇ on double stuffer rugs, when part of the

Do-it-yourself method for a second warp beam and back beam. Cement blocks placed on floor hold flat (so it won't turn) a piece of wood to use as a beam. Warp is wound around a rectangular piece of wood like a 2 × 4; additional wood strips can be added for greater diameter. A second back beam can be made with lease sticks kept in position on top and rear of back beam so warps don't touch each other.

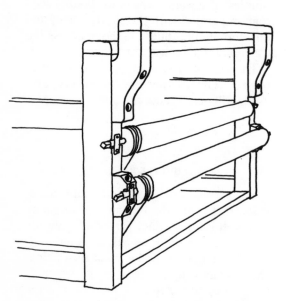

Second warp beam attached with brackets to rear corner posts of loom, and second back beam with its brackets. Note raised position of this beam.

warp serves as a "stuffer" and is not interlaced with weft yarns;

◊ when making puckered or seersucker-type fabric.

Those are just a few of the reasons for having two warp beams. The weaver will find that a loom equipped with a second warp beam can solve many problems of warp tension when a variety of yarns are used in the warp, and can help achieve special effects.

The warps to be put on each beam should be prepared individually and should not touch each other: this is the reason for the additional back beam. This second back beam is mounted higher than the first. It can also be used when a raised warp is necessary to help reduce excessive warp tension sometimes occurring on looms with a rising shed. Dressing the rest of the loom is the same as if there were only one beam.

SECTIONAL WARP BEAM

Sectional warping is ideal for warps of great length: small, manageable sections of the warp are wound onto the warp beam directly from spools. Loom equipment for this type of warping is attached to the warp beam (two other accessories are also often used: a *tension box* and a *counter*). The sectional

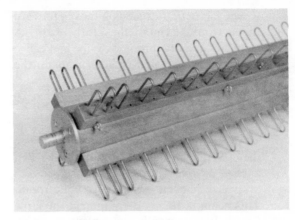

Equipment for making a regular beam a sectional warp beam. Wood strips (rakes) with metal dividers are attached to the warp beam.

warp beam is optional with many looms. Some older "rug" looms have standard sectional beams. On new looms you can add the equipment to your existing beam and remove it when not needed.

CLOTH PROTECTOR

A very simple but practical device to add to any loom is a *cloth protector*. A few looms have one as standard equipment. It is simply a piece of narrow, flat, smooth wood that is attached with a spacer to the front of the breast beam. This protects the

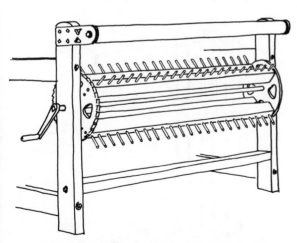

A standard sectional beam on a "rug" loom. A regular warp beam can be made from some of these sectional beams by removing the pegged boards and turning them over. Note the round back beam typical of this style of loom.

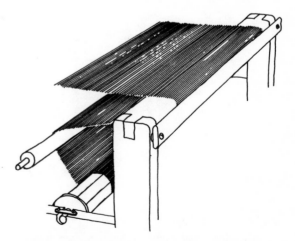

Cloth protector on breast beam protects woven fabric during weaving process. Also, knee beam keeps woven fabric out of the way, giving more knee or leg space for the weaver.

woven fabric from wear as it moves forward to be wound around the cloth beam. A weaver's activity during weaving can cause unnecessary abrasion or attract lint to the weaving at this point.

KNEE BEAM

An additional beam placed high between the breast beam and the cloth beam is called a *knee beam*. The woven fabric passes around the beam, giving more knee room. This beam is standard equipment on some looms. It is especially convenient on small, compact looms.

SHED REGULATOR

A *shed regulator* is a device that can be attached to counterbalanced looms to produce a clear shed when the tie-up is unbalanced. The tie-up on a four-harness loom is unbalanced when an odd number of harness frames is attached to one treadle. In this instance, the warp yarns open at an uneven height in the shed.

The parts of a shed regulator are two rollers, cords, springs, and necessary screws and bolts to attach it to the loom frame.

The working principle is that the existing harness frames and rollers are hung from another roller placed higher; the weight of the harness frames is balanced by springs

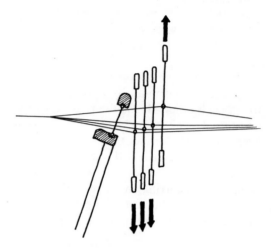

A shed that is not clear on a counterbalanced loom, the result of an unbalanced tie-up (any three harness frames attached to one treadle).

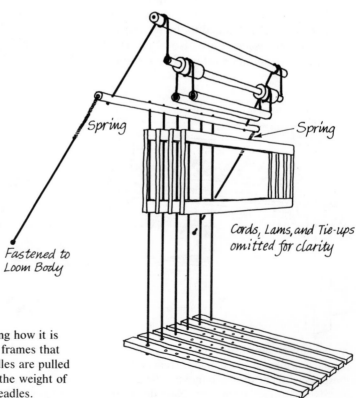

Spring

Spring

Fastened to Loom Body

Cords, Lams, and Tie-ups omitted for clarity

A Leclerc shed regulator, showing how it is attached to a loom. The harness frames that are not pulled down by the treadles are pulled by a spring action that balances the weight of the harness frames, lams, and treadles.

attached to a second roller and then to the loom body. This second roller has cords attached to each treadle. The springs balance the weight of the harness frames, lams, and treadles. During the weaving process the harness frames tied to the treadle are pulled down while the opposite harness frames are pulled up by the spring action. This shedding motion is similar to that of a countermarche loom.

A shed regulator is also convenient in a balanced tie-up when yarns in the warp are fine or tend to stick together. (A balanced tie-up on a four-harness loom is when any two harness frames are attached to one treadle.)

TREADLES

The style of the loom determines the location of the treadles. They may be attached in the front or at the rear of the loom; each way has certain advantages. On looms with four or more harnesses, treadles and lams work together and both have to be considered when deciding which is best for you. The purpose of the treadles is to move the harness frames up or down with ease and accuracy. The lams are the intermediates, or the mechanical device used to accomplish this purpose. Some jack-type looms do not have lams.

Both front- and rear-mounted treadles need to be tied up to the lams at a point that will allow the lams and harness frames to

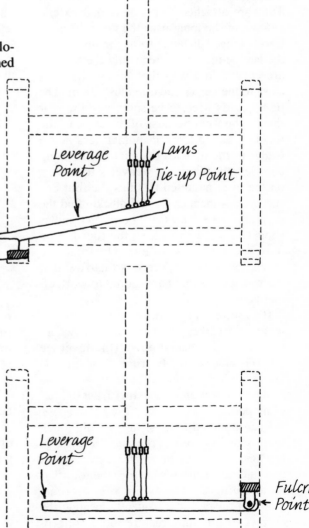

Above: Loom frame showing front-mounted treadles.
Below: Loom frame showing rear-mounted treadles.

move up or down smoothly and evenly. The point where each treadle ties to the lams should be as close to the center line of the harness frames as possible to help equalize the foot pressure needed to move all harness frames evenly. This difference is more noticeable on narrow looms than on wide ones because of the shorter distance from the lam fulcrum point to the leverage point or the center line of the loom. On some narrow looms this is remedied by pivoting the lams from a point outside the loom body or using "floating" lams that pivot from either side, allowing maximum distance from leverage point to fulcrum point.

Front-mounted treadles are usually pivoted from a point outside the loom body. They are attached to brackets that extend in front of the loom near the floor. This allows a longer distance from the fulcrum to the lam tie-up point. Frequently the treadles are curved in a way that brings the ends close to the center line (see illustration). The tie-up cords need to be shorter in the rear than in the front because of the angle of the treadles. Some loom manufacturers add a wedge to the treadles to equalize the tie-up cord length. Since the weaver's foot rests on the front-mounted treadles the foot can slide across them easily and quickly find the correct treadle. The space between treadles should be wide enough so the foot fits on only one treadle at a time. On some old looms the treadle space is so narrow that the weaver must be bare-footed to work effectively.

It requires more force to move front-mounted treadles because the point where the treadle is pushed down (the leverage point) is close to the fulcrum. Less force is needed on rear-mounted treadles, since the foot pressure is applied farther from the fulcrum point.

Rear-mounted treadles are usually much more sensitive to foot pressure because of the longer distance between leverage point and fulcrum. During weaving, the foot that is not being used does not rest on rear-mounted treadles; consequently locating the correct treadle may require more concentration on the part of the weaver. Tie-up

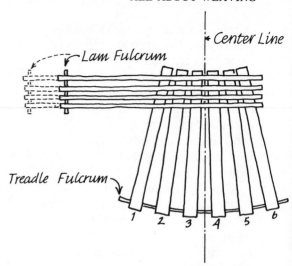

Treadles are curved toward the center line of the loom to minimize the difference in the effort needed to depress them. Treadle 1 will require more force to press down than treadle 6. By curving the treadles closer to the center line and placing the lam fulcrum farther away, treadle 1 will work more easily. This problem is more apparent on narrow floor looms than on the wider looms.

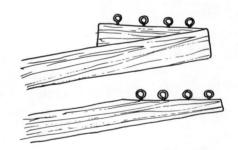

Treadles that have been modified to equalize the distance from the lams to the treadles, from the front to the back harness frames. *Above:* A wedge is added. *Below:* The treadles are cut at an angle.

---

cords on rear-mounted treadles are usually of equal length because the treadles are quite often mounted higher and in a horizontal position when "at rest."

It is generally true that all treadles, whether mounted at the front or the rear of the loom, perform satisfactorily, providing the harness frames, lams, and tie-ups are properly adjusted.

2

Characteristics of Yarns

Yarn is the fundamental element in weaving. Working with the color and the texture of yarn is what makes weaving an ever-exciting challenge to our senses of sight and of touch. All yarn has a visual and tactile texture quality.

Yarns for the handweaver are generally classified by fiber, size or count, ply, twist, and sometimes color. Actually, getting fully acquainted with the characteristics of yarn is probably the most difficult task that confronts a weaver. That each fiber behaves in a unique manner and that yarn is spun in many ways, receives color differently, and works up differently are just a few of the challenges; the availability of appropriate yarns is also something that all weavers must cope with. But what stimulation one may receive from visiting a well-stocked yarn shop or receiving a package of yarn by mail! Ideas for one's work very often stem from the sensual impact of a specific yarn.

The simplest and most direct surface the loom produces is texture. It can be rough or smooth, shiny or dull. In weaving, make every effort to capture the qualities that make a yarn beautiful. When looking at weaving, the eye sees first the degree and type of surface texture, not the manner in which the piece was woven on the loom.

Each time a different yarn is used, try to make the most of its particular identity. Quite often this requires you to find new ways to use the loom. For many years weavers have used materials other than yarns to achieve surface enrichment. Use

Shelves of weaving yarn inspire ideas for creative weaving.

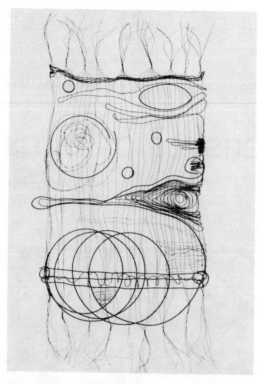

Weaving by a college student on a simple frame loom using many sizes and types of wire.

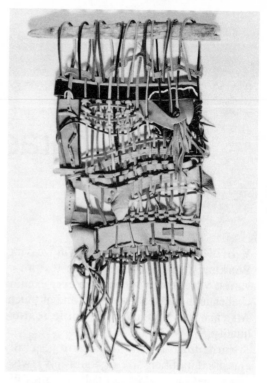

Weaving on a simple frame loom, using leather for warp and weft, by student Cassandra Tellier.

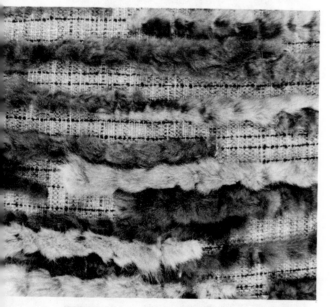

Pillow with strips of fur. To cut fur, use a razor blade and work on the skin side. When weaving, use only every fourth or sixth warp end to tie down the fur picks (or weft inserts) without obscuring the texture of the fur.

your ingenuity in adapting natural as well as manufactured materials for weaving.

Fibers

Yarn is a continuous strand of fibers; some yarn is spun, which is a grouping of short fibers called *staple fibers,* while other is *filament yarn,* usually artificial fibers of infinite length twisted together to make the yarn.

As in all phases of handweaving, there are basic rules with yarn, and if they are followed the weaver is sure to develop a familiarity with the qualities of yarn and then through experimentation find yarns and sources that are suitable for an individual way of weaving.

Basically, yarns are of three kinds of fiber: vegetable, animal, and artificial or man-made. Vegetable-fiber yarns most used by handweavers are cotton, linen, ramie, jute, sisal, and hemp. Animal fibers include wool, animal hair, and silk. Some of the artificial fibers are rayon, acrylic, nylon, and polyester.

At first it is advisable to use natural-fiber yarn. Start with cotton, then wool and linen. In general, natural-fiber yarn is easier to handle and the results are predictable. Using inferior yarns in the beginning is not a good idea. You will find they are difficult to work with, the color is not always true, and your end result will suffer. You will not be using a large quantity at first, so the cost for quality yarn is negligible compared to the satisfaction with the resulting product. Characteristics that are desired in a piece of weaving are determined principally by the fiber and yarn selected.

Take advantage of fibers and yarns that are common in the area in which you live. In that way you may well find better quality and variety and the information you need about these fibers.

Another important factor: always use yarns that are manufactured for use by handweavers. Yarns that are produced for power looms in mills can be found in odd lots and are generally inexpensive, but they are often difficult to use for handweaving because of the type of spin, the finish put on them, and the fibers or materials from which they are made. Handweavers handle yarns differently from the way a power loom does, so yarns are made expressly for their use.

Knowledge of how and when to use certain fibers and the variety of yarns made from them comes from experience and familiarity with the medium; it seems almost instinctive after a while. There is a difference in rhythm, tension, and beating as you work with the various fibers. You will not find in any publication exact directions for using every yarn in all weaves and techniques because of the variety of yarns and fibers available and the endless ways of using them. In this book, rules for the sett of yarn for warp—how warp ends are to be spaced in the reed—are given in the section on warping. In the following descriptions of fibers there are guidelines you can apply to almost all weaving circumstances.

Cotton

Cotton is known the world over. The word itself comes from the Arabic *qutun*. It is a vegetable-seed fiber composed of unicellular hairs attached to the seeds of species of the genus *Gossypium*. This fiber can be from ½ inch (1.3 cm) to over 2 inches (5 cm) in length and the diameter is very small. The color of cotton is usually light to dark cream. The chemical composition is almost pure cellulose. Under the microscope a distinct feature of the cotton fiber is its twisted appearance.

Cotton plant, showing flower and boll beginning to open.

The cotton plant grows from 2 to 6 feet (0.6–1.8 m) high. The blossom falls off and in its place grows a green boll, which is the seed pod. In this boll are many dark seeds wrapped closely in a mass of hairy cotton fibers. When the boll is fully grown it turns brown and slowly opens. The cotton fibers come out in fluffy puffs.

After the cotton is picked, the first process is ginning, which removes the seeds. The cotton is then processed, as all fibers are, to remove impurities, straighten the fibers, and draw them out into a *roving* ready for spinning into yarn.

The quality of cotton yarn depends on the length and fineness of fiber. Cotton is generally classed by the geographical region of growth. It is grown in the warm regions of the world. Egyptian and United States cotton is a long, strong, fine fiber of good luster. Indian and Asiatic cottons are short, coarse fibers with little luster.

Cotton is an excellent yarn for the beginning weaver; it has high resistance to friction and is quite elastic. It has a lower tensile strength (resistance to breaking) than silk or linen but is stronger than wool. Cotton is stronger when wet. It also takes dye readily.

Some cotton yarn is *mercerized*. In this process the yarn is saturated with sodium hydroxide to change its appearance and properties. The fibers swell to a cylindrical shape and then shrink. Since the yarn is processed while under tension, the fibers tend to straighten out. The fibers become semitransparent and shiny, making the yarn smoother, heavier, shinier, and stronger than unmercerized cotton.

Cotton fiber can also be treated to resemble wool or have the appearance of silk; it is difficult sometimes to determine the fiber content of a specific yarn (tests to determine fiber content are discussed later in this book).

Flax/Linen

Linum usitatissimum is the botanical name for flax, the fiber from which linen yarns are spun, which derives its name from the Anglo-Saxon word *fleax*. *Flax* and *linen* are separate words, but they are as closely related as two can be without being synonymous.

Flax plant, which has a blue flower. The fiber from which linen yarn is spun comes from the stem.

Fiber flax grows much like wheat. The best climate is temperate, with ample rainfall. After the plant is harvested the fibers must be separated from the straw, and this is first done by *retting,* a sort of rotting process. There are two methods: dew retting,

which is spreading the harvested flax in the fields to allow the dew and sun to work on it, and water retting, which is done in tanks or brooks.

Scutching is next, a process to break the dried, brittle straw away from the supple fiber. The flax is passed between toothed gears, causing the brittle straw to break away.

The combing process called *hackling* follows. Handfuls of scutched flax are fed into a machine, which combs first with coarse and then with finer teeth. The flax is now in a continuous chain form and is called *flax line sliver*. The waste from the hackling process is called *machine tow*. Line fibers are at least 10 inches (25 cm) long; tow fiber is shorter. The fiber is now ready for spinning—it is this fiber that inspired the term "flaxen hair." Water-retted flax has a truly beautiful golden color and is lovely to handle.

A nineteenth-century hackle. The flax was pulled through the combs, cleaning out remaining pieces of straw and short fibers and putting the long fibers parallel ready for spinning.

Next the spinning process makes the fibers parallel and reduces the continuous chain to the required diameter. The flax line sliver is now drawn out or rubbed into a single strand with very little twist. In this form it is called *roving*.

There are three types of *flax line spinning:* dry, wet, and gill. As implied, *dry spinning* is without water. It produces yarns that are soft, hairy, more absorbent, and slubbier than wet-spun. Sizes of dry-spun are usually on the coarse or heavy side and rarely finer than 20 lea grey. (In linen, *lea* is the count or size.)

Wet spinning involves passing the roving through a trough of water heated to 160–180° F (72–82° C). This softens gums and waxes inherent in flax, allowing individual fibers to split or slip. It also reduces the diameter of the fiber, allowing more fibers in a given diameter—the more fibers, the stronger and more even the yarn. All sizes over 25 lea grey are wet-spun. Wet-spun flax is characteristically smoother and more even than dry-spun.

In *gill spinning* the drawing process continues, to produce a sliver very nearly ribbon-thin. The sliver is carried to the spinning rollers by gills, which are needles arranged much like a wire brush. After the sliver passes over a dampening roller, twist is accomplished in the usual manner. Gill spinning produces the soft suppleness of dry-spun, but the yarn is less hairy and more even.

Flax *tow yarns* are spun from the waste of the hackling machine process, using water-retted flax. Tow fibers are less than 10 inches (25 cm) long, and the yarn spun of tow usually contains straw, is uneven, and is much weaker than line yarn.

The term *grey* as applied to linen yarn means that the yarn or fiber remains in its natural state. Grey linen yarn, containing pectins, waxes, gum, and other impurities, gives off the offensive odor of the barnyard. You can smell it on the spool, so it is easy to detect. The odor disappears when the yarn is exposed to air but returns when it is damp. While the dark brown color may be attractive to the eye, the true nature of grey yarn must be considered. Grey yarn should not be used where there is any possibility of exposure to moisture other than in laundering. Because it will retain moisture, it becomes subject to mildew and rot.

Boiling is a highly specialized chemical treatment that removes gum and impurities. The yarn must be neutralized so that it will be neither acid nor alkaline. This yarn has been termed "natural" by the industry. In the boiling process there is 10 to 20 percent weight loss.

Linen is characteristically slubby (a slub is a thick section), and even the best of wet-spun line yarns will have the occasional slub and bit of straw. Tow yarns are slubbier in nature. "Slubby," or "lumpy," tows are purposely spun with exaggerated, pronounced slubs, giving a homespun look. Single tow yarns are usually confined to use as weft yarns. When a natural fiber is used as a warp yarn, it is usually plied and used under low tension with short beating to avoid friction. However, single-ply linen in both warp and weft produces fabric that is soft and smooth when properly finished.

Flax absorbs about 20 percent of its own weight in moisture without getting wet on the surface. Linen yarns are the strongest of all natural fibers. Linen has little if any stretch and does not shrink. It is notoriously hard to dye.

It is generally recognized that the very best quality linen yarns come from the United Kingdom: the dry-spuns from Scotland and wet-spun and finest sizes from Northern Ireland.

Ramie, Jute, Sisal, and Hemp

These plant fibers have physical and chemical properties similar to those of flax. They are mostly grown in the tropics and produce coarser yarn than linen.

The *ramie* plant produces the finest yarn because it has a very long fiber. Most ramie comes from China, so it is sometimes called China grass. This fiber produces yarn stronger than cotton of the same size, and its strength increases twofold when wet. It will not shrink and is immune to mildew, which attacks other natural fibers.

The ramie fiber is difficult to prepare for spinning into yarn. The silk-like fibers lie between the plant bark and a pithy core and are not easy to separate.

Ramie yarn is very attractive, somewhat resembling linen. However, unlike linen, it *does* dye very easily and is colorfast. This fiber has good absorption. It has a very smooth surface and is therefore less susceptible to dirt and can be easily washed or cleaned.

Its tensile strength is greater than that of linen, hemp, or cotton and can be maintained for long periods, which makes ramie excellent for warp yarn.

Jute plants grow 12 feet (3.6 m) tall. They produce a yarn that is heavy but soft and easy to work with and takes dye very easily. Most jute comes from India.

Sisal is a hard leaf fiber from the sisal plant. This fiber is light yellow or white and is very strong and durable. *Binder twine* is sisal fiber. Its primary purpose is to bind bales of hay and straw. Handweavers use binder twine to add stiffness to weaving and in pieces that will be exposed to the weather. Sisal is native to Indonesia, East and West Africa, and Haiti.

Hemp plants produce fibers from 3 to 8 feet (0.9–2.4 m) long that are used mostly for rope but can also be spun and woven. It is believed to be the first plant cultivated for its fiber. First grown in China, it is now found in almost every country of the world.

Hemp plant, which has small greenish flowers.

Although the above-mentioned fibers are coarse, they go through a process similar to that used for linen to prepare them for spinning into yarn.

Wool

The most indestructible fiber ever discovered, wool is probably the one most used by handweavers. The term *wool* is generally applied to the fine, soft fibrous covering of sheep, but can also refer to the hair of the angora or the cashmere goat, the camel, alpaca, and vicuña. We commonly use the terms *wool, hair,* and sometimes *fur* for the same fiber. They are closely related, but, to be exact, the term *hair* is used when the individual fibers are coarse and straight; if they are fine and thick, they are *fur;* and if they are fine and kinky—with a rough surface making them easy to mat or stick together—they are *wool.*

Animal fibers:
1. Wool—fine and kinky fibers that stick together.
2. Fur—fine, thick fibers.
3. Hair—coarse, with straight fibers.

Like all fibers, wool goes through many operations or processes to become yarn. It is first sorted to separate the different grades. After reaching the mill it goes through a number of stages to convert the raw fiber to spun yarn.

1. **Washing.** During washing or scouring, the wool is moved gently by rakes through a series of tubs containing a soap and water solution. Then it is rinsed in clear water. During the washing process the wool loses 30 to 70 percent of its weight as the natural grease and dirt are removed. Then the wool is passed through squeeze rollers and dried.
2. **Dyeing.** Putting color in wool can be done at several different points in the overall processing. Bulk wool can be

dyed immediately after washing in large steel pressure kettles. It can also be dyed after it is spun into yarn; the spindle on which the yarn is wound is dipped into dye vats. Or the fabric can be dyed after it has been woven. In this case, it is passed over a series of rollers that distribute the dye.

3. **Blending.** There is great variety in natural color and quality of wool. To obtain uniformity in the spun yarn, various lots must be mechanically mixed or blended. At this time, oil and water are sprayed over the wool to keep the fibers pliable.

4. **Carding.** This process combs the wool and aligns the fibers. The wool is drawn through rollers covered with fine teeth. The wool fibers are straightened and pulled into a thin web. The web is divided into strips and rubbed together to form *roving*, a single strand of loose fibers with very little twist. Woolen fabric can be made from this roving; it is relatively thick, fuzzy fabric.

5. **Combing.** To produce worsted yarn for fabric that has a crisp, smooth surface, the wool is combed. The web goes through additional machines to further straighten and line up the fibers and remove short pieces. The fiber is then condensed into a thin strand.

6. **Drawing.** For worsted yarn, the fiber is further reduced to a thin, slightly twisted roving.

7. **Spinning.** Spools of roving are put on spinning frames and the roving is pulled through rollers that further draw out the fibers. It is then wound on revolving bobbins that apply a twist to the roving and make yarn. This yarn is now ready for the weaving process.

The principal advantages of wool yarn are its strength, elasticity, texture, and color. Even the finest spun wool is very strong. Wool fiber can be drawn out to more than one half its length and then return to its former length without damage. The fact that wool tends to stretch can present problems for the novice handweaver, but they will be overcome through experience.

Wool has beautiful natural color but is also one of the easiest fibers to dye because of a central canal that permits the dye to penetrate the fiber.

Wool has the finest texture. The outer scales tend to interlock with each other, binding the fibers together. Wool can be spun into yarn that is smooth or rough, fine or heavy; it is said to have "life."

A wide variety of projects can be woven with wool yarn. It is ideal for clothing, rugs, table pieces, and wall hangings. It is easily cleaned with proper care. If you want to spin your own yarn, wool is ideal. The best wool is produced in climates that are cold and damp. Wool is a universal fiber.

Silk

Silk is a continuous protein filament produced by the silkworm larvae when constructing their cocoons. The finest fiber of silk is produced by the silkworm that feeds on mulberry leaves. Silkworms are difficult to raise. They are fed for seven weeks on mulberry leaves. From two hundred trees about five pounds of silk can be produced. There is a lot of work involved in tending the trees, feeding the worms, and reeling the silk from the cocoons. An unpleasant odor also accompanies the process, as each cocoon contains the remains of the worm.

Silk fiber, when unwound from the cocoon, is double: two filaments are glued together with a gum secretion called sericin. One cocoon produces up to 1,500 yards (1,370 m). Raw silk does not have all the sericin removed and thus is yellowish in color. To remove the sericin from raw silk, you simply boil the fiber in a very strong solution of mild soap. Boil for about one hour at 200° F (94° C). This will not injure the fiber. Then rinse in hot water to remove the gum and sap.

The length of the silk filament makes twisting or spinning unncessary. Silk has many remarkable qualities: even though it is extremely fine, it is one of the strongest fibers and is quite elastic.

Silk yarn for handweavers is not as readily available as other natural fibers. Heavy silk, usually raw silk, is as easy to weave as mercerized cotton. Very fine silk, however, falls into another class and should be attempted only by the very experienced handweaver. Some special equipment, such as small-eyed heddles, is helpful when weaving fine silk. A high degree of skill is required to handle this yarn, mainly because it is so fine and tends to slip. Warp yarns must be close sett (close together) and the weft firmly beaten because the weave will become loose after washing. If the warp becomes electrostatic, it should be moistened with water to maintain a good shed, or vertical separation of the threads for the shuttle to pass through.

Synthetic, Artificial, or Man-made Fiber

Man-made fibers were successfully introduced early in the 1900s. *Rayon* was the first such. It is said to have been invented for the sole purpose of imitating silk. Rayon is made from cellulose, the fibrous substance in plant life, so it is not a true synthetic fiber. Rayon yarn can resemble other fibers, such as cotton and wool. It is easy to dye, has high natural luster, and is luxurious and economical.

True synthetic fibers are made by chemical synthesis or compounds. Raw materials such as nitrogen, oxygen, hydrogen, and carbon are combined with other ingredients to form long-chain polymers from which fibers are made and texturized. Their advantages are that they are strong, soft, and very resistant to wear, heat, and decomposition. It was the development of the texturizing processes (making a smooth fiber rough, kinky, sticky, hairy, slubby, or whatever) that made the use of synthetic fibers so popular. Before that, most synthetics were available only in a smooth or silk-like texture and very limited colors. Some trade names of synthetic fibers refer to the texturizing method, not the chemical composition.

The handweaver will find that synthetic yarns are economical and readily available but more difficult to handle than natural-fiber yarns. Some tend to be too rigid when

stretched, yet weak when tied in a knot. The touch or feel of most synthetic fiber is not as pleasant as that of a natural fiber and the color is not always true. Some yarns also tend to be "sticky"; that is, they cling together, making their use as warp yarns sometimes troublesome. New developments may correct some of these problems.

Synthetic fibers are generally made to have qualities and characteristics for specific purposes; however, because of current labeling practices, quite often the handweaver finds it almost impossible to take advantage of the qualities of an individual synthetic yarn.

How to Distinguish Fibers

Many yarns available for handweaving do not bear labels giving fiber content of that particular yarn, and a weaver may not be able to distinguish with a glance at a yarn one fiber from another. Fibers are mixed in spinning, and chemical treatments such as mercerizing and dyeing change appearance and properties, making the fiber identification of a specific yarn difficult.

There are, however, a few tests you can perform to identify fiber content. They are appearance, physical properties, burn test, and microscope. You may have to use several tests to determine the fiber content of some yarns, and certainly you will have to make at least two tests on yarn that has a fiber mixture.

Appearance: If a yarn is shiny, it could be rayon, silk, or perle cotton. If it is glossy, it might be silk or mercerized cotton; if slightly glossy, linen or wool. If it appears dull, it is probably cotton.

Physical properties: This test usually applies to tensile strength or resistance to breaking. The simplest test for strength is pulling the yarn between both hands. If it breaks easily it could be wool, rayon, or linen tow; cotton would be a little harder to break; linen, ramie, or silk are almost impossible to break; and many synthetics, such as nylon, *are* impossible to break by hand. A yarn fiber that has no elasticity is linen.

Burn test: This is the quickest and easiest way to determine a natural from a synthetic. Take a small piece of yarn, about 4 inches (10 cm), and burn the end of it. When it cools, pinch the burned end between your fingers. If it crumbles to ash, it is a natural fiber; but if the burned end is a hard bead, then it is a synthetic fiber. The odor of burned yarn will help to identify the fiber further. Wool and silk smell like burned feathers or hair; when burned, they form a black bead that very easily crumbles to ash. Cotton, linen, hemp, and rayon burn with an uneven flame, form no bead, and smell like burning paper. Nylon yarn melts, burns with a small flame, and forms a dark, hard bead. Orlon also melts but has a bright white flame, smokes, and forms a hard bead.

Microscope examination: By looking at yarn under a microscope you can determine content by the appearance of the fiber. Wool has visible scales on all sides and marks across the fiber; cotton or jute has ribbonlike fibers with ends spread, tapered, or cut at an angle; linen or hemp have marks across the fiber-like stalks, while bent fibers have broken curves and tapered ends; rayon has regular fibers with no marks.

At first, study known samples of yarn to distinguish their different smells, and to get acquainted with their characteristic behavior.

Flax, silk, cotton, wool, and synthetic fiber, as seen greatly magnified.

Yarn Count or Size

The *count* of yarn is the numerical designation to indicate size. It is the relationship of length to weight, a measure of fineness or thickness of yarn.

There are several methods of yarn count. One, used for most spun yarns, is based on the number of standard lengths per standard weight. The following table shows the number of yards of yarn in 1 pound of cotton, linen, wool, and worsted.

Size	Cotton	Linen	Wool	Worsted
1	840 yds.	300 yds.	256 yds.	560 yds.
2	1,680 yds.	600 yds.	512 yds.	1,120 yds.

The lower numbers mean heavier yarn, while the high numbers refer to fine yarn. Note that, for instance, a number 1 yarn means a different length in each type of fiber.

Another method of yarn count is based on the number of standard weights per standard length. The measure is in *deniers* and is used for silk and man-made fibers. The low number is finer yarn, while the higher number is the thicker yarn. The denier system has become standard all over the world. Denier is the number of unit weights of 0.05 gram per 450-meter length, being equivalent numerically to the number of grams per 9,000 meters.

Another numbering system known as the *Tex System* is intended to replace the many diverse methods in existence. The Tex number of a yarn is the weight in grams of a 1-kilometer length.

To convert within 1 percent an English number to metric, divide the English number of yards per pound by 500. Example: number 8 cotton is number 13 metric. Number 8 cotton has 6,720 yards per pound, so:

$$\frac{6,720}{500} = 13.4, \text{ or } \#13$$

Handweavers must rely on yarn manufacturers to furnish the correct information concerning nature, composition, size, and yardage of their yarns. For a given project it is important to know the yardage of the yarn in order to figure the quantity required.

Ply

When a number of single strands of yarn are twisted together, they form *ply* yarn, which may be two-ply, three-ply, and so on. The size of yarn and number of ply are usually written like a fraction, the yarn size above the ply count.

Yarn is plied for several reasons: for strength, for color effect, or to combine different fibers and/or textures. For warp, ply yarn is superior to single yarn, especially for the beginner. The feel and appearance of the woven piece greatly depend on whether single or ply yarn is used in warp, in weft, or in both.

A two-ply yarn is twice as thick as a single-ply; therefore the yardage is just half. For example, if you wish to figure out the yardage for size 5 two-ply cotton, start with the fact that size 1 cotton has 840 yards per pound, so size 5 would have 5 × 840, or 4,200 yards. Since it is two-ply, the yardage is half, or 2,100 yards per pound.

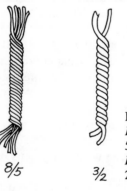

Plied yarn:
Left: Size 8 yarn, 5 ply (8/5).
Right: Size 3 yarn, 2 ply (3/2).

Type of Twist

The *twist* of yarn will affect its texture. Twisting is the process of spinning raw fibers into yarn. Yarns are spun to obtain strength, smoothness, uniformity, and novelty.

All fibers, natural or synthetic, are available in different forms. Cotton and wool come in short lengths called *staples,* and silk is produced in a long strand called *continuous filament.* Synthetic fibers are produced in either staple or continuous-filament form. Staple fibers are spun or twisted into yarn, while continuous filament needs no further spinning or twist.

Twists in yarn are classified according to direction and amount or pitch of twist. *S* and *Z* describe the direction. By holding yarn in a vertical position you can determine the direction. If the spirals conform to the central portion of the letter *S*, we call it *S-twist, left-*

S and Z twists show direction yarn is spun.

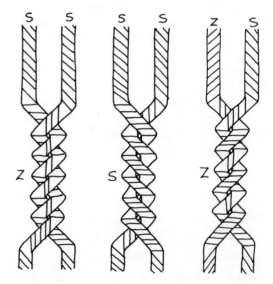

Yarns spun and plied with various combinations of S and Z twists. Similar twists produce a softer yarn, while opposing twists cause the yarn to be tighter and harder when plied.

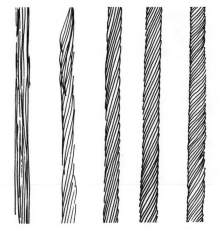

The amount of twist in yarn determines its strength. No twist shows the fibers parallel; this is very soft, weak yarn. With more twist in the yarn, it becomes stronger and harder.

A variety of novelty yarns are spun by combining yarns of varying amount and direction of twist and plying some of them with an uneven tension. Different colors and fibers can be combined for additional interest within one yarn.

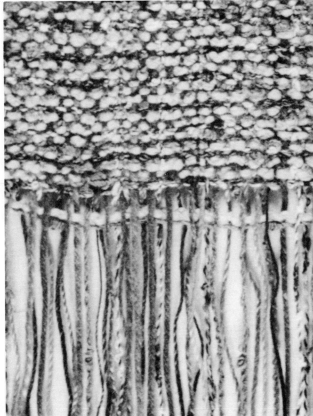

A variety of novelty yarns in warp and weft are used in this fabric.

hand, or *counterclockwise twist*. And if the spirals conform to the central portion of the letter Z, we call it *Z-twist, right-hand,* or *clockwise twist*. The direction of twist in yarn can affect the appearance of the woven piece. Yarns of the same twist in warp and weft can produce a stiff fabric, while a much smoother fabric results when warp and weft have opposite twists. Plied yarns are usually doubled or folded with an opposing twist to prevent overtwist and hardening of the yarn.

The amount of twist in yarn can range from none at all to a very tight twist, whether S or Z. No twist is when the fibers lie parallel. This yarn is weak, very soft, and normally used for weft only. A tight-twist yarn is very strong and hard and is used mostly for warp.

The term *novelty* applies to yarns twisted in a manner that gives them an unusual or special effect, which may be of surface, texture, or color. Such yarns may have nubs, flakes, loops, beads, lumps, or color combinations.

Novelty yarns can be produced by combining or plying yarns of different size and color. Also, in spinning, textural effects can be achieved by using varying amounts of fiber and applying uneven tension to the yarn as it is spun.

Color

The process of putting color in yarn is called *dyeing*. One can dye unspun fiber, yarn, or the woven fabric itself. *Stock-dyed* means that the fiber has the color put in before spinning; *yarn-dyed,* that the yarn is dyed after spinning; *piece-dyed,* that the woven fabric is dyed. For the handweaver, stock-dyed yarns are most satisfactory. If fibers such as linen that do not receive color easily are yarn-dyed, sometimes the color does not penetrate thoroughly.

Packaging

Yarn for handweaving is *put up*—packaged or made available—in several ways: on cones, on tubes, in balls, and in skeins. A cone can sit on the floor while you are preparing the yarn for your warp, and the yarn will pull directly from it without becoming tangled. A tube can be put on a spool rack so it will rotate freely as the yarn is drawn off. A ball of yarn can be put in a bowl or other container while it is being used. You should never let a cone, tube, or ball of yarn roll around the floor. It could collect dust or lint, and also the amount of spin in the yarn could be affected.

Yarn that comes in skeins must be handled in a different manner. There are two different types of skein: a pull skein, where the yarn can be pulled directly out of the skein for use, and another type that must be put on a winder, or swift, to be used.

A tube of yarn.

A ball of yarn in a bowl.

Yarns that are put up in skeins are nearly all handspun, but some less expensive yarns are also packaged this way. Very good quality wool keeps best stored in skeins. In this form the wool is not stretched and thus will retain its natural elasticity. To be able to handle a skein of yarn properly, you should have a piece of equipment known as a *swift*. There are several types. The *umbrella swift* is attractive in design, can be used upright as well as on its side, and is adjustable for any size skein. While in use, it must be mounted (usually by a clamp) on some stationary base. A *squirrel cage winder or swift* sits on the floor and can be moved to any location for convenience. It is also adjustable. The drums must be parallel, or yarn will pile against the flange of the drums and not unwind easily. *Antique skein winders and clock reels* are beautiful pieces of equipment. Some are adjustable to accommodate any size skein; many, however, are not, so that most commercial skeins of yarn will not fit them.

Unless a skein comes untied, it can be easily opened and put to use if you follow a few simple procedures.

To open a skein means to untwist it, stretch it between your hands, or put it on

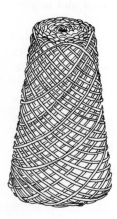

A cone of yarn.

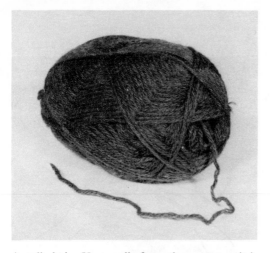

A pull skein. Yarn pulls from the center as it is used.

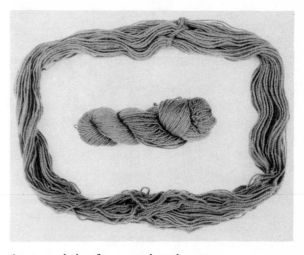

An open skein of yarn ready to be put on a swift, and a skein twisted and folded for storage.

An umbrella swift, adjustable for any size skein of yarn. ▼

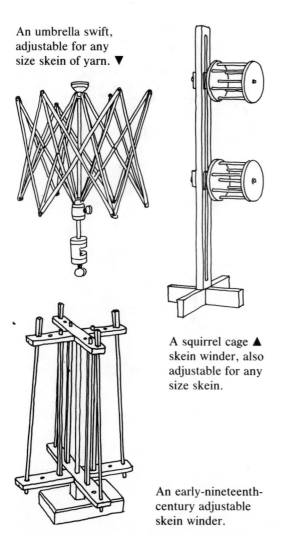

A squirrel cage ▲ skein winder, also adjustable for any size skein.

An early-nineteenth-century adjustable skein winder.

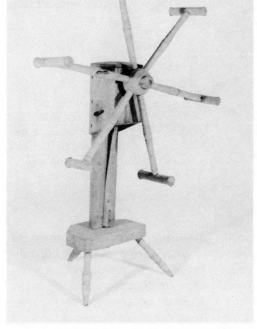

A nineteenth-century clock reel. This type was used to make skeins from hand-spun yarn. It is not adjustable. Each turn is counted by the clock mechanism.

The strands are tied to keep the ends in order: the tie goes in and out.

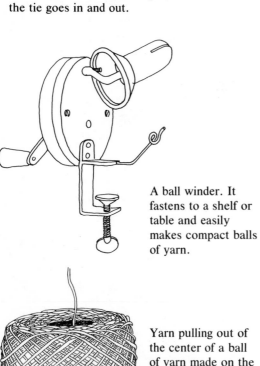

A ball winder. It fastens to a shelf or table and easily makes compact balls of yarn.

Yarn pulling out of the center of a ball of yarn made on the ball winder. The ball has a flat top and bottom for easy storage.

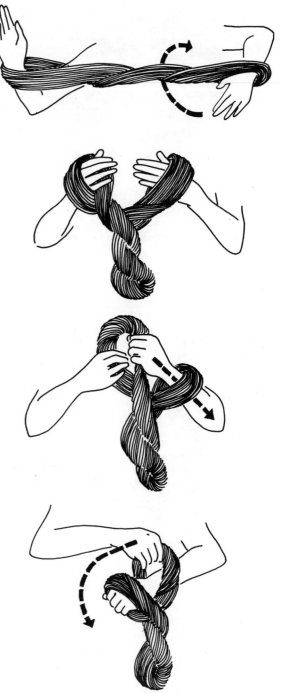

Steps in twisting a skein of yarn ready to be stored for future use.

a swift. Make sure it is opened in the right place and that all yarn goes in the same direction; that is, the yarn must not turn and go in the opposite direction at the ties in the skein. The ties do not completely circle the yarn but twine in and out. Now put the yarn on a swift and make it taut. Find the ends of the yarn. Quite often they are attached to the ties; both ends may be in one section of the ties or on opposite sides of the skein.

Other ties are not attached to the yarn but merely hold it. Remove any holding ties, untie the ends, and start unwinding the yarn with one end. Turn the skein over until the yarn unwinds freely. Never try to straighten it by pulling one end of the yarn through the skein.

If you don't use all the yarn in the skein, tie it together again, remove it from the skein winder, twist the skein, and tuck one looped end into the other loop. It is ready to be stored for future use. A tied skein may be tangled if it is "opened," that is, untwisted, but it is not snarled. If a skein is untied and one end passed through a part of the skein, it becomes snarled. A tangled skein can be straightened; a snarled skein is hopeless.

We all know how to make a ball of yarn by winding the yarn around our fingers, but a very neat ball can be made with a device called a *ball winder*. The balls made on a winder will feed from the center and will stack nicely for storing.

Yarn Treatment

In handweaving, nearly all treatment or finishing of yarn is done after the weaving is completed. Occasionally, however, it is advisable to process the yarn before it is woven. You may want to test colorfastness and shrinkage or put a dressing (conditioner) on "hard to handle" yarn.

Soft water at about 110° F (44° C) is appropriate for wool. If washing wool, use soap with a low pH and always keep water at the same low temperature for wash and rinse. The important thing is to avoid "shocking" wool. Do this by avoiding quick temperature changes or hard squeezing or shaking. Act as though you were hand-washing fine clothing. Washing improves linen and does not affect cotton, but wool is lightly felted: in washing, fibers lock together and some shrinkage occurs.

If using very fine yarn, loosely twisted yarn, yarn that fuzzes, or homespun yarn, you will find that putting on a dressing makes it easier to handle. Always put yarn in skeins and tie them properly or have a prepared warp securely tied. Immerse the yarn in a dressing made by boiling flaxseed in water until you have a thick gelatinous liquid. Use approximately one part flaxseed to eight parts water. Strain out the flaxseed before putting the yarn in the liquid. After the yarn is thoroughly wet, remove it from the liquid and let it dry before putting it on the loom. The piece woven from this yarn should be washed in gentle suds to remove the dressing.

Flaxseed can be purchased at a drugstore. The flaxseed can be boiled in fresh water as many as four times; a small quantity of seed makes a large amount of dressing. Keep the seed in a tightly covered jar ready for use. Use full strength for fine yarn. Dilute with water to the consistency of thin starch for strong yarn.

3

mmmmmmmmmmmmmmmmmmmmmmmmmmm

Handspinning and Natural Dyeing

Even though there are beautiful, good-quality yarns readily available, it is natural for handweavers to want to create their own yarn. It is said that if the loom is the most important tool of the trade, the spinning wheel has second place. By hand-spinning, it is very easy to make yarn exactly as you want it: thick or thin, smooth or slubby, tight or loose (soft), and of any desired fiber. Spinning is a logical part of the craft of weaving.

All you need to start is a drop spindle. A *spindle* is a shaft with a weight. Spinning on a drop spindle is relatively slow, but you have control of the size of yarn you make. Spinning on a spinning wheel is much faster, and the process of handling the fiber is just the same as with a spindle.

When first attempting spinning, it is ideal to start with the small investment of a drop spindle. You can have the experience of spinning many different fibers as well as learning how to clean, store, and prepare these fibers for spinning. Then, if you enjoy spinning, you can purchase a spinning wheel suited to your style and manner of spinning.

Preparing Wool for Spinning

Wool is the easiest fiber to hand-spin and generally the most accessible. Wool fiber can be purchased from a local sheep raiser, at many local shops, and by mail order. If you are lucky enough to live near a Wool Grower's Co-operative warehouse, then you can actually see the wide variety of textures and natural shades that are available in wool fiber. You will also get firsthand information concerning breeds of sheep and grading of wool fiber.

All the wool from one sheep is called a fleece. Within one fleece there are a number of different kinds of wool. The illustration shows an open wool fleece with tip ends (outer wool) facing up. By close examination, it is easy to see the kinds of wool from

Lightweight whorl drop spindle, excellent for using when learning to spin.

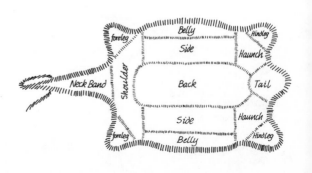

PLAIN-WEAVE FABRIC WITH HAND-SPUN YARN.

Wool.   Silk (woven by Christina Smucker).

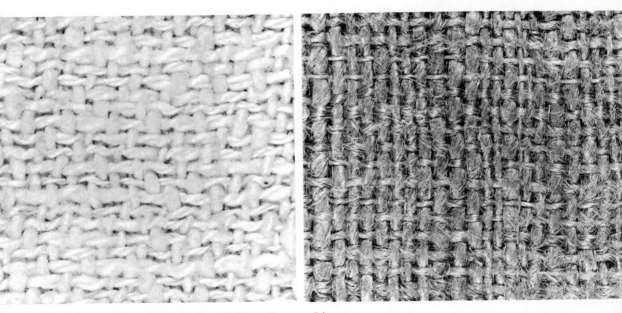

Two-ply cotton (woven by Corinne Whitesell).   Linen.

the different parts of the body. Generally the best wool is the sides, shoulders, and forward part of the back, and sometimes the neck wool. The belly has very soft, fine wool that is not strong. The tail and hind legs have strong wool that, if not too dirty, is the easiest to spin. The foreleg and haunch wool is

not of much use. The back wool tends to be weak, but the fiber has nice length. For a given project the wool should be used from one area because of the differences in the way it spins, its affinity to color, tensile strength, and felting qualities. (Felting occurs when heat, moisture, and pressure are applied, causing the fibers to interlock with each other, forming a compact material. Wool fibers felt differently depending on their structure, curliness, length, and size, or thickness.)

When the fleece is sheared from the sheep, it is put in a bundle by folding each side by thirds lengthwise, rolled up, and secured with the neckband; the cut side is out. It is easy to open a fleece by unrolling it.

Since the many breeds of sheep produce many varieties of wool, there are wool fibers for spinning very fine, soft yarn or heavy, coarse yarn.

Sheep Breeds and Grades by Count*

American, or		
Delaine Merino	64–80	Fine-wool breeds
Rambouillet	62–70	
Corriedale	50–60	
Columbia	50–60	
Panama	50–58	Crossbreed-wool breeds
Romeldale	58–60	
Targhee	58–60	
Southdown	56–60	
Shropshire	48–56	
Hampshire	48–56	
Suffolk	48–56	Medium-wool breeds
Oxford	46–50	
Dorset	48–56	
Cheviot	48–56	
Lincoln	36–46	
Cotswold	36–40	Long-wool breeds
Romney	40–48	

*Count refers to the number of 560-yard hanks spun from one pound of wool top (commercially cleaned and combed wool fiber). The count for each breed can vary, in each animal, outside these generally accepted limits.
Figures from American Sheep Producers Council

Staple is the term to indicate the lengths of fiber. When choosing your fleece, look for a staple that is at least 4 inches (10 cm) long, is not brittle or discolored, and is reasonably free of foreign matter. It should also feel free and airy and have luster (some breeds have more than others).

The natural grease in wool is called *lanolin,* and if the fleece is old, the lanolin is what makes it yellow. We generally refer to wool fleece as being white or black, but a black fleece can be many shades of grays and browns. Within each fleece there are also several shadings of one color that all blend well together.

After choosing the fleece you must prepare the fiber for spinning. You can remove the grease before or after spinning. If the wool is reasonably clean and free of foreign matter, it is easier to spin with the grease still in it. However, if it is quite dirty or you find the odor objectionable, then wash it before spinning.

Remember, to wash wool, use soap with a low pH and treat the wool gently, as you would hand-wash delicate clothing. *Never* put it in a washer or dryer. Use water of the same temperature for wash and rinse. You can damage the fibers by temperature shock and abrasion.

When wool is washed and stored for a period of time it will become dry and difficult to spin. It is possible to put an oil dressing (spinning oil) on the wool to make it manageable, as if it contained some of the natural lanolin. For every 10 pounds (4.5 kg) of wool to be oiled, mix 1 cup of olive oil, 1 tablespoon of ammonia, and 6 cups of cold water. Do not substitute baby oil or mineral oil for olive oil. Spray the wool, allowing the solution to penetrate the fibers.

Now the fibers are ready to be combed or carded, to straighten and arrange them. The method used determines the textural qualities of the spun yarn. *Carding* separates and evenly distributes the fibers. *Combing* straightens and arranges the fibers parallel to one another and in the direction of the yarn when spun. Carding is done with hand cards by the spinner, but combing generally is not a hand technique.

Worsted is the term applied to yarn spun from combed wool. Yarn spun from carded wool is softer but weaker, while yarn spun from combed wool is stronger and smoother. They can both be spun with a hard (tight) or soft (loose) twist.

To hand-card wool, use two *hand cards.*

They are identical, but mark them for the right and left hands and always use them that way because the teeth get worn in a certain direction with use and a switch will loosen them. Cards are rectangular-shaped pieces of wood with handles, backed on one side with wirelike hooks or teeth embedded in leather, composition-coated cloth, or cardboard. A good pair of hand cards will last a long time if properly cared for.

A variety of hand cards:
Left: Sturdy cards with a flat bed, which are easy to use.
Right: Curved-bed cards, which are nice for shaping the carded wool on the back.
Center: A flicker; used singly, this carder teases small amounts of wool at a time.

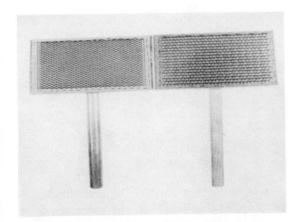

Wires or teeth on hand cards:
Left: Coarse for carding strong coarse fibers—helpful in removing foreign matter and best for unwashed wool.
Right: Fine for delicate fibers and washed wool—will better separate the fibers.

Steps in the Hand-Carding Process

1. Take the left card, place it on your left knee, and grasp it with the left hand, palm up. The handle is pointing away from the body. With the right hand, stretch a loose handful of fibers on the card, attaching them to the hooks. Cover the entire surface with a layer, aligning the fibers as much as possible. (If the fiber has been washed, it is difficult to line up the fibers.)

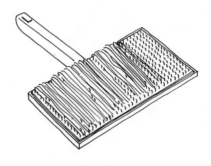

2. Grasp the right card in the right hand with palm down. Put it on top of the left card and brush it over the left card by pulling toward the body. Repeat this brushing motion several times. The fibers will begin to align and most will be on the right card.

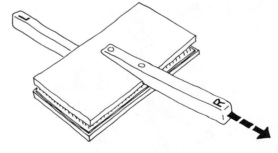

3. Change the position of the right card and move it across the left card. This puts all fibers on the left card. Brush again as in step 2.

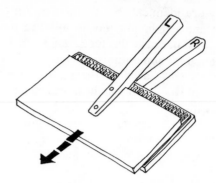

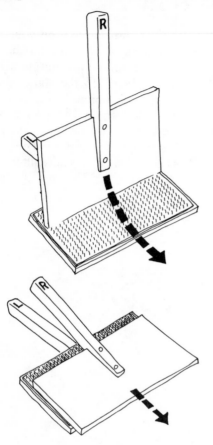

Repeat these steps several times until the fiber is well brushed on both sides. Briefly, the steps in carding are: brush, put fiber on left card, brush, put fiber on right card, and repeat as long as necessary (this depends on the fleece), ending with the fibers on the left card.

Now gently move the fibers from left to right card and from right to left card several more times until the fibers rest loosely on the right card. For the most part the fibers lie perpendicular to the length and are fluffy.

5. With the back of the left card, gently curl or roll the fibers toward the handle of the right card. This roll of fiber is the *rolag*. Air has been put into the fibers. The rolag is now ready to be spun into yarn.

4. Put the right card on your right knee and, with the left card on top, move it across, putting the fibers on the right card. Brush again as in step 2.

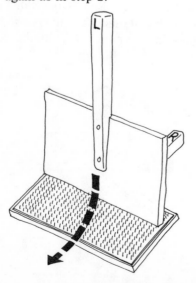

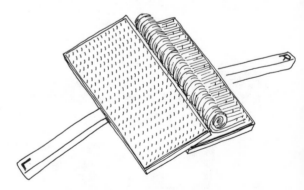

To use the *flick carder:* Clench a "lock" of wool in one hand. In the other hand, loosely hold the carder by putting the thumb on top next to the index finger. This eliminates tension in the hand. Now gently "flick" the wrist and slap the wool. Do not comb or brush through the fibers. Flick one end of the wool three or four times, then turn it 180 degrees and flick the other end.

The fibers will be free and airy, no longer sticking together, and ready for spinning. When first using the flicker, rest the hand and wool on a flat surface. This will help eliminate the possibility of hitting your fingers with the carder.

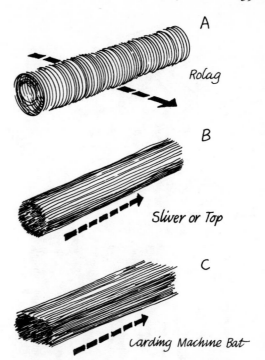

Direction of fibers after carding or combing:
   A. Rolag—carded wool.
   B. Top, roving, or sliver—combed wool.
   C. Piece of a bat—made on the bench carder.
Rolag and top are sometimes called sliver.

Combed wool is generally prepared commercially and can be purchased in roving or top form: this is a continuous sliver with all fibers parallel. *Roving* is a strand usually the size of a pencil; *top* is a larger group of fibers forming a strand about 1½ inches (3.8 cm) in diameter.

Another piece of equipment that prepares fibers for spinning is the *bench carder*. It has two drums covered with wire teeth, like those on the hand cards. The wool fibers are teased or pulled apart and gently fed onto the drums, which are turned by a crank. The fibers are stretched and pulled in the same direction as the drums rotate. To remove the fibers from the drum, use a knitting needle to lift them from the carding cloth. Lift and pull apart small sections of the fibers as the needle slides across the drum.

The fiber comes off in a *bat* form and is spun by separating strips in the direction of the fiber. This wool closely resembles combed wool. It can also be pulled apart against the direction of the fiber in single strips, or in an alternating manner to create a long strip. The fibers are now in a form more like carded wool, but it is very difficult to pull the bat apart in this manner. Never

Top, which is commercially cleaned and combed fiber, is available in almost all vegetable, animal, and synthetic fibers.

Close-up of wool top.

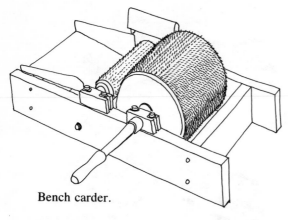

Bench carder.

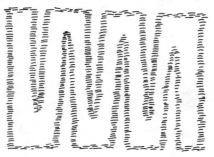

A bat of wool made on a bench carder can be put in strips in one of several ways for spinning.
Top: The fibers are like carded wool.
Bottom: The fibers are parallel to each other, as in combed wool.

use scissors to cut wool fibers in unspun form.

A bench carder must be well adjusted or it will pull and tear the wool fibers. This method of preparing fibers for spinning is not quicker than hand carding, but it is an easier way of handling short fibers and of

carding together fibers of different colors and textures in blending your own yarns.

When spinning yarn for a given project, do not mix hand-carded and bench-carded fibers. They each spin differently and will produce dissimilar textures.

Spinning is much easier for the beginner if the wool is carded. Wool can, however, be spun without carding or combing. It should be reasonably clean, and the fibers should be in order just as they were sheared from the sheep.

Take special care when storing wool fleece. It is best stored in cardboard cartons lined with heavy brown paper and sealed. Moths are attracted to it, so it is best to include some mothballs. Plastic bags are not recommended for storage because the wool can sweat and pack very firmly, necessitating more carding or combing. Any moisture can also cause mildew and mold that is impossible to remove. *Note:* If the wool is not thoroughly dry, oxidation can cause a rise in temperature so great as to set the wool on fire by spontaneous combustion.

If wool has been washed it can be mothproofed with oil of eucalyptus. Just add a few drops of the oil to enough cool water to be soaked up by the clean, damp wool. After the wool is thoroughly dry it can be stored, but the mothproofing process must be repeated each time the wool is washed. The eucalyptus has a clean, fresh scent.

It is advisable that you have a tetanus immunization if you are working with unwashed wool. Tetanus, or "lockjaw," infection can occur from wounds contaminated by earth or manure. A simple cut on your hand could become infected.

How to Spin Wool on a Drop Spindle

A *drop spindle* is simply a stick with a notch at one end and a weight called a *whorl* at the other end. The whorl can be wood, clay, a potato, a stone, or any object that has enough weight. The spinner attaches the fibers to the notch and allows the whorl to pull the fibers down in a twirling or spinning

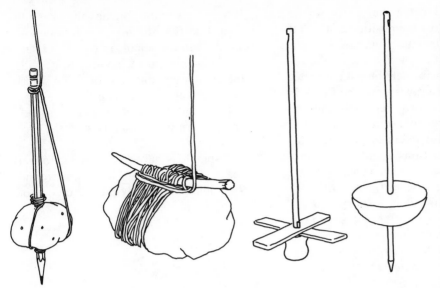

A variety of drop spindles: *Left to right:* Homemade spindle, using a potato and a pencil; primitive spindle, using a stone and a twig; Turkish spindle (spun yarn is wound in a figure-eight manner around the crosspieces, and then they are pushed off the spindle and the yarn is in ball form); heavy, well-balanced spindle.

motion. The spinner draws out the fibers and with the fingers forms them into a yarn while the spindle twists them into a continuous strand. When the spindle reaches the ground, the spinner winds the finished yarn around the spindle, attaches the yarn to the notch, and repeats the process.

When starting, use a spindle with a light-weight whorl. The downward pull of the weight tends to make the fibers pull apart and the yarn breaks. When you have experience in spinning, a heavier whorl is preferable as it spins more easily and allows more range in types of yarn that can be spun. Wool is the easiest fiber to spin on a drop spindle.

Here are the steps in spinning on a drop spindle:

1. Take about 2 yards (1.8 m) of yarn and tie one end around the spindle above the whorl. Wind the yarn on the spindle until 18 inches (45 cm) is left. Now pass the yarn over and under the whorl and around the spindle at the bottom. Bring the yarn to the top and secure it around the notch with a hitch.

Hitch to secure yarn at top of spindle.

2. Lay a rolag over the back of the left hand. With the right hand holding the spindle yarn, lay it over the rolag, holding it with the first finger and thumb of the left hand.

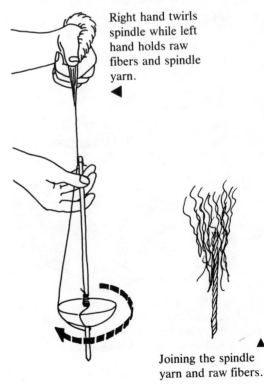

Right hand twirls spindle while left hand holds raw fibers and spindle yarn. ◀

Joining the spindle yarn and raw fibers. ▲

3. With the right hand, take hold of the spindle near the notch and give it a twirl or spin to the right.

4. The right hand then moves up to grip the fibers just below the position of the left hand. The thumb and finger of the right hand draw out a few fibers from the rolag, which is being held by the left hand. This action of drawing out the fibers is called *drafting*. (The term has another and distinctly different meaning for weavers: it also refers to pattern notation, or instructions about use of harnesses and treadles in the actual weaving of cloth.) The unspun fibers will twist around the yarn and the spinning process begins. Always pinch the fibers with the index finger and thumb so the twist does not move into the rolag, making it difficult to pull out the fibers.

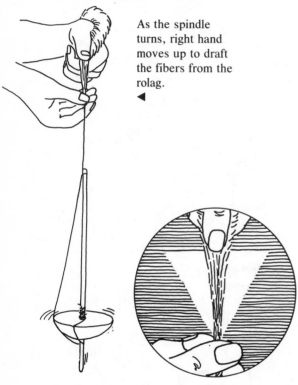

As the spindle turns, right hand moves up to draft the fibers from the rolag. ◄

▲
Drafting: the triangular-shaped area, as the raw fibers are drawn from the rolag before the spin moves into these fibers. Sometimes called the "Spinner's Triangle."

5. Continue to draft the fibers and twirl the spindle, letting the fibers spin, forming the yarn. The process is rhythmical. Draft the fibers only once with each twirl of the spindle.

6. When the spindle touches the ground, turn it so that the notch points downward. Turn the spindle in your hand, letting the spun yarn wind around it, with the greater amount of yarn at the whorl end and tapering to a point near the notched end. Leave about 14 inches (35.5 cm) of yarn unwound and start the process again.

7. The spindle is full when it begins to feel heavy. Wind the last bit of yarn around the middle and gently push the cone of yarn: it will slip off the spindle.

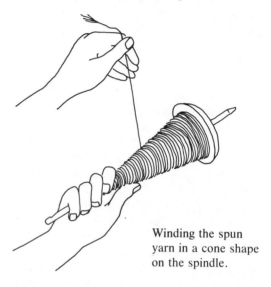

Winding the spun yarn in a cone shape on the spindle.

How to Spin Cotton on a Spindle

Cotton fiber can be purchased in a form to be carded or combed or in roving or top form ready for spinning. One advantage of cotton is that it is a much cleaner fiber to handle than wool. The disadvantage is that it has a short staple, making it difficult to spin on a drop spindle because the weight pulling down makes the yarn pull apart and break. A lightweight spindle held horizontally in your hand works best for cotton. The spindle should have a small, lightweight whorl and a hook on the end beneath the whorl. Your fingers must be very nimble to spin cotton, but it is relaxing work. Being compact, a cotton spindle is very portable.

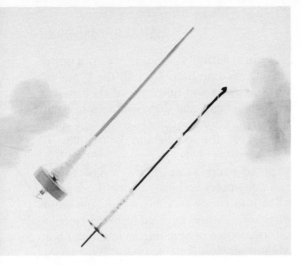

twirls the spindle. The spinning begins. The left hand gently holds the fibers, letting them pull out, or draft, as the right hand continues to twirl the spindle. The spin must not be allowed to enter the fibers before they are drawn out. If it does, they are almost impossible to separate and spin.

Cotton spindles:
Left: Lightweight wooden spindle with hook on the bottom.
Right: A well-balanced metal spindle. Yarn is spun from hook on top while bottom rests on a surface to relieve the weight pulling down when spinning short fibers.

Position of spindle, held with thumb and *middle* finger of right hand. Left hand holds unspun fiber. Right hand twirls the spindle and left hand drafts the fiber.

1. Attach a piece of yarn to the spindle, wind it around a few times, and take it over the side, under the whorl, and around the hook.

Lightweight cotton spindle with spindle yarn, ready to start spinning.

3. When the spun yarn exceeds your lateral reach, unhook it, hold the spindle in an upright position, and tightly wind the yarn around the spindle in a cone shape. Leave about 10 inches (25 cm) unwound. Turn the spindle to the slanting position again, fasten the yarn to the hook, and start spinning. When the spindle is full, the cotton yarn can be removed by pushing the cone off the end of the spindle.

2. Hold the spindle in a slanting horizontal position in the right hand, grasping it with the thumb and middle finger. With the left hand, hold the cotton fibers between the second and third finger. The thumb and third and fourth fingers control the fibers. The fibers are held over the yarn attached to the spindle and the right hand

Position of spindle as spun yarn is wound in cone shape for storage until removed.

Linen

Linen yarn is easy to spin, but the spinning process is quite different from that for wool or cotton. Generally you spin linen, not on a drop spindle, but on a spinning wheel. Flax fiber for spinning can be purchased in bundles. It has been retted, combed, and hackled, which makes it clean and easy to spin. You can grow your own flax plants, but the same processes described for commercial linen yarn must be followed to put the flax in the proper form for handspinning.

Getting Acquainted with Spinning Wheels

A spinning wheel will spin yarn in a similar manner to the drop spindle, but the process is much faster because it not only spins but puts up the yarn—some types of wheel wind the yarn on bobbins for storage.

Before actually starting to spin on a wheel, become familiar with the types of wheel, names and functions of their parts, and advantages and disadvantages of each type. There are basically two types of spinning wheel: the spindle and the treadle.

The *spindle wheel* is the simplest. It has acquired many names that are descriptive of its character and use, among them great wheel, walking wheel, big wheel, and wool wheel. This wheel evolved from the spindle and is capable of spinning any animal fiber or short-staple vegetable fiber. Easy to use, the wheel has only two disadvantages: its large size and the difficulty of plying yarn.

Like a drop spindle, the wool wheel has a spindle, but it is turned on its side and is supported by bearings (usually leather). The whorl becomes a pulley and is driven by a single band that goes around a groove in the circumference of the whorl and then around the large wheel, or drive wheel. When the wheel is turned, the pulley and spindle also turn. The number of turns is in relation to the diameter of the pulley and the wheel.

An early-nineteenth-century wool wheel with minor's head.

SPINDLE HEADS FOR THE WOOL WHEEL.

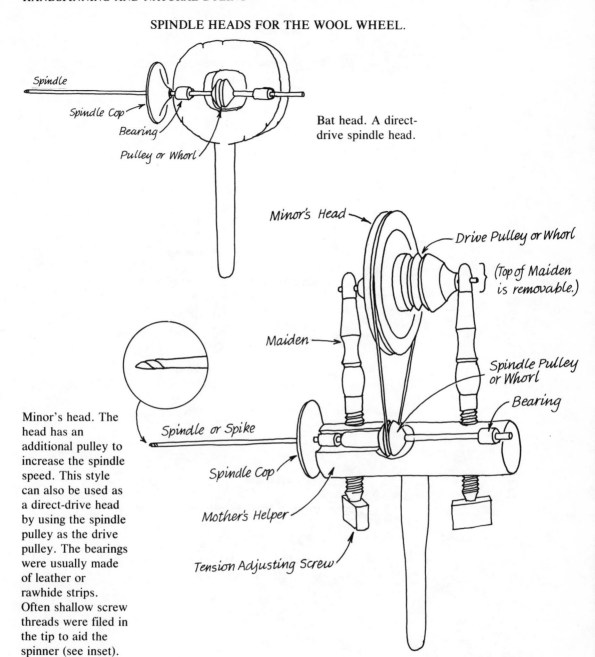

Spindle

Spindle Cop

Bearing

Pulley or Whorl

Bat head. A direct-drive spindle head.

Minor's Head

Drive Pulley or Whorl

(Top of Maiden is removable.)

Maiden

Spindle Pulley or Whorl

Bearing

Spindle or Spike

Spindle Cop

Mother's Helper

Tension Adjusting Screw

Minor's head. The head has an additional pulley to increase the spindle speed. This style can also be used as a direct-drive head by using the spindle pulley as the drive pulley. The bearings were usually made of leather or rawhide strips. Often shallow screw threads were filed in the tip to aid the spinner (see inset).

To spin on the wool wheel, stand beside it with the spindle in front of you and the wheel at your right side. Attach an 18-inch (45 cm) piece of yarn to the spindle and, with the left hand, hold the yarn at a 45-degree angle. With the right hand, start the drive wheel in motion by pushing clockwise on one spoke. This will cause the spindle to turn and the yarn (held at an angle) will wind up the spindle until it reaches the end, where it will flip off. A rolag is attached to this yarn. Then draft the fibers, allowing them to twist and form yarn.

The yarn will continue to flip off the end each time the spindle turns, and each time it flips off, one turn of twist is put in the yarn. Holding the yarn more in line with the spindle will give a looser twist, and an angle

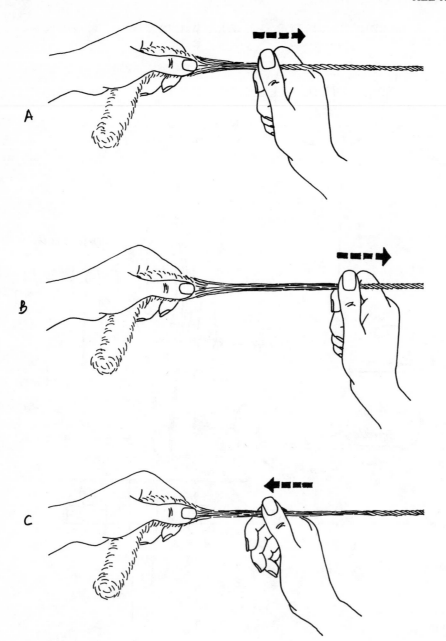

Drafting action

A. Drafting fingers pull fresh fibers from rolag. The hand holding the fresh fibers never allows the twist to move into that area.

B. Fresh fibers continue to be pulled from rolag, but drafting fingers pinch fibers so twist does not move into drafting area.

C. When the drafting is complete, the drafting fingers release their pinch and the hand slides up the drafting area and the twist follows. When the drafting hand reaches the rolag, the process starts again.

of close to 90 degrees will make a tight twist. This is an ideal way to spin short fibers because they require more twist for strength.

As it is spun, the yarn extends back from the spindle; it does not wind up at this time. The wheel continues to turn, called *free-wheeling,* for several turns; this requires delicate adjustment. Large wheels that have more mass will freewheel longer. When the wheel slows, the right hand moves over and pushes the wheel to keep it turning.

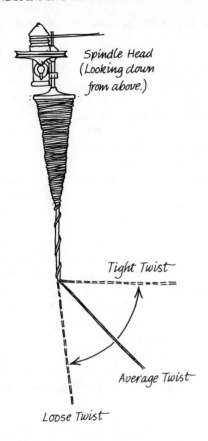

Spindle Head
(Looking down
from above.)

Tight Twist

Average Twist

Loose Twist

The spindle head of a wool wheel. The angle at which the yarn is held to the tip of the spindle determines the amount of twist.

Examples of wheel finger, a tool used when spinning on the wool wheel. Held in the right hand, it extends the spinner's reach to the wheel.

As the yarn is spun the spinner walks (thus the name *walking wheel*) back from the spindle as long as the wheel can be reached with the right hand to keep it turning. A wheel finger is a useful device to extend the spinner's reach. Drafting then stops and the wheel is *backed off,* or turned counterclockwise until the yarn that had wound around the spindle to the end is now at a 90-degree angle to the spindle and close to the spindle cop. As the wheel is again turned

clockwise, the spun yarn is wound for storing in a cone shape on the spindle until there is about 18 inches (45 cm) of yarn between the hand and spindle. The left hand moves the yarn again to a 45-degree angle to the spindle, the yarn twists around to the end of the spindle, and the process starts over.

The wool wheel has admirable advantages, for it allows the spinner to control the size of yarn, and the same twists per inch (TPI) can be made in a given length of yarn when the spinner knows the number of turns the spindle makes to one turn of the wheel. Here is a way of determining this:

How to determine spindle speed of direct-drive spinning wheels

$$\frac{\text{Diameter of wheel (inches)}}{\text{Diameter of spindle pulley (inches)}} = \begin{array}{l}\text{Number of}\\\text{spindle}\\\text{revolutions}\\\text{per full}\\\text{turn of wheel}\end{array}$$

EXAMPLE:

$$\frac{38''}{^{3}/_{4}'' \text{ diameter}} = 50+ \text{ revolutions, or a 50:1 ratio}$$

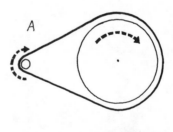

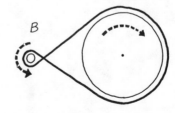

The drive band on a wool wheel.

A. Open-band spinning. As the wheel turns to the right, or clockwise, the spindle also turns to the right and Z-twist yarn is spun.

B. Cross-band spinning. A cross is put in the drive band so that when the wheel is turned right, or clockwise, the spindle turns left, or counterclockwise, and S-twist yarn is spun.

Yarns with different direction of twist (S or Z) can be spun easily on this wheel. When the wheel is turned clockwise, or to the right, the spindle turns to the right, causing the yarn to twist from right to left, making a Z twist. This is termed *open-band spinning*.

To spin S-twist yarn, the spindle must turn to the left. This is accomplished by crossing over the drive band before it goes around the spindle whorl. This causes the spindle to turn to the left, and the yarn to twist from left to right, making S-twist yarn.

It is important to keep proper tension on the drive band. To do this, a *tensioner* is part of the design of these wheels. If the drive band is too loose, the spindle will not turn.

There are many different styles of spindle wheel. They are very simple machines and have been most often made by local woodworkers: this accounts for the variety in style, especially of older examples. Contemporary models still show some variations.

The Treadle Spinning Wheel

There are a number of styles of antique and contemporary treadle spinning wheels.

You will find that the wheel, the bobbin, and the orifice (the opening through which the spun yarn passes at the end of the spindle) will vary in size from wheel to wheel. A large wheel will take less effort in spinning because of the wheel size and ratio; a large bobbin will accommodate large quantities of yarn; and a large orifice (or open end of spindle) will allow heavier yarn to be spun.

The basic reason a treadle spinning wheel "spins" and winds yarn on the bobbin is that the bobbin rotates faster than the flyer. The slower the bobbin rotates in relation to the flyer, the *more* the twist. The faster the bobbin rotates in relation to the flyer, the *less* the twist. Adjustment of the different speeds of the bobbin and flyer determines the amount of twist in the yarn. A spinning wheel is a sensitive instrument, and all parts must work together.

Two styles of contemporary treadle spinning wheel. *Left:* Haldane castle wheel. *Right:* Haldane saxony wheel. *Photo courtesy of The Hidden Village.*

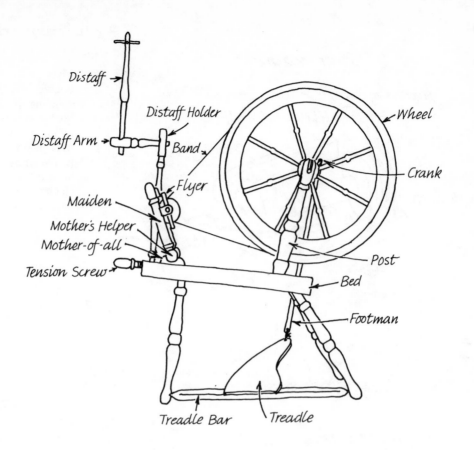

Distaff, Distaff Holder, Distaff Arm, Band, Flyer, Maiden, Mother's Helper, Mother-of-all, Tension Screw, Wheel, Crank, Post, Bed, Footman, Treadle Bar, Treadle

PARTS OF THE TREADLE SPINNING WHEEL

Flyer: A horseshoe-shaped wooden piece permanently attached to the spindle. Wire hooks are attached to guide the spun yarn to the bobbin.

Maidens (2): Upright pieces of wood with attached leather bearings where the metal spindle rests.

Spindle shaft: Metal rod with eye in one end that fits in the leather bearings on the maidens. Near the other end, threads are cut for the flyer pulley to be screwed on.

Flyer pulley, or whorl: Round wooden pulley with two or more grooves of different diameters for the drive band. The different grooves are used to adjust the speed of the flyer. The flyer pulley is securely screwed to the spindle.

Bobbin: Wooden part on which the spun yarn is wound. It is slipped on the spindle before the flyer pulley. The bobbin must turn freely on the spindle. The beveled end of the bobbin goes against the flyer, and the other end, which has a pulley groove, is next to the flyer pulley. The other drive band passes around this groove.

Drive band: One strong, continuous string that passes twice around the wheel. It passes once around one of the grooves in the flyer pulley, which turns the flyer and gives the twist to the fiber. It also passes around the groove on the end of the bobbin and turns it. This cord should be soft and pliable, preferably of cotton. To give smooth action, the join should be bound or sewn together rather than knotted.

Crank: Metal part attaching the wheel axle to the footman.

Mother-of-all: Wooden part holding the mother's helper. It is attached at the base by the tension screw.

Mother's helper: Horizontal wooden part to which the maidens are attached.

Tension screw: Wooden screw with a handle that passes through the bed and is threaded on the mother-of-all. By turning this, you move the mother-of-all and thus adjust the tension of the drive band. Turning toward you (clockwise) tightens the drive

Flyer Assembly

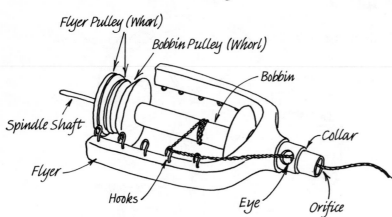

Flyer Pulley (Whorl)

Bobbin Pulley (Whorl)

Bobbin

Spindle Shaft

Collar

Flyer

Hooks

Eye

Orifice

Flyer assembly for double-drive-band spinning wheel. The bobbin is removed by unscrewing the flyer pulley, which is frequently a left-hand thread (turn clockwise to unscrew).

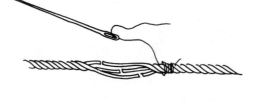

Method of binding a spinning wheel drive band.

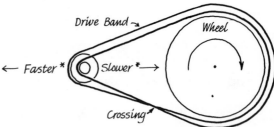

Drive Band

Wheel

← Faster *

Slower *→

Crossing

* Bobbin Speed

band, and away (counterclockwise) loosens it. This is a crucial adjustment in spinning.

Footman: A wooden stick or sometimes a leather thong attached to the treadle by a cord or leather tie and to the crank on the wheel.

Wheel posts (2): The wooden pieces on each side of the bed that hold the wheel in place. Slots at the top hold the crank, which runs through the center of the wheel. Pegs hold the crank in place.

Distaff: A staff that holds the flax during spinning.

Aside from style and size differences, there are two types of tension adjustment:

1. **Double drive band:** This wheel has a single length of cord running from the wheel to the bobbin pulley, back to the wheel, around the bobbin, and back to join the first end, where it should be bound together rather than knotted.

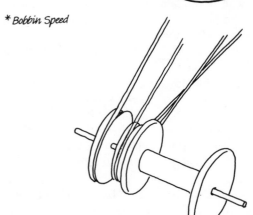

Double-drive-band mechanism. Increasing or decreasing tension on the drive band will cause the bobbin to go faster or slower, allowing fine adjustment of the spindle and bobbin pulley speeds. When the tension is loose, the bobbin will spin more slowly (giving more twist in the yarn) because the drive band will slip.

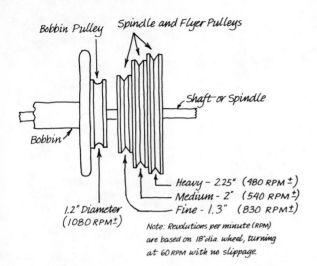

Bobbin Pulley   Spindle and Flyer Pulleys

Shaft or Spindle

Bobbin

1.2" Diameter
(1080 RPM±)

— Heavy – 2.25" (480 RPM ±)
— Medium – 2" (540 RPM ±)
— Fine – 1.3" (830 RPM ±)

Note: Revolutions per minute (RPM)
are based on 18" dia. wheel, turning
at 60 RPM with no slippage.

Different sizes of spindle pulley provide a wide assortment of speeds for spinning fine to heavy yarns. The difference between the diameters of the bobbin pulley and the spindle pulley determines the amount of twist in the yarn, the amount of spun yarn winding on the bobbin, and how fast it winds.

Tension on the drive band is adjusted by the tension screw, which moves the mother-of-all to give faster or slower speed to the bobbin and spindle.

2. **Single drive band:** This wheel has a single band that runs around the wheel and bobbin pulley or flyer. A separate cord goes from a spring or rubber band around the bobbin groove or flyer pulley to a peg that is tightened to put a brake on the bobbin or flyer for "tension" or speed adjustment. Two types—flyer lead and bobbin lead—are shown; in both mechanisms the drive band is the most important factor in controlling the amount of twist. With the flyer lead, if the spinner holds back on the yarn the bobbin moves with the flyer and can cause overspin. With the bobbin lead, if the spinner holds back on the yarn the flyer moves with the bobbin and results in underspin.

Wheels with either double- or single-drive-band type of tension adjustment are satisfactory; it is a matter of personal preference. In both cases the tension controls the rate of winding on the spun yarn; the

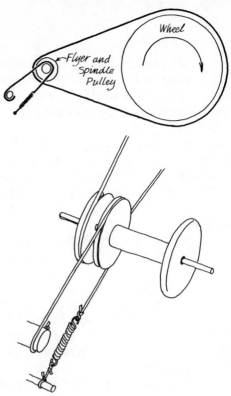

Single-drive-band spinning mechanism: flyer lead—the flyer is driven by the drive band, and a separate adjustable friction band controls tension on the bobbin.

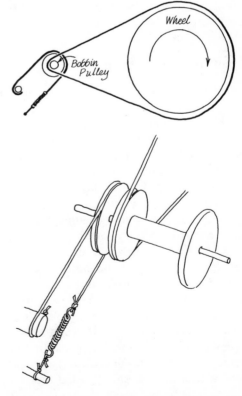

Single-drive-band spinning mechanism: bobbin lead—the drive band drives the bobbin pulley, and a separate band controls the flyer tension.

tension screw must therefore be in a convenient position for easy, efficient adjustment. Old wheels, which we classify as antique wheels, almost always have a double drive band.

To get acquainted with your wheel, sit squarely in front of it with the open end of the spindle (orifice) toward you and practice treadling. Relax; sit back in the chair, which should be a bit lower than the normal chair seat height.

Place the right foot on the treadle, press with the ball of the foot, and move from the ankle.

To start the wheel, gently give a spoke a push to the right, clockwise, with the index finger. Do not grab the rim of the wheel: a spinning wheel does not respond to sudden jerks or rough treatment. When the crank is at the top and starting down, press with the ball of the foot on the treadle. Keep the wheel going by pressing lightly with the foot on the treadle. Remember, treadling is an ankle motion—the whole body should not move. When you are able to keep the wheel going slowly and evenly in the same direction, start to spin. Do not let the wheel run backward.

How to Spin Wool

To start spinning, tie a piece of yarn to the bobbin. With the right thumb, turn the bobbin to the right to wind the yarn around it several times. Put the yarn over the hooks of the flyer and pass it through the eye of the spindle and out through the orifice.

If you are right-handed, lay the end of the yarn on a rolag held in the left hand, between the thumb and first and second fingers. Start the wheel to the right, or clockwise, and twist the yarn and rolag so the fibers catch together. The right hand holds the yarn about 6 inches (15 cm) from the orifice and gently draws the fibers from the rolag in the left hand. The amount of fibers released for spinning is controlled with the right hand by opening and closing the thumb and first finger. This action is (as described under spinning with a drop spindle) called drafting.

A sampler woven to record different types of fiber, spin, and color. *Photo by Charles Vorhees.*

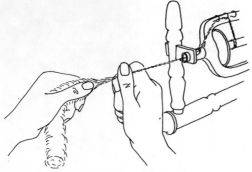

Position of hands of right-handed person in relation to spinning wheel while spinning.

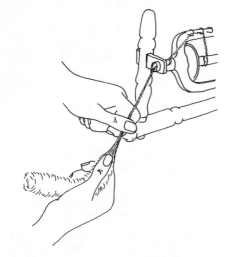

Position of hands while spinning when one is left-handed. Note angle of spun yarn in relation to spindle.

Again, the fiber pulls out in a triangular shape.

At first proceed slowly; the hands and feet should move at the same pace. The fibers twist together as the spin moves from the left hand to the bobbin. Keep your fingers moving to allow the twist to move to the unspun fibers. As long as the wheel turns, you must allow yarn to run continuously onto the bobbin. Do not jerk; keep the action smooth and easy.

When one section of the bobbin becomes full, move the yarn to the next hook so the yarn is evenly distributed on the bobbin.

When the bobbin is full, remove the drive band from the bobbin pulley and pull the spun yarn out of the spindle eye and orifice.

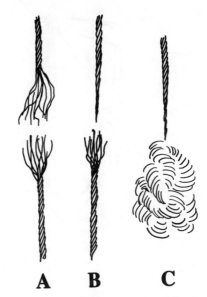

A   B   C

If the yarn breaks while spinning, it is very easy to rejoin the fibers. Never tie a knot. The fibers reach out and seem to want to cling together.

A. Two open ends are easy to join: overlap the ends and hold them together until the twist joins them.

B. An open end and a tightly spun end can be joined in the same manner, although it is not as easy.

C. Unspun fiber and a spun end are the easiest and most effective way of making a continuous yarn if it breaks while spinning.

Niddy noddy. This early-nineteenth-century tool is the simplest device to use in making a skein of yarn. It is portable, inexpensive, and quaint in design. It is very easy to make a skein on, but difficult to draw yarn off. Three corners are slightly turned up to hold the yarn, but the fourth corner is straight to make it easier to slide off the skein.

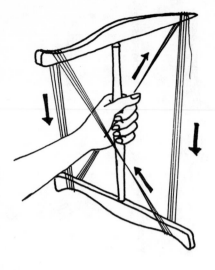

To make a skein of yarn on the niddy noddy, attach the yarn with a simple knot to the straight corner and wind the yarn from corner to corner. The center post is held with one hand and with wrist action the device is turned as the yarn is wound around. Fasten the ends and tie the skein in two places. Slide the skein off, first at the smooth end (where it was started). The skein can now be twisted and stored or washed and/or dyed.

Niddy noddy, niddy noddy,
Two heads, one body,
Here's one, 'tisn't one,
Twill be one, by and by.
(Here's two, etc.)
— old English lyric, Anon.

The yarn can then be smoothly drawn off. Wind it in skeins for washing or dyeing. Skeins also make measuring of quantities much easier.

By turning the wheel to the right, or clockwise, you have spun yarn with a Z twist. To make two-ply yarn, you need two strands of spun yarn. This yarn can be on separate bobbins or in balls, but must be allowed to unwind freely. Put the yarn attached to the bobbin around a hook and through the spindle eye and the orifice, and attach the two strands of spun yarn to it. Now start spinning, but turn the wheel to the left, or counterclockwise. Hold the two strands of yarn so they run freely through your fingers and both are under the same tension. The two strands of yarn are being plied with an S twist.

How to Spin Flax

Spinning flax is unlike spinning wool. It is not more difficult, but the two fibers have distinct characteristics and so cannot be handled in the same manner.

The flax fiber is spun most easily if it is dressed on a distaff. A distaff is a part of some spinning wheels or can be an independent piece of equipment.

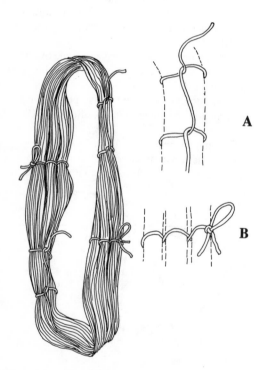

A

B

A skein must be properly tied before it is removed from a niddy noddy or any style of skein winder. This prevents tangling.

A. Fasten each end by hitching twice around the skein.

B. Use a strong piece of cord and twine it loosely three times around the skein. Tie it securely, but do not pull the skein yarns tightly together. Twine at two places on the skein.

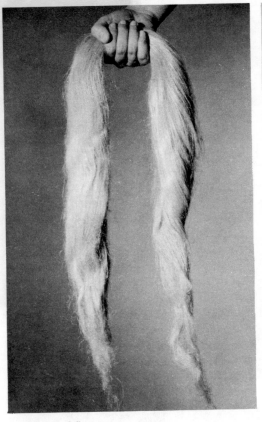

A bundle of flax.

Spinning wheel with distaff.

Many styles of distaff:
    A. Made from a dogwood branch.
    B. Lantern-shaped.
    C. A typical style.
    D. Made of reed and shaped.
    E. A green dogwood branch bent and joined at the top.
    F. Freestanding distaff made from a branch. This is ideal if the spinning wheel
doesn't have room to attach a distaff.

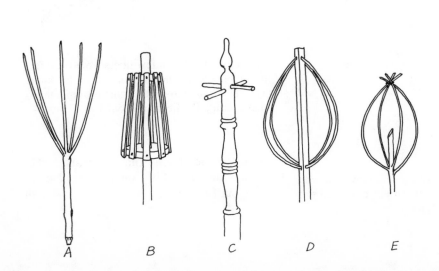

A   B   C   D   E   F

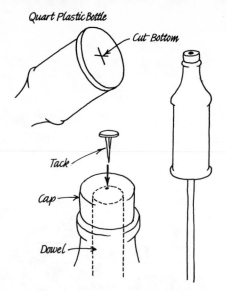

Homemade distaff, consisting of plastic bottle and dowel.

Flax can be purchased in bundles of varying weights. It is easy to work with about 2 ounces (56 g) at a time. Carefully divide the bundle into several smaller bundles. You can see where it will separate easily; divide it there, being sure the fibers do not tangle.

DRESSING THE DISTAFF

1. Take hold of one end of the 2-ounce (56 g) bundle and give it a shake. Do the same with the other end to loosen the fibers.

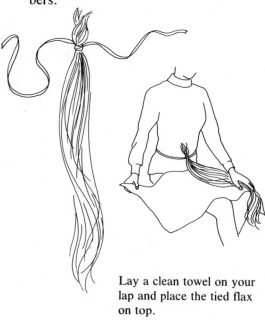

Lay a clean towel on your lap and place the tied flax on top.

Now take the bundle of flax and tie it about 6 inches (15 cm) from one end with the center of a ribbon about 2 yards (1.8 m) long. Now sit in a chair without arms, tie the ribbon around your waist, and lay the flax in the center of your lap.

2. Hold the other end of the flax bundle in your right hand and move it as far left as possible. With your left hand hold a few fibers from the edge of the bundle flat on your knee. Move your right hand (holding the bundle) back to the right side, keeping the arm outstretched, and a thin layer of fibers will spread across your lap. By raising the arm holding the bundle as it moves, you can pull the fibers out of your grasp more easily.

Repeat this process, as the fibers pull out in a fan shape; they must not lie in a straight line from the waist. Change hand positions, and continue working back and forth until all the fibers are finely spread and lying in layers on your knees. All the fibers should be crisscrossed; none should be straight.

The left hand pulls a few fibers from the edge of the bundle and holds them flat on the knee. The right hand moves the bundle from left to right, letting the fibers pull out.

3. Untie the ribbon from your waist and lay the fan-shaped flax on a table. Place the distaff on the flax with the top near the tied ribbon.

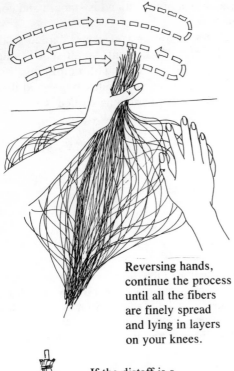

4. Starting at one side, gently roll the flax around the distaff so the distaff is completely enclosed. Tie the ends of the ribbon around the flax: cross them in opposite directions around it, crossing them first on one side and then on the other. Tie a bow at the bottom of the distaff. Tuck any stray fibers up underneath and put the distaff on the wheel. The flax is now ready to spin.

The ribbon is tied around the flax to secure it to the distaff.

Reversing hands, continue the process until all the fibers are finely spread and lying in layers on your knees.

If the distaff is a straight post, attach tissue paper in a cone shape to hold the flax on the distaff.

The flax bundle is on a flat surface; the distaff is positioned on the flax with the top near the tied ribbon.

Have a small bowl of water handy to keep the thumb and first finger of your left hand damp while spinning. Pull the starting yarn from the bobbin so it is close to the distaff. Take a few fibers between the thumb and first finger of your left hand. Twist them around the yarn and start the wheel, as ex-

Spinning flax: The left hand pulls a few fibers from the distaff. With the right hand, fasten them to the starting yarn on the bobbin. Note the bowl of water to keep the fingers of the left hand damp.

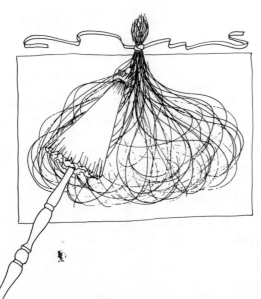

plained under "Getting Acquainted with Spinning Wheels." The flax fibers will gradually pull down from the distaff and start twisting.

While you are spinning, the left hand remains close to the distaff, with the thumb and first finger pulling the fibers from the bundle. As the fibers twist, they run through the thumb and first finger of the right hand, which clears away any knots or thick fibers.

Work slowly and gently and do not let the fibers twist above the left hand. Keep the distaff neat. After spinning the fibers from one area for a while, turn the distaff and pull the fibers from another area. Always work with the lowest fibers. When you reach the first crisscross of the ribbon, untie it and retie it higher, out of the way. By following these few rules, you should be able to spin all the fiber with no waste.

Keep the tension medium-loose on the spinning wheel and don't treadle too fast. Let the spun yarn pass directly to the bobbin. Keep the left fingers damp and move them slightly backward and forward. The spun yarn should be round in diameter, not flat, but smooth and glossy, with no "whiskers."

When the bobbin is full, remove the yarn and make a skein. If you wish to soften the yarn, boil it in a soap bath several times.

How to Spin Top

Top, which is commercially cleaned and combed fiber, is spun by the handspinner in a slightly different manner. Top comes in a long, continuous ropelike strand but is not spun or twisted. The fibers in top are parallel to one another, and it has a smooth and uniform appearance.

To spin worsted, simply strip a piece of the top lengthwise and spin it by letting it feed onto the bobbin as the flyer rotates. It is not necessary to draft these fibers if the piece is thin enough. Yarn spun this way requires more twist and is smooth and consistent.

To spin top as you would carded wool, pull apart (do not cut) small sections approximately 5 inches (12.5 cm) long. Lay this piece over your index finger and draft the fibers as in spinning carded wool.

To spin top in the same way as carded fiber, break off a length and lay it over your index finger. Attach the starting yarn as in spinning any fiber. Allow the wheel to draw the fibers from the center of the length of top.

Spinning Problems and Remedies

1. Yarn breaks: you are permitting too much wool to pass through your fingers too quickly. Or the tension is too tight; in this case, loosen the tension.
2. Yarn gathers in tight corkscrews and doesn't wind on bobbin: the tension is too loose and must be tightened. The tension is crucial. Also, too much fiber may have passed through your hands and become stuck in the orifice or hung up on a hook. Loosen this yarn so it will run easily to the bobbin.
3. Yarn twists too much: treadling is too fast or drive band is too slack. Tighten the tension screw.
4. Yarn underspun (not enough twist): bobbin is revolving too rapidly. The drive band must be slackened by loosening the tension screw.

The tension adjustment is the most crucial part of your spinning.

Tighten Tension When:
1. yarn is not winding on bobbin;
2. you are spinning bulky or thick yarn;
3. bobbin fills up and the greater diameter of the bobbin requires more tension.

Loosen Tension When:
1. unspun fibers are being pulled from your hands before they are adequately spun;
2. you are spinning fine yarn;
3. you are starting a new bobbin.

A continuous rhythm can be achieved through the movements of your hands and feet. With patience and practice you can spin the type of yarn you want.

Conditioning the Wheel

A well-designed and well-balanced wheel is a pleasure to use. Spinning will not be tiring if the wheel is kept in good working order.

Periodically it should be cleaned and lubricated. Remove the spindle from between the maidens. (Usually one maiden rotates.) Unscrew the bobbin screw, remove it, and pull off the bobbin. Now put petroleum jelly or olive oil on the metal spindle. Remove the wooden pegs in the posts and raise the wheel. Lubricate the axle and the crank where the footman is attached. A general rule is to lubricate all moving parts. Put the pieces back and see that the wheel revolves easily. Turn the maiden gently so the spindle shaft turns smoothly.

When starting to spin, have a lot of patience. To learn to spin any fiber, it is important to understand the basic principles and then do a lot of practicing. Realize that in no way can hand-spun yarn replace commercial yarn, nor can large quantities be spun economically. The advantage is the personal satisfaction of creating a sensitive, unique, beautiful product.

If you have given spinning a fair try, and even had help from someone who is proficient, but still do not enjoy it and find it makes you tense, then just accept that you may simply not have the temperament to spin.

Spinning is for me most relaxing. Many happy hours can be spent spinning while you listen to favorite music, watch TV, or even carry on a conversation with friends. Knowing your equipment, a sensitive feel in your hands, and a relaxed attitude are the necessary ingredients for successful spinning.

A relaxed time for the author and her pets.

Dyeing

Vegetable, or plant, dyeing is one of the ''fun'' aspects of handweaving. It is not necessary for the handweaver to put color in fiber by dyeing, because commercial yarns are available in a wide range of colors. There is great satisfaction, however, in gathering natural materials, extracting the dye pigment, and putting it in fiber.

It is questionable whether vegetable-dyeing fibers is practical for everyone. A proper place to work and a knowledge of the use of the *mordants,* or chemicals used to set the color, are essential. The color of any one dyebath may be a surprise, and there is small possibility of getting exactly that color again. But then, this is why vegetable dyeing is exciting. For the hand-weaver who needs a large quantity of yarn of one color, and who must be certain it is colorfast, vegetable dyeing is not practical.

Contrary to popular belief, a recipe is not necessary for vegetable or plant dyeing. Any natural vegetable material can be used for color, and the same mordants are used for almost all natural dye materials. The use of mordants varies, however, for different fibers.

The basic rule for vegetable dyeing is: Try any vegetable material for dyeing, but carefully follow the rules for using each mordant. The color from each may be a pleasant surprise or a disappointment. Factors that affect the color from natural materials include the age of the plant or part of the plant (bark, for example); the species; the soil it was grown in; the amount of sunlight and moisture during the growing period; and the chemical content of water used for dyeing. Some people even maintain that the phase of the moon under which the material was gathered affects the color.

Safety precautions to follow when vegetable-dyeing are:

1. Work in a well-ventilated area.
2. Keep lids on kettles to avoid inhaling fumes.
3. Wear rubber gloves.
4. Do not cook food in a kettle that has been used for dyeing.
5. Do not dye in an area where food is prepared.
6. *Never* use *any* utensil used in dyeing for food preparation.

These are the steps in vegetable dyeing:

1. Gather the vegetable material to be used in dyeing. It can be used fresh or dried and stored for later use.
2. Break or cut large pieces of your chosen vegetable material into smaller ones. (In some instances the color or dye is more easily extracted from smaller pieces.) Put the pieces in a kettle and cover with water. An enamel kettle gives the best results, since chemical mordants may react undesirably with aluminum or other metal pots.
3. Cover the kettle and boil the material for at least an hour to extract the color. Turn off the heat and allow to cool; it can stand overnight. Do not inhale fumes from the boiling kettle.
4. Strain out the vegetable material and discard. The liquid is the *dyebath,* or "brew."
5. At the same time that the dyebath is being prepared, mordant the fiber to be dyed, following the steps given below.
6. Put the mordanted fiber in the dyebath. The wool fiber and the dyebath must be at the same temperature because wool is easily damaged by temperature "shock." Simmer the fiber in the dyebath for about an hour, or until the fiber is the desired color. The fiber can stay in the dyebath until cool, or overnight.
7. Remove the fiber from the dyebath, rinse well, and hang up to dry. When you are using certain mordants, the fiber must be washed with soap; for specific instances, see directions for using mordants on the following two pages.

Hang hand-spun yarn, after dyeing, to "set twist" by weighting just enough to straighten the skeins. This helps to even out the spin or twist.

HANDSPINNING AND NATURAL DYEING

Both spun yarn and unspun fiber can be dyed, and you can dye them together in one dyebath. Unspun fiber can be spun after it is dyed. Spun and unspun fiber of the same color make an interesting texture contrast in a weaving, as unspun fiber reflects the light differently.

Mordanting. A mordant is a chemical used to fix the color in dyeing. Different chemicals can be used as mordants to bring out a different range of color from one dyebath. Each chemical mordant is used in a slightly different way; for best results, follow the steps described for each mordant. Fiber can be mordanted separately, or mordanting and dyeing can be done in the same kettle. See the last page of the color section for examples of dyed wool.

The steps in mordanting are:

1. In a cup of warm water, dissolve the required amount of mordant.
2. Add the dissolved mordant to a kettle of warm water, or to the dyebath if dyeing and mordanting are done at the same time.
3. Stir until thoroughly dissolved.
4. Add the wet, clean fiber to the warm water in the kettle.
5. Cover the kettle and simmer for the required time.
6. Do not inhale fumes from the steaming kettle, and wash your hands after using mordants.
7. Use each chemical mordant carefully, according to the following instructions.

Here are the five most common mordants and directions for using them with wool fiber. Mordants can be purchased from shops specializing in spinning and dyeing supplies (see list in back of book). They are available in some drug and farm supply stores as well. I have also seen them on the drugs and sundries shelves of large supermarkets. Amounts given are for 4 ounces (113 g) of wool and 1 gallon (3.8 l) of water.

Alum—Potassium Aluminum Sulfate
Use 1 ounce (28 g) or 1¾ tablespoons.

Add mordant to water; thoroughly dissolve. Add wet wool fiber. Simmer for 1 hour. Stir gently occasionally. Remove fiber from kettle, and squeeze out excess water. Do not rinse. Dye fiber immediately, store damp for dyeing next day, or dry and store for later use. Too much alum will make fiber sticky. Alum (aluminum ammoniate), used in preserving food, can also be used as a mordant. It can be purchased at the grocery store and is safe, especially if working with children. It is ideal for a first dyeing project.

Chrome—Potassium Dichromate
Use ⅛ ounce (3.5 g) or ½ teaspoon.

Add mordant to water; thoroughly dissolve. Add wet wool fiber. Keep lid on kettle, as chrome is light-sensitive and letting light in can cause uneven dyeing. Simmer for 1 hour. Stir occasionally. Remove wool and wrap in a towel, squeezing out excess water. Dye immediately, keep wool damp in towel and dye next day, or dry and store in a dark place to use later. Chrome softens the fibers.

Tin—Stannous Chloride
Use ⅛ ounce (3.5 g) or 1 teaspoon.

Add mordant to water; thoroughly dissolve. Add wet wool fiber. Simmer for 1 hour. Stir occasionally. Remove wool from bath immediately. Wash in warm soapy water and rinse. Dye immediately, or dry and store to use later. Wash again in soapy water after dyeing. Too much tin causes the fibers to become brittle.

Blue Vitriol—Cupric Sulfate
Use ¼ ounce (7 g) or 2 teaspoons.

Add mordant to water; thoroughly dissolve. Add wet wool fiber. Simmer for 1 hour. Stir occasionally. Remove wool, and squeeze out excess water. Do not rinse. Dye immediately, or dry and store to use later. This mordant is available in farm supply stores.

Iron—Ferrous Sulfate
Use ⅛ ounce (3.5 g) or 1¼ teaspoons.

Add mordant to water; thoroughly dissolve. Add wet wool fiber. Simmer for 1 hour. Stir occasionally. Remove wool, and squeeze out excess water. Rinse thoroughly. Dye immediately, or dry and store for use later.

Iron dulls the color; this is called *saddening*. It is used on top of previously dyed fibers to produce somber greens.

After basic dyeing has been tried, it is time to experiment. Some additional tips follow.

Top-dyeing may be necessary, if the color from one dyebath was unsatisfactory. Mordant the already dyed fiber in a different mordant and dye in another dye material over the original color. This can be the way to get a specific color. Find out by experimenting.

Fugitive colors are dye materials that lack colorfastness. Mordants will not set the color. In vegetable dyeing, most reds are fugitive. If the fibers do dye red, the color will probably fade in time.

Sometimes no mordant is needed. Some natural materials contain tannin or tannic acid, and tannin *is* a mordant, so no additional mordant is needed. Black walnuts and oak galls are the most common materials containing tannin. These dye materials are called *substantive*.

Before using vegetable-dyed fibers in a piece of weaving, test the fastness of the color. Simply put a portion of the dyed fiber in direct sunlight. Put another portion away from any light. After several days, compare the two to determine if the portion in the sunlight has lost any color.

Glauber's salt (sodium sulfate) can be added to a dyebath to ensure that the fibers are evenly dyed. This is called *leveling*. Colors may be deeper because Glauber's salt also increases dye absorption and ex-

hausts the color in the dyebath. Use 2 ounces (56 g) per pound (450 g) of dry fiber.

Colors can be brightened—or made to "bloom"—by adding a metallic salt, stannous chloride (tin), to a simmering dyebath. Remove the fiber, stir in the metallic salt, and then return the fiber to the dyebath. Follow directions for using tin as a mordant.

Tartaric acid or cream of tartar is used to make clear, bright colors. If it is not used, colors will appear dull and lusterless. Use 2 tablespoons (30 cc) to 1 gallon (3.8 l) of water whenever you want a bright color.

Do not put off vegetable dyeing because of lack of chemical mordants. Beginning dyers can use readily available substitutes. For example, for copper mordant, put a couple of handfuls of copper pennies in 1 gallon (3.8 l) of dyebath, and 4 ounces (113 g) of wool, and simmer for 1 hour. Use an iron kettle as a substitute for ferrous sulfate (iron). In an iron kettle, simmer for 1 hour 1 gallon (3.8 l) of dyebath and 4 ounces (113 g) of wool. You can also use iron nails for iron mordant in the same manner as pennies for copper.

Easily accessible natural dye materials will give earth tones such as yellows and browns. Materials that give a red color are not good to start with because, as explained earlier, the color is not always fast.

Sources of dye materials and the colors obtained from them are wide-ranging. From the kitchen: onion skins, herbs, and spices will give a color range of yellow through rust; tea and coffee will give tan and warm brown; carrot tops and parsley will give soft yellows and greens. From the outdoors: marigold blossoms will give yellow, gold, and rust; barks will give beige, yellow-tan, and warm brown; leaves, weeds, and hedge trimmings will give warm gray, gray-green, and olive brown.

The world of vegetable or natural dyeing is wide open. Use materials that are readily available to you, have the courage to experiment, and have fun.

4

∿∿

Warping Methods

The quality of any weaving depends on the excellence with which the warp is prepared for the weaving process. It is essential that the warp—the lengthwise yarn strands—be carefully prepared and *dressed,* or put on the loom.

Each strand of yarn in the warp is referred to as an *end*. It is the length of each end that determines the length of the woven piece. Preparing the warp ends, or winding a warp, involves measuring each end to the correct length and arranging them in the right order.

Calculating the Warp

Careful planning comes first. Winding the warp can be time-consuming. Also, the composition, color sequence, length, and so forth, of the warp are for the most part difficult to change once it is set up (the plan for the weft or crosswise yarns can be more easily altered).

Before starting to prepare the warp, there are several decisions to be reached. The first is what is going to be made—for example, should it be tightly woven or airy? Then comes the choice of yarn.

Next you must decide how to space, or *sett,* the yarn in the reed, to know how many warp ends will be needed for each inch (or centimeter). At this point, decide how wide the finished weaving will be. To determine the total number of warp ends, multiply the number per inch (or centimeter) by the planned width of the weaving.

And last, decide how long the woven piece should be. A word of caution: to be realistic, you must add to both the width and the length of the warp, for something will be "taken up" through the weaving process.

Choose yarns appropriate for the item being made. Rugs will require heavy, coarse yarns such as 10/5 linen or any tightly twisted cotton or wool yarn. An item of clothing would require more loosely twisted, soft, supple yarn of any fiber. Yarn that is smooth, is plied, and has long fibers is the easiest to use for warp.

To determine how to sett the warp in the reed, there is one general rule to follow. Wind the warp yarn around a ruler within a 1-inch (or 1-centimeter) measure, setting each winding right against the previous one. Count the number of times it goes around in 1 inch (or centimeter). *Half* of this number is how many ends to have per inch (or centimeter) for a *balanced* weave (see the illustrations). For a *weft-faced* weave (where the weft yarns are predominant), use fewer than half of this number. For a *warp-faced* weave (where the warp yarns cover the weft yarn), use the whole number.

There are no set rules or reference tables to tell exactly how to sett in the reed all the yarn types available to the handweaver. The preceding rule is a general guide; experience is what you must rely on. One other helpful rule is that wide warps should be sett a bit closer (more ends per inch or centimeter) than are narrow warps. All warps tend to

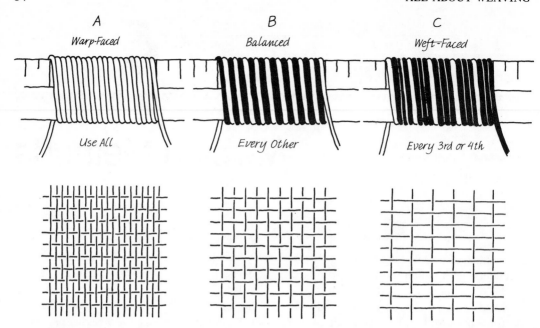

To determine the sett of the warp, wind the warp yarn around a ruler.

A. Warp-faced weave: the total number of times the yarn goes around in a given measure (inch or centimeter) is how many ends to use in the same measure in the warp.

B. Balanced weave: one half the number of times the yarn goes around in a given measure is used in the same measure in the warp.

C. Weft-faced weave: a third or fourth of the number of times the yarn goes around in a given measure is used in the same measure in the warp.

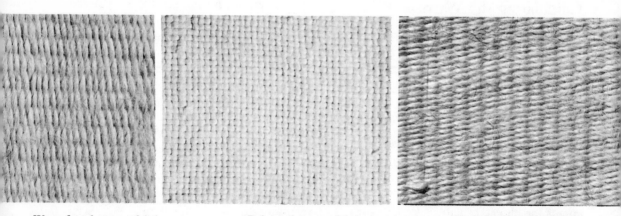

Warp-faced-weave fabric.   Balanced-weave fabric.   Weft-faced-weave fabric.

pull in somewhat during weaving, and warp sett a little closer tends to hold its width more easily. A wide warp is much more difficult to keep full width than a narrow warp.

The length and width of the warp must be greater than the size of the finished weaving. This is a result of shrinkage, take-up of the warp and weft yarn as they go over and un-

der during weaving, and the wastage because part of the warp must be fastened to the front of the loom and because there is a portion at the end that cannot be woven.

The width of the warp, allowing for shrinkage and take-up, should be about *10 percent more* than the width of the required size of the weaving (this can vary according to the type of weave, yarn, and each individual weaver's work habits).

The length of the warp will also be *10 percent longer* than the project, *plus* 1 yard (0.9 m) for the loom. The type of weave and the weaver are variables here too, but perhaps the greatest factor is the yarn. The warp is woven while under tension, and if the yarn is stretchy there will be considerable take-up when the tension is released.

Although I again stress that experience will be the best guide in calculating warp length and width, I must add: never economize on the amount of yarn used for warp length. The expense of a little extra warp is nothing compared to the inconvenience of a warp too short to complete the project. In such a case there is no remedy, whereas you might be able to devise some small project (such as an eyeglass case) to use up extra warp.

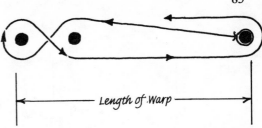

Placement of pegs to make cross in warp and to get length of warp.

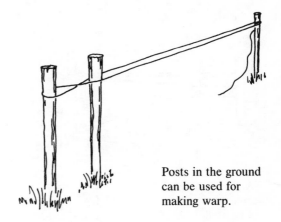

Posts in the ground can be used for making warp.

Warping Equipment

There are several methods, involving different pieces of equipment for winding yarn in preparation of a warp. With each method, the efficiency you can obtain will vary. By being familiar with each piece of warping equipment you can use it to its best advantage, and a proper warp can be prepared. All warping methods described can be accomplished by one person. Always have confidence in your own resources.

Basically, warping equipment should provide a means of measuring all warp ends to the same length and arranging them in order, one after the other. To do this, warp ends are placed alternately under and over two pegs, forming a cross, which prevents warp ends from getting out of sequence as they are extended around pegs to achieve the desired warp length. There are various pieces of equipment by which this can be achieved. Quite often a weaver will have equipment for preparing warp in at least two different ways. No one method is universally superior.

The simplest device for warping is a set of posts in the ground. Place two posts close

together at one end to make the cross and a third post at the distance necessary for the length of the warp. Walk the yarn back and forth around the posts until you have the required number of warp ends.

When working indoors and preparing a short warp—under 5 yards (4.5 m)—take a piece of hardwood and attach to it two ¾-inch (2 cm) dowels or pieces of broom handle about 8 inches (20 cm) long. On another piece of hardwood place a single dowel. Attach these pieces with C-clamps to stationary points, such as a table, shelves, windowsills, or other furniture. The distance between the two pieces should equal the length of the warp. To make a longer warp with this basic equipment, put three dowels in the first board and use the second board with the single dowel as a turning point. In this way the warp can be doubled in length.

These simple warping methods are satisfactory for short warps and when using sturdy yarn for a narrow warp, but more refined equipment must be used when preparing longer and wider warps with finer yarn. The principle, however, is the same.

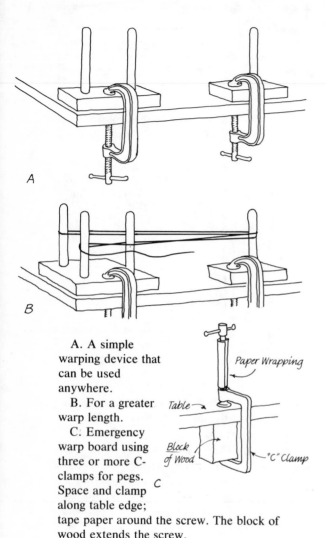

A

B

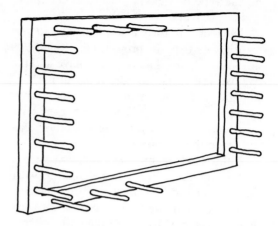

Warping frame.

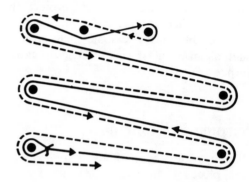

A. A simple warping device that can be used anywhere.

B. For a greater warp length.

C. Emergency warp board using three or more C-clamps for pegs. Space and clamp along table edge; tape paper around the screw. The block of wood extends the screw.

Paper Wrapping

Table

Block of Wood

"C" Clamp

C

Using a warp frame—start at lower left peg.

To wind a warp on a frame, board, or reel, first trace the path with a tape measure from peg to peg to determine the exact length of the warp. Now fasten the end of the warp yarn to the peg farthest from the cross, and wind the yarn back and forth around the pegs. Where the cross is to be made, go over the first peg, under the second peg, and around the end peg. On the return, go over the peg you went under before and under the one you went over. Retrace the path of the warp and just pass around the peg where it started. Continue going back and forth in this manner until there are the required number of warp ends (see page 92 for methods of counting warp ends).

If working on a frame or board, be sure to fasten it securely to the wall at a level convenient for your reach. Stretching or stooping while winding warp can be very tiring.

If warping several colors, as for stripes, do not cut the yarn when a new color is started. Simply leave the first color hanging from the last peg and start the new color by tying it to the peg. Do the same with the next color. To use the first color again, pick up the hanging yarn and continue warping. The warp yarns will be crossed at the last peg, but it doesn't matter because this is the end that is cut when the warp is removed from the warping board. When these yarns are cut, they will fall into order and no longer be crossed.

A *warping board* is a good purchase because it requires minimum space and is reasonably priced. It is not, however, satisfac-

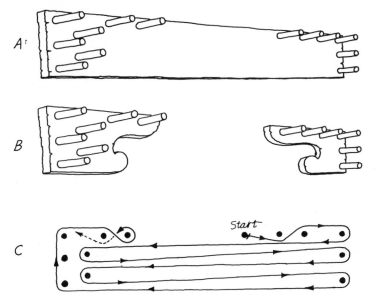

Warping boards:

A. A warping board showing arrangement of pegs.

B. A warping board in two parts using same arrangement of pegs. By placing each piece farther apart a much longer warp can be made.

C. This schematic drawing shows how to prepare warp on these two warping boards. The warp has a cross at both ends.

tory for very wide warps. The length of the pegs is about 6 inches (15 cm), so they will not accommodate a large number of warp ends. If the pegs were longer, they would bend under the tension of the warp. The size (thickness) of the yarn being used for the warp affects how many warp ends can be prepared at one time. Prepare the warp in several sections if the warp board will not hold all the warp ends. A warp board or frame usually has a maximum capacity of 20 yards (18.3 m) in length. If making your own equipment, be sure to use hardwood. The pegs will become loose in softwood because of the warp tension.

A *warping reel* is required for making longer warps. The yarn goes around the reel to get the desired length. For long warps it is beneficial to make a cross in the warp at both ends. You will find that there are two or more pegs close together at the top and at the bottom of the reel. The reel turns while the warp yarn is held in one position, which is less tiring than warping on a board where the arm must go back and forth, carrying the yarn from peg to peg. The disadvantage of a reel is the space it requires. Some reels sit on a table, some on the floor. Most models can be folded for storage and can be easily disassembled. There are both horizontal and vertical warping reels.

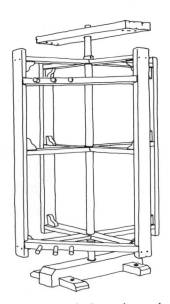

A large old-time vertical warping reel permanently attached to floor and ceiling.

When you are warping on a board, frame, or reel there should be little tension on the yarn as it comes from the tube, cone, ball, or skein. All strands of yarn must run freely as they slide through the thumb and first two fingers. You can use either hand. The warp should not sag between the pegs, nor should it be under such tight tension that it bends the pegs inward. As it goes around the pegs

Horizontal warping reel designed and manufactured by Thought Products, Inc.

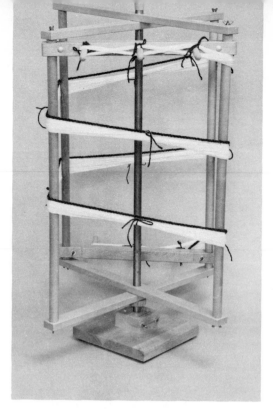

Table-model vertical warping reel with warp tied ready to be removed. The dark yarn in the warp traces the warp length. It remains on the reel as a guide when the warp is wound in several sections. *Photo by Charles Vorhees.*

Horizontal warping reel with special attachment for guiding the warp yarn. *Photo courtesy Nilus Leclerc, Inc.*

of the frame or board, the hand that is not holding the yarn pushes the warp toward the frame, piling it up, for it cannot be evenly spread along the peg—there would not be room for all the warp ends. If the cross is

properly made, the ends are still all in order. Try to finish warping in one session, for yarns tend to stretch when left under tension for a period of time.

Up until now we have talked about using

Spool rack with guides. The yarns release freely from the spools through the guides to the warping equipment.

of wood with two rows of staggered holes. The warp ends are threaded alternately through the holes of the paddle. With the paddle held in the right hand, the odd-numbered warp yarns are on the left and the even on the right of the paddle. The rigid heddle-type paddle is threaded with the even warp yarns through the slits and the odd through the holes.

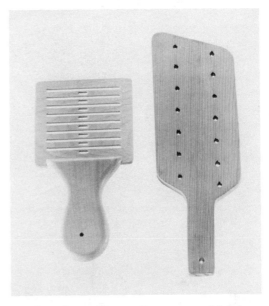

Paddles used when winding a warp with four or more strands of yarn at one time:
Left: Rigid heddle style.
Right: Easily made paddle with rows of staggered holes.

just one strand of yarn at a time to wind the warp. In this way the yarn at the cross is in order: one over, one under. The warp yarns certainly cannot become twisted when put on in this way, but it is a very slow method of warping. It becomes necessary to use multiple strands of yarn when winding a warp either for speed or when using a variety of color and texture of yarns. If you put on two warp ends at once, the time preparing the warp is cut in half. Yarn in this case comes from two sources.

Having two warp ends going over and under together to form the cross will not cause the warp ends to be tangled when they are put on the loom. If, however, you use four or more strands of yarn at once, the warp ends will no longer be parallel but will twist around one another, resulting in a difficult, unsatisfactory warp. To satisfactorily wind a multiple-strand warp (four or more strands), use a *paddle* or pick up the cross with your fingers. Both these processes will take some practice but are well worth the effort.

Learning to Use a Paddle

There are two styles of paddle, one like a small rigid heddle, the other a flat piece

To create an even tension as the spools of yarn unwind, place them on a spool rack with the yarn coming alternately from the top of the even-numbered spools and from the bottom of the odd-numbered spools.

A paddle is easiest to use when warping on a reel. More practice is needed to feel at ease using it on a frame or board.

The object is to have the warp yarns alternate as they go over and under the pegs that form the cross. By raising and lowering the rigid heddle-style paddle, two sheds are made. As the first peg of the cross is approached, raise the paddle: the odd warp yarns are on top of the peg and the even

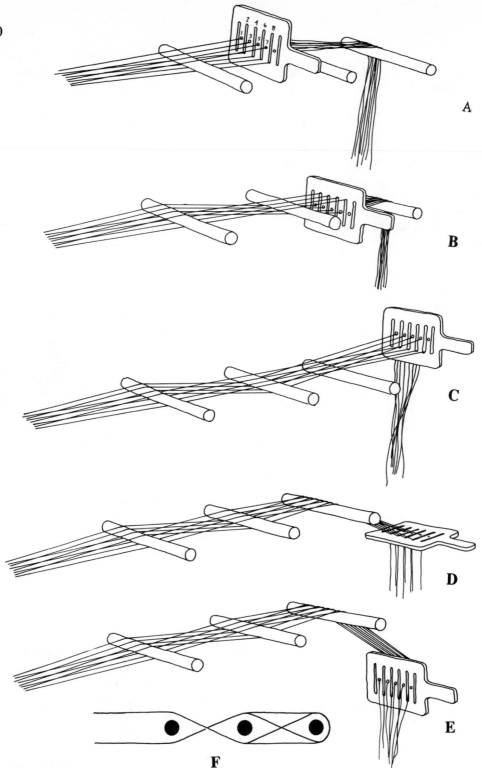

Winding a warp with a rigid heddle-style paddle:

A. Raise the paddle, putting odd warp yarns on top of the first peg, making one shed.

B. Lower the paddle, putting the even warp yarns on top of the second peg, making the opposite shed.

C. All warp ends go around the end peg.

D. Turn the paddle 180 degrees.

E. The paddle is in position to return and make the same sheds on the same pegs.

F. The cross in the warp that is made when using a paddle.

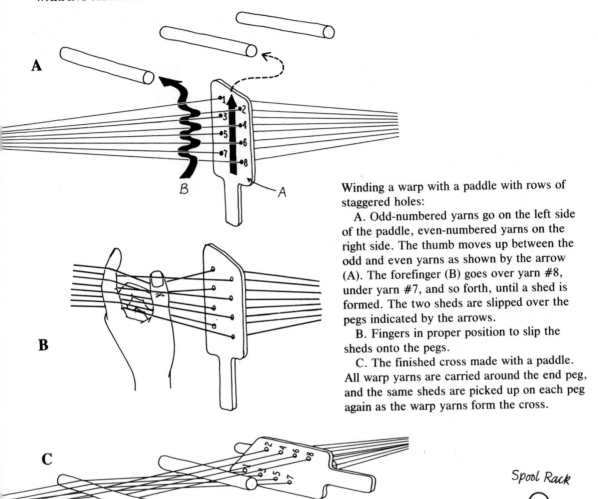

Winding a warp with a paddle with rows of staggered holes:

A. Odd-numbered yarns go on the left side of the paddle, even-numbered yarns on the right side. The thumb moves up between the odd and even yarns as shown by the arrow (A). The forefinger (B) goes over yarn #8, under yarn #7, and so forth, until a shed is formed. The two sheds are slipped over the pegs indicated by the arrows.

B. Fingers in proper position to slip the sheds onto the pegs.

C. The finished cross made with a paddle. All warp yarns are carried around the end peg, and the same sheds are picked up on each peg again as the warp yarns form the cross.

on the bottom. Then lower the paddle at the second peg, reversing the position of the warp yarns: the even will be on top and the odd on the bottom. All the warp yarns go around the end peg, and the paddle is then turned 180 degrees and the sheds are opened as the cross is made once again. This time the position of the odd and even warp yarns are the same as before on each peg.

By understanding the basic principle of using a paddle, and with time, patience, and practice, warps can be prepared with speed and efficiency using any number of warp yarns.

Yarn unwinds from the top of the spool for the even-numbered warp yarns in the paddle, and from the bottom for the odd-numbered warp yarns.

Long Warps

A long warp should have two crosses, one at each end. A long warp is over 8 yards (7.3 m). Almost all warping equipment has at both ends the pegs necessary to make a cross. The cross previously discussed, which consists of the crossing of single yarns over and under in the figure-eight manner, is called the *porrey cross*. This cross of sin-gle yarns is necessary for threading the hed-dles of the loom. The *portee cross* is at the opposite end of the warp. It consists of groups of yarns forming a figure eight; for instance, a group would be all the strands in a paddle. The portee cross is used for ar-ranging the warp on the loom. Each cross is placed in the raddle (see Chapter 5, "Dressing the Loom"), which aids in keep-ing the width of the warp as it is beamed on the loom.

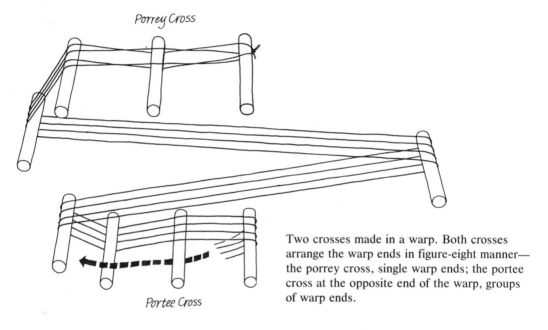

Porrey Cross

Portee Cross

Two crosses made in a warp. Both crosses arrange the warp ends in figure-eight manner— the porrey cross, single warp ends; the portee cross at the opposite end of the warp, groups of warp ends.

Counting Warps

After determining the length of the warp and putting it on the frame or reel, it is not necessary to think about the length again. But the warp ends must be counted to be sure the right number is prepared for the width of the weaving. I have found two ef-fective methods. The first is to count out loud as each cross is made; to be successful, you must not be interrupted. Remember that when you are working with one strand of yarn, two warp ends are wound each time a complete circle i made on the frame or reel. For the second method, take another strand of strong yarn a different color from the warp and put it around each portee cross. The yarn separates each cross, mak-ing the counting very easy, as you can mul-tiply the number of crosses by the number of warp ends in each cross, which is the group of yarns forming a figure eight or all the strands used in a paddle.

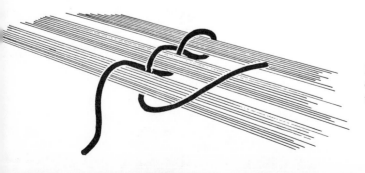

Method of counting to ensure correct number of ends in the warp.

Removing the Warp

After the warp yarns are properly wound and counted, it is necessary to group and tie the warp so that when it is removed it will remain intact and not tangle.

Use lengths of strong yarn of a color different from that of the warp itself for the ties. A half-bowknot is used so it is easy to untie and remove when the time comes. Do not use a knot that will be time-consuming to pick apart, nor one that must be cut—you would not want to cut a warp yarn inadvertently.

Tie the warp at the looped ends near the crosses, at the top and bottom of the two pegs at the crosses, and at least once each yard (or meter). Check to be sure each group is tied properly. With a short warp needing only a porrey cross, cut the warp ends at the opposite end from the cross. A warp that has a cross at both ends can be removed from the warping equipment without cutting either end. The manner in which the warp is beamed on the loom (see Chapter 5, "Dressing the Loom") will determine which end is cut.

The warp is now ready to be removed from the warp frame or reel; it can go directly to the loom or can be stored for later use. There is no need to straighten out, comb, or adjust the tension of the warp between the warping equipment and the loom. If the warp is not going to be used immediately, chain it and put it in a bag so it will not become soiled or snagged. Include in the bag a slip of paper stating the number of warp ends and the length of the warp.

To chain, take hold of the cut end, form a loop as shown, and keep pulling *loose* loops through each succeeding loop. Take a different-colored piece of yarn and tie together the last loop and the warp loop that was around the end peg. The tie of a different color denotes the first one to be removed when the warp is ready to be used.

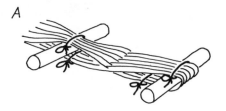

A

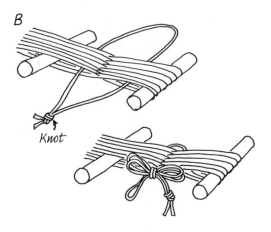

B

Knot

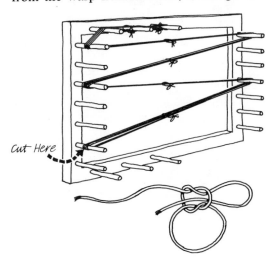

Cut Here

Group and tie the warp before removing it from the frame. Use a half-bowknot made by tying a bowknot and pulling one end through so there is only one bow. To untie the knot, pull the short end.

A. Tie the warp at the top and bottom of each peg, marking the cross.

B. Another method of tying the cross. Take a strong piece of cord about a foot longer than the width of the warp. Put the ends of the cord through the cross and knot the two ends together, then tie a bowknot. While dressing the loom, untie the bowknot and the cord can stay in the cross until the process is completed. This ensures that the cross will not be lost.

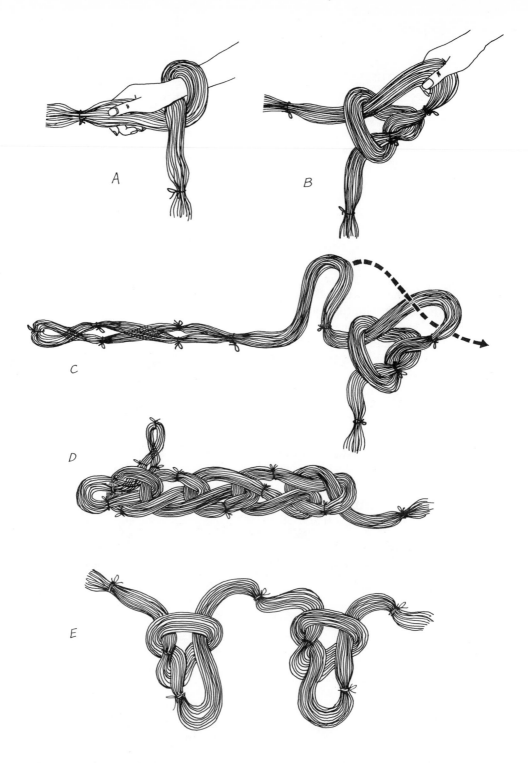

Method of chaining the warp:

A. With the cut end of the warp, form a loop over the hand.

B. Pull the warp through this loop to form another loop.

C. Repeat this looping to the end of the warp.

D. The completed chained warp. Bring the last loop and the loop at the end of the warp together and tie with a different-colored yarn.

E. Alternative method of chaining the warp. Simply tie slip knots in the warp. Release one knot at a time as needed while warping.

Wide Warps

If you are preparing a wide warp or one in which all the warp ends cannot be accommodated at one time on the equipment, it is necessary to wind the warp in two or more sections. The only problem encountered here is ensuring that each section is the same length. To do this, take a heavy strand of yarn of a different color and put it on the frame or reel, the exact length of the warp. Leave it there as a guide as each section is warped.

Knots in Yarn

Knots in the warp yarn can be very troublesome and must be removed. If you feel a knot slip through your fingers as you wind the warp, stop and go back to the end top or bottom peg, whichever is closest. Cut the warp end there and make a new knot at the peg. A knot at either end of the warp will not interfere with the weaving, but knots in the middle will not pass easily back and forth through the reed during the weaving process.

Sectional Warping

There is another method of preparing a warp that is quite different. It involves putting the warp yarns directly on the loom as

Warp yarns being put on the loom by the sectional warping method. *Photo courtesy Nilus Leclerc, Inc.*

they are measured and counted. This method is called *sectional warping* because individual sections of the warp are wound at one time. Each section is usually 1 or 2 inches (2.5–5 cm) wide.

Sectional warping is excellent for long warps, when using rather fine untextured yarn, and when many colors are used irregularly or in long repeats.

The equipment required for sectional warping is:

Sectional warp beam: This is special equipment that can be attached to the warp beam of most looms. It is often a permanent part of old looms. It consists of strips of wood with wooden pegs or metal rakes attached at 1-inch or 2-inch (2.5–5 cm) intervals. There are generally four of these strips. For accuracy in measuring length of warp, it is important to know the circumference of the warp beam after these strips are attached.

Spool rack: This rack must be portable and capable of holding at least forty spools. Guides for the yarn are helpful.

Spools for rack: These can be wood, plastic, or cardboard and should be capable of holding 600 to 800 yards (550–730 m) of yarn. At least forty are needed; they should fit the spool rack.

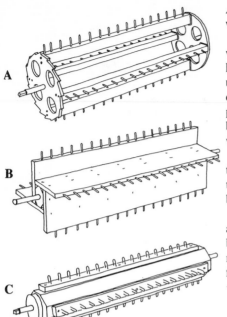

A variety of sectional warping beams:

A. Permanent sectional warping beam. On some looms it is possible to unscrew these strips at the ends and turn them so the pegs point inward; then the beam can be used for regular warping.

B. Pegs were inserted in the ends of four boards and then attached to a regular beam.

C. Wood "rakes" are attached to a regular warp beam. These strips can be removed and the beam used for regular warping. ◀

Spool rack with guides for the yarn. ▲

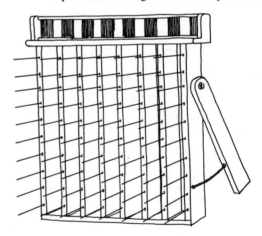

A sturdy spool rack with reedlike thread guides at the top.

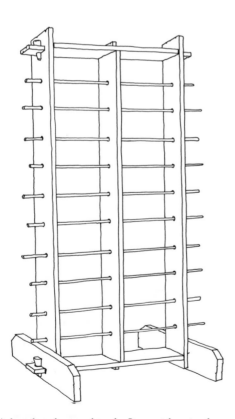

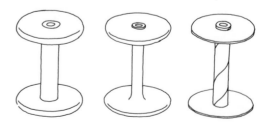

A handmade spool rack. It must be sturdy and not easily tipped over. This one can be disassembled for storage.

Wood, plastic, and cardboard spools to fit spool rack. One spool is needed for each warp end in one section when sectional-warping.

Tension box: This attaches to the back beam and should be adjustable to fit any size of beam. It consists of dowels that the warp ends go over and under to adjust tension and a reed to keep the warp ends evenly spaced.

Metal thread guides: These eight guides are optional equipment but are helpful in guiding the warp yarn onto each section of the beam.

Bobbin winder: This piece of equipment is not necessary but is a big aid in winding

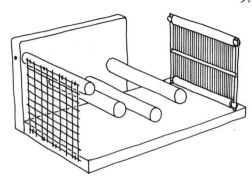

A simple tension box.

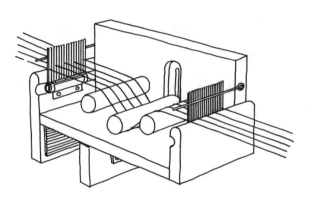

Tension box, adjustable to fit on any size of back beam, where it must be securely attached.

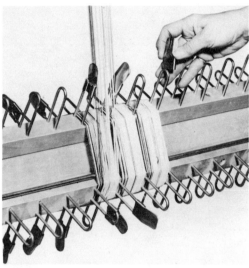

Warp being wound on a sectional warp beam. Metal thread guides can be put on the rakes to guide the warp yarn onto each section. Eight guides are used on each section. *Photo courtesy Nilus Leclerc, Inc.*

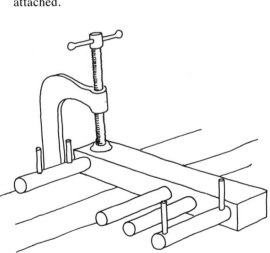

An easily constructed tensioner attached to the warp beam with a C-clamp. The yarn is guided onto each section of the beam with metal thread guides.

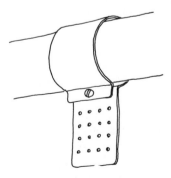

Thread guide for a round back beam; it slides easily for correct position and can be used without a tension box providing the yarn unreels evenly from the spools.

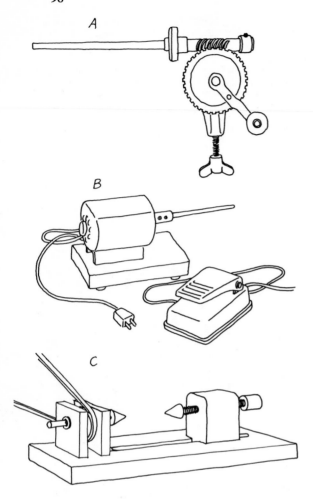

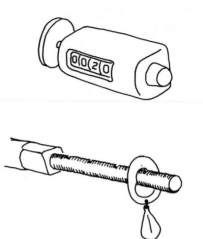

Counters to tally the number of yards of warp being wound on a sectional beam.
Top: Mechanical counter—the length of the warp yarn is recorded as the yarn passes around the wheel.
Bottom: A simple device that fits on the end of the warp beam and measures or counts the number of times the warp beam goes around, therefore measuring the length of the warp yarn.

Bobbin or spool winders:

A. A hand-crank model that is secured to a table.

B. Electric model with foot-controlled variable-speed rheostat.

C. Motor- or hand-crank-driven model. Any size of spool or bobbin can be used, since it is held between two points.

Dividers or spacers used to keep warp yarn separated.

Dividers: These are small pieces of wood or plastic placed in the warp as it is wound on the beam to ensure even tension by keeping the warp yarn separated. This is also optional equipment.

To prepare a sectional warp, have the loom equipped with a sectional warp beam and follow these steps:

the spools of yarn for the warp. An electric winder with a variable speed control is the most useful.

Measuring device or counter: This is optional equipment but certainly convenient. It attaches to the tension box and measures the length of the warp yarn being put on the loom. Without a counter, you must keep track of each revolution of the beam to get the desired warp length and to be sure each section is the same length.

1. Plan the warp. Determine the length and number of ends per inch. Also plan any color sequence.

2. Wind the warp yarn on spools. In sectional warping you are winding the warp in 1- or 2-inch (2.5–5 cm) sections at a time, depending on the sectional warp beam. One spool of yarn is needed for each warp end in a section. EXAMPLE: If

you are preparing 2-inch (5 cm) sections and the warp plan calls for 10 warp ends per inch, 20 spools are needed. The amount of yarn on each spool is determined by the length and width of the warp. EXAMPLE: If the warp is 20 inches (50 cm) wide and 10 yards (9.14 m) long and there are 2-inch (5 cm) sections, each of the 20 spools should hold at least 100 yards (91.4 m) of yarn.

$$(20 \div 2 \times 10 = 100)$$
$$(50 \div 5 \times 9.14 = 91.4)$$

Be generous. To wind the spools, use a bobbin winder and run the yarn through the counter to measure the length of yarn for each spool.

3. Arrange the spools on the rack. Place the spool rack directly behind the loom and arrange the spools, in order of any planned color sequence, so each unwinds in the same direction.

4. Thread the tension box. Place the tension box on the back beam directly above the section of warp being wound. Fasten it securely. Place the warp ends over and under the pegs of the box and thread them in order through the reed in the box.

5. There are varying methods of fastening the warp to the beam. The easiest method I have found is a cord with a loop at the end tied to each section. The warp ends for each section are grouped and tied to this loop. Many sectional beams are equipped with screw eyes or a rod to fasten the cords. The cord serves a similar purpose as the apron on a regular warp beam. This method allows the maximum amount of warp to be woven at the end.

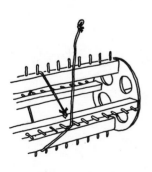

Cord on every section of warp beam is used to attach each group of warp yarns.

6. Now the warp can be wound on the beam. Be sure the yarn is in line from the spool rack, through the tension box, and onto the section being wound. Turn the crank on the beam the number of revolutions to get the planned length of warp. A counter will accurately measure the length; otherwise, count the revolutions and multiply by the beam circumference. In this case, work uninterruptedly for an accurate measurement. Be sure all warp ends are running freely, under even tension from the spools. To prevent warp ends from cutting into each other on the beam and to ensure even tension, place dividers through the warp as it is being wound around the beam—one divider every two or three revolutions of the beam.

7. Wind the second section. When the required length of warp is on the beam, put a piece of masking tape across the warp ends just beyond the reed of the tension box. Be sure to keep all ends in order, one beside the other. Now manually pull the warp about 10 inches (25 cm) through the tension box. Cut the warp behind the masking tape (closest to the tension box). Do not let the free warp ends slide out of the tension box. Tape the end of the warp to the section just wound so it doesn't flap around when you are winding succeeding sections. Now tie the loose warp ends to the loop of cord in the next section and proceed in the same manner until the full warp is wound.

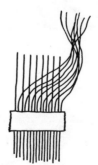

Tape on the warp ends keeps them in order.

In sectional warping, the warp is prepared and beamed on the loom in one operation. You are ready now to proceed with threading the heddles (see Chapter 5, "Dressing the Loom").

Using Prewarped Spools

Some makes of loom have a hexagonal metal warp beam. Spools of ready-warped yarn can be put on this beam. The spools have a hexagonal hole in the center so they will not slide around the beam. The warp has been put on the spools under even tension and to an accurate length measure. After these spools are placed on the beam, the warping and beaming processes are eliminated and you are ready to thread the heddles (see Chapter 5, "Dressing the Loom"). The spools each provide 2 inches (5 cm) width of warp.

The variety of yarn available on prewarped spools is limited, but they certainly serve a purpose. No warping equipment is needed, and warping and beaming time is eliminated.

The hexagonal beam is generally available only for table looms, but with the proper resources a hexagonal beam could be adapted to larger floor looms.

With a very simple piece of equipment (shown in the illustration below) the empty spools can be rewound with warp yarn. The process is very similar to sectional warping.

Loom with prewarped spools.
◀

Equipment used with prewarped spools:
   A. Device used to rewind spools with warp.
   B. The hexagonal metal warp beam.
   C. Prewarped spool.
   D. Empty spool. ▼

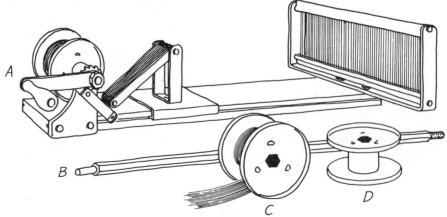

A

B

C

D

Warping Simple Frame Looms

On very simple frame looms the processes of warping and dressing the loom are done at one time. The warp is quite often one continuous strand of yarn, in which case it is wound back and forth around the object used as a loom. Be careful to keep the yarn taut and under even tension. Two ways of putting warp on a frame loom are:

1. Fasten the yarn to the bottom of the frame, then put the warp yarn all the way around the frame by going up the front, over the top of the frame, down the back, and under the bottom of the frame; then start over again. You can weave two pieces, one on the front and one on the back, or you can put the warp yarns together as you weave.

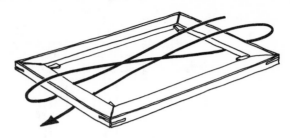

An artist's canvas stretcher used for a frame loom with the warp in a figure-eight manner. The wedges need not be used.

Twining is done on a closed shed. A double strand of yarn goes over and under, crossing between each pair of warp ends.

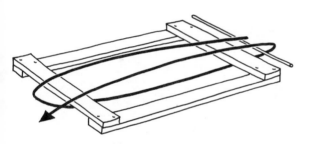

Easily constructed frame loom with warp going all the way around the frame. Bar at end is removed during weaving to relieve tightness of warp caused by take-up.

2. The second method is to wind the warp around the frame in a figure-eight manner. Fasten the yarn to the bottom of the frame, put it through the center, over the top from the back, through the center again, and around the bottom from the back; start again by going through the center. It is easier to keep even tension on this warp, and the warp ends are easier to separate to make a shed, or opening for the weft yarn to pass through. To keep the warp ends evenly spaced, place a row of twining or chaining across the warp at the beginning of the weaving. After the weaving is finished, place another row of twining or chaining across

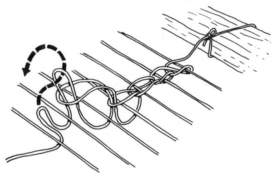

Chaining is done on a closed shed. Take a piece of strong yarn about five times the width of the warp. Fasten the yarn to the side of the loom and put the yarn underneath the warp ends. Pull up a loop beside the first warp end, use a crochet hook or put your thumb and forefinger through the loop, and pull up another loop between the first and second warp ends through the first loop. Tighten the first loop, and continue in this way across the warp. To finish, pull the end of the yarn through the last loop.

the end; leave the first row in place. This makes neat edges on the weaving.

Loom size does not matter when you are warping and dressing a frame loom. Many weaves and techniques can be done on frame looms, but it takes more time because the loom is not performing many functions,

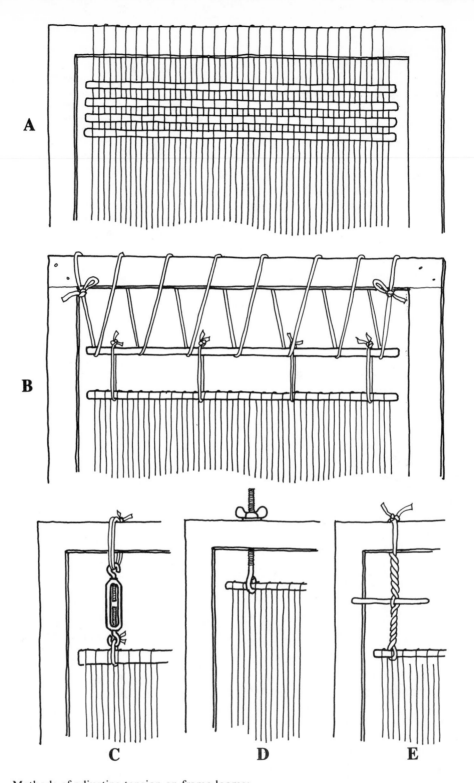

Methods of adjusting tension on frame looms:

A. Put a loose warp on the frame. Insert wood or thick cardboard strips in the warp. Use as many as needed to make the warp tight. As the weaving progresses and the warp gets too tight, remove the strips one at a time to relieve the tension.

B. Attach an additional stick or dowel to the bar that holds the warp. Lash the second bar to the frame. As tension increases on the warp, release the lashing.

C. Attach the bar that holds the warp to the frame with a turn buckle. Start with it tightly screwed. Gently unscrew it to release the tension on the warp.

D. Put holes in the frame and insert eye bolts. Unscrew to release warp tension.

E. Fasten the bar that holds the warp to the frame with cord. Twist with a stick to adjust the tension.

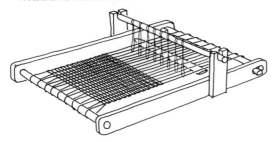

A frame loom with string heddles and a stick used to make sheds.

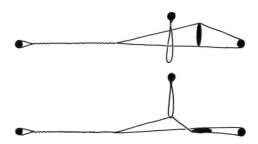

How sheds are made with string heddles:
Top: Shed stick turned on end, making one shed.
Bottom: String heddle pulled up, creating opposite shed.

such as separating the warp ends to allow the weft to pass through. Very large projects can be undertaken on what is basically a frame loom. To aid in separating the warp ends, string heddles and a shed stick can be used. The string heddles are tied to every other warp end, making one shed, and the stick is inserted under the opposite warp ends. When this stick is turned on end, the opposite shed is opened. Rigid heddle frames can also be used in frame looms to make the shed.

When weaving on a large frame loom for quite a distance there will be considerable take-up, causing the warp to become very tight. While warping a frame loom, you can use several different methods to help relieve this tightness and still keep an even tension when weaving. Wood or cardboard strips inserted in the warp can be removed when the warp becomes tight. Or a means can be provided for allowing the bar that holds the warp to be extended from the frame to relieve the tension.

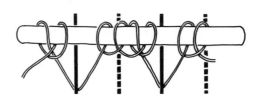

Method of tying string heddles on a bar for frame or tapestry loom: Starting at the left, make a clove hitch on the bar, go under the first warp end, make half hitches and then another clove hitch, go under the third warp end, and make another series of half hitches. Repeat across the loom, putting a string heddle around every other warp end.

5

vvvvvvvvvvvvvvvvvvvvvvvvvvvvvvvvvvvvvvvvvvvvvvvvvvvvvvvvvvvvvvvvvvvvvvvvvvvvv

Dressing the Loom

Getting the warp on the loom ready for weaving is appropriately called *dressing the loom*. The five processes involved are:

1. Beaming the warp—winding the warp on the warp beam.
2. Threading the heddles.
3. Sleying the reed—pulling threads through the reed.
4. Tying on the warp—fastening the warp to the cloth beam.
5. Spreading—evenly distributing the warp ends across the loom.

The above processes are not necessarily listed in order, as there are several methods of dressing a loom. The beginning weaver should try the different methods and then pick the one most suited to the circumstances and equipment. The individual style of working, the type of yarn, and the weave or technique used can determine the method; each weaver will have a favorite. The most important point is the end result, a well-dressed loom.

Have confidence that the processes described here can be carried out by an individual working alone. It is nice to have help, but being aware of your own skills and understanding the theory behind the processes will enable you to put the warp on the loom by yourself—and this is actually recommended.

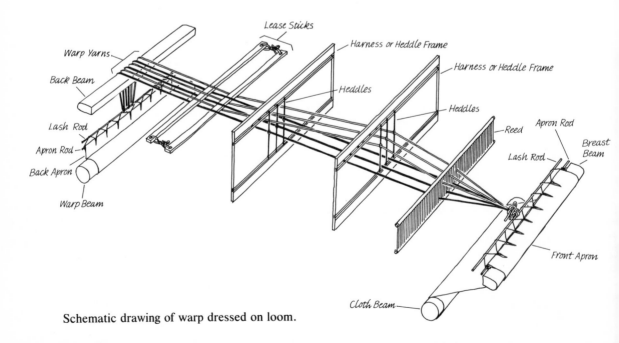

Schematic drawing of warp dressed on loom.

Dressing the Loom from the Back Toward the Front

BEAMING THE WARP

This process involves fastening the warp to the warp beam apron and winding the warp around this beam. The object is to have the warp evenly tensioned and evenly spaced on the beam to the width of the intended weaving.

The equipment needed for beaming is:

1. **Lease sticks:** These are usually made of wood; you will need at least two. They should be 6 inches (15 cm) wider than the weaving width of the loom. They must be smooth, slender, springy (bend easily), have rounded edges, and have a large hole in each end.

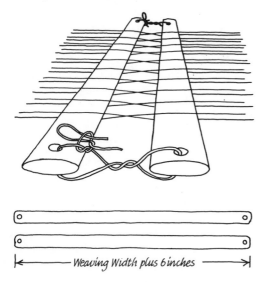

Top: Lease sticks in the porrey cross, their ends securely tied. The twist in the cord that ties the sticks together keeps them about ½ inch (1.3 cm) apart.
Bottom: A pair of lease sticks.

2. **Raddle:** This is similar to a reed but open on one long side and containing fewer dents, or slots, per inch (or centimeter). Very old raddles were all wood, with 2-inch (5 cm) sections and a "cape"

to cover the open top; they were called *order reeds.* Newer models have metal teeth with ½-inch (1.3 cm) sections. To use the raddle, set it in the batten in place of the reed. The handtree acts as the cape. Homemade versions are simply a smooth piece of wood with finishing nails set in, evenly spaced, for teeth. To prevent the warp from coming out of the spaces, take a strong piece of string, tie it to the first nail, and then wind it around each nail, across the warp ends, as the warp spacing progresses. If you do not use the raddle in the batten, clamp or tie it on the back or breast beam or shuttle race, or find a place and a method of securing it on your particular loom.

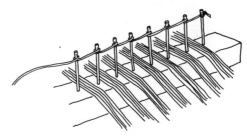

Method of using string to close top of raddle so warp ends will not fall out.

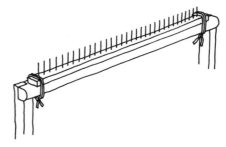

Raddle securely fastened to the back or breast beam.

3. **Heavy brown paper, corrugated cardboard, or sticks:** The paper or cardboard must be wider than the warp and sturdy and smooth (no tears). The length should be 1 yard (0.9 m) less than the warp length. It can be used over and over. The sticks should be smooth and wider than the warp, and you will need four to six for each yard (0.9 m) of warp.

The steps in beaming the warp are:

1. Get the loom ready for beaming. Remove the reed and batten handtree. If the harness frames are easy to remove from the loom, remove them. Otherwise push the heddles to the extreme right and left edges of the frames, evenly divided on each side. If you are using the full width of the loom, it is best to remove the frames. Lay the warp through the center of the loom, the looped or porrey cross end toward the back.

2. Mark the weaving width with masking tape on the back beam and the apron. This is simply a guide; remove the tape when the warp is beamed. Some old looms have notches, scribe marks, or pegs on the beam to use as a guide.

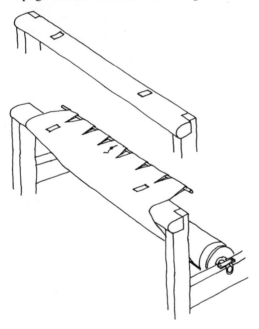

Masking tape on back beam and apron marks warp width. The yarn must be centered on the beam. A brightly colored piece of yarn sewn to the center of the apron is also helpful.

3. Unroll the apron and bar from the warp beam and place them on top of the back beam.

4. If the warp is chained, untie the last tie (the one of a different color) and place your hand through the warp loop.

5. Slide out the lash rod (sometimes called the apron bar) and place the looped end of the warp on this bar. Keep the warp within the measured area for the width of the weaving. If the lash rod is fastened to the apron at intervals, evenly space the warp in each area.

6. Walk to the front of the loom, take hold of the warp in a bunch, pull it toward you, and shake it gently to straighten it out. Do not comb your fingers through it or remove any ties.

7. From the back, find where the porrey cross is tied. Put the lease sticks through on either side of the cross—they will be in the same places as the pegs were on the warping equipment. Securely tie the ends of the lease sticks, keeping them up to ½ inch (1.3 cm) apart. Check again to be sure the lease sticks will not slide out of the warp, and then remove the ties that marked the cross in the warp. There should be four ties. Pull the short end of the half-bowknot to untie it quickly and easily.

8. Now anchor the lease sticks to the loom so they do not flop from side to side. Some looms have devices to hold the lease sticks, or you can tie them to the castle supports with cords.

9. Gently move the warp ends apart at the cross, spreading the warp to the weaving width.

10. If the warp is over 20 inches (50 cm) wide, use a raddle to keep the width of the warp. Put it in the batten in place of the reed. With tape, mark the warp width, centered, on the raddle. Raddles are usually marked off in ½-inch (1.3 cm) sections. Look at one edge of the warp as it comes across the lease sticks. Take the number of warp ends from the edge that constitutes ½ inch (1.3 cm) of the warp. Place these ends in the first section of the raddle. EXAMPLE: Warp is planned with ten warp ends per inch; place five warp ends in each section. Be sure to take the warp ends in order: the first passes over one lease stick and under the other stick; the second, in the opposite position. Place all the warp

The warp fastened
to the center of the
back lash rod. The
lease sticks are
inserted in the
porrey cross, then
securely tied
together and
anchored to the
loom. *Note:* in this
illustration, for the
sake of clarity, the
heddle frames are
not pictured.

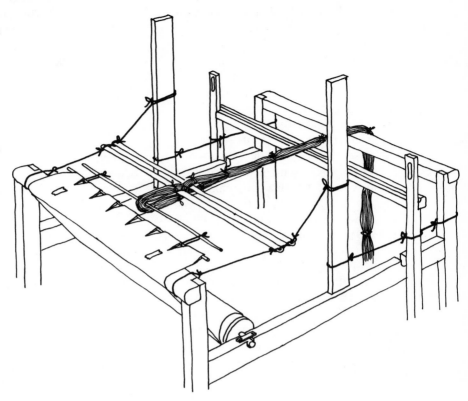

The warp spread to
the weaving width
and lashed to the
apron rod. The warp
is evenly spread in
the raddle, which
will maintain the
warp width during
beaming.

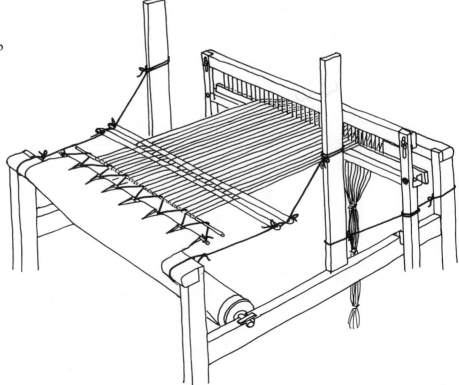

ends in the raddle. Then replace the batten handtree or cape, or put string around the nails (depending on the type of raddle), to prevent the warp ends from coming out of the raddle.

11. Remove additional ties from the warp if they prevent it from spreading to its full width. Shake the warp again from the front and spread it to its full width.

12. Standing at the right side of the loom, facing the back, start turning the warp beam. On most looms the beam turns clockwise. Be sure the brake on the beam holds; the beam must not be allowed to unwind (turn forward, or counterclockwise). Turn the beam until the lash rod meets the beam.

13. Now check for uneven tension by gently patting the warp across the top near the cross. It is easy to feel warp ends that are loose and spongy or very taut. Find the cause—usually strands of the yarn twisting around one another—and correct any loose or tight warp ends.

14. As the warp is wound around the warp beam, insert heavy brown paper, corrugated cardboard, or wooden sticks between layers of the warp to prevent one layer on the warp beam from cutting into the lower layer. If this happened,

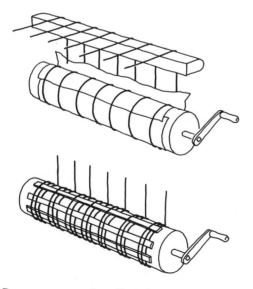

Paper, corrugated cardboard, or wooden sticks are wrapped with the warp as it is beamed.

some warp ends could be caught and pulled out, causing them to sag during weaving. Whichever material is used between the layers of warp, be sure it is wider than the warp, for the warp must never be allowed to fall off the edges of the material.

15. Continue beaming the warp, undoing the ties as you go. Check continuously for even tension on all warp ends. Beam under low tension; you will tighten the warp later as you weave. Stop turning the beam when the end of the warp is at least 10 inches (25 cm) in front of the harness frames. The ends can fall out of the raddle now, for it has served its purpose. Remove the raddle from the loom.

THREADING THE HEDDLES

This process involves putting each warp end through the eye of a heddle. The order in which the heddles are threaded determines the pattern of the weave. Here I will describe the basic method of threading called *straight draw*. (For specifics on threading according to a particular plan, see Chapter 7, "Drafting.") If the loom was beamed by the sectional warping method or if prewarped spools were used, now proceed with threading the heddles. There will be no lease sticks, but the warp ends are threaded in order as they come off the tape.

There are several kinds of heddle: string, wire, flat steel, inserted-eye, and continuous-filament polyester heddles. A string heddle has a large eye, making it easy to thread; it will not cause unnecessary abrasion on the warp ends because it "gives"; it is noiseless and lightweight (necessary for some looms, especially countermarche) and with a frame is easy to make. String heddles are impractical on table looms because there tends to be a certain amount of stretch with them and the shed on a table loom is not deep enough to accommodate this. Wire heddles are the least expensive; they are easy to thread, with a large eye; and they slide easily on the heddle bar but will bend. Flat steel heddles are sturdy, have a small

Top: Frame for tying string heddles. Loop string around peg A, tie knots at pegs B and C. Complete heddle by tying ends together around peg D.

Bottom: Drawing of frame, showing that the center line of the heddle is not the center of the pegs. ▶

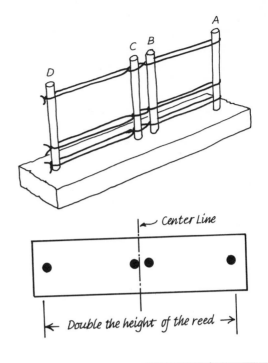

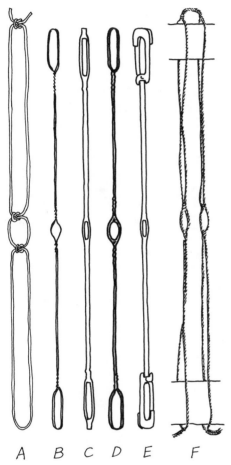

A B C D E F

Styles of heddle: A, string; B, wire; C, flat ▲ steel; D, inserted-eye; E, repair heddle (can be inserted anywhere on the harness frame to correct an error in threading); F, continuous-filament polyester heddles, shown on the heddle bars.

A variety of reed and heddle hooks. Hooks vary according to yarn being used and size (depth) of loom. ▶

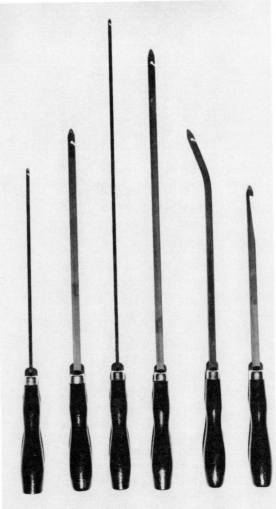

eye, and generally cost more. Inserted-eye heddles cost about the same as flat steel but have a large molded eye, eliminating abrasion of the warp ends. They are otherwise similar to wire heddles. Continuous-filament heddles are made of knotless, braided polyester. The heddles are joined in a continuous 100-heddle bundle and are easily put on the heddle bars. These heddles do not stretch, they slide easily on the heddle bars, and there is little friction between warp and heddle. Continuous-filament heddles are available in a variety of eye lengths.

A large-eye heddle is easy to thread and would seem suitable for either heavy or fine yarn. However, a small eye is in fact more satisfactory for fine yarn, since it permits a clear separation of warp ends. Heddles are made in standard lengths. The different styles are readily available and can be interchanged on most looms.

You will find a reed and heddle hook handy. This is a flat piece of metal with a hook on the end and a comfortable wooden handle. This hook is optional equipment: you can thread the heddles without it.

A mistake in threading the heddles is very easy to make and time-consuming to correct. Accuracy is of utmost importance, for it directly affects the quality of the weaving.

To thread the heddles:

1. Find a comfortable position for working—you can work from the front, back, or side of the loom. The size and style of loom influence your decision. Remove any parts of the loom necessary to get as close to the heddle frames as possible. Reaching and stretching while threading the heddles can be very tiring.
2. The lease sticks should be close to the back harness frame, in a position level with the eyes of the heddles. They can be suspended from the loom frame or held between cords fastened to the loom on either side of the warp. The warp ends are hanging from the sticks, and from the front of the loom it is easy to see the order of the warp ends. Thread the heddles from the right, the left, or the center; this is a personal preference. Use the heddles in the center of each frame. Push the ex-

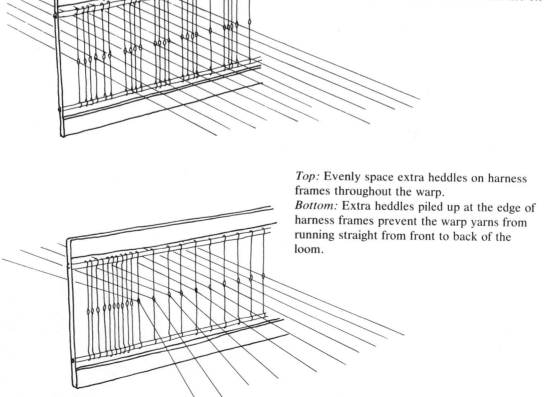

Top: Evenly space extra heddles on harness frames throughout the warp.
Bottom: Extra heddles piled up at the edge of harness frames prevent the warp yarns from running straight from front to back of the loom.

tras to the extreme right and left on each harness frame.

If you are using the full width of the loom but not all the heddles, let the extras hang unthreaded, evenly spaced throughout the warp. The edge of the warp (selvage) must lie in a straight line from the warp beam to the cloth beam, and if heddles are piled up on the edges the warp cannot be straight. It is easy to remove unneeded heddles from the frames, but time-consuming to replace them.

3. Thread the heddles in a straight draw— the basic threading pattern. In a four-harness loom, the first warp end will go in a heddle on harness 1 (closest to the front), the second in a heddle on harness 2, the third in a heddle on harness 3, and the fourth in a heddle on harness 4. Repeat this order until all warp ends are used.

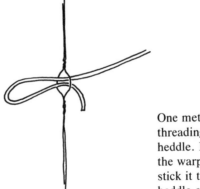

One method of threading the heddle. Fold over the warp end and stick it through the heddle eye.

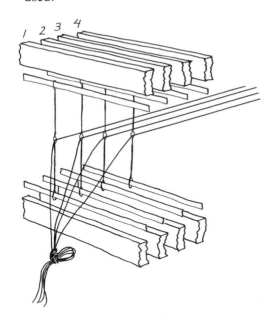

Four harness frames threaded in a straight draw. Each group of warp yarns is tied in a slipknot.

4. To thread the heddle, pick up the warp end, fold the end over, and stick the fold through the eye of the heddle. Or use the reed and heddle hook to hook the yarn and pull it through the heddle eye.

5. When a group of threaded warp ends constitutes a multiple of four, group and tie the ends in a slipknot in front of the harness frames. By grouping the warp ends in fours you can check for errors. The slipknot prevents the warp ends from falling out of the heddles, and it is easy to untie for the next process.

SLEYING THE REED

The reed evenly spaces the warp ends and helps maintain the desired width of the weaving while you are working. To *sley a reed* means to put the warp ends through the spaces, or dents, of the reed. The reed is a comblike structure with both sides closed and with metal teeth. It is called a reed because originally the teeth were of reed or bamboo. There are regular steel as well as stainless-steel reeds. A reed is useless if it is rusty, so in damp climates stainless steel reeds or reeds treated to prevent rust are a good investment.

Reeds are described according to their length, height, and number of dents per inch (or centimeter). The new international standard is dents per centimeter, but most American reeds have been measured in inches. The number of dents is usually imprinted on the metal piece on the end of the reed. If it isn't marked, count the spaces within a specific measure. Most handloom reeds are 5 inches (12.5 cm) high but are also available in heights from 4 to 6 inches (10–15 cm).

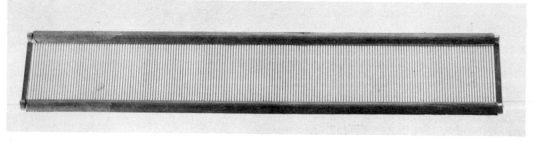

A present-day reed.

Reed Dent Conversion

Metric to inches

Dents per cm	2	2½	3	3½	4	4½	5	5½	6	6½	7	7½	8
Dents per inch (approx.)	5	6	7½	9	10	11½	13	14	15	16½	18	19	20

1 centimeter = .394 inch

SLEYING

Use the same hook with which you threaded the heddles or use a reed hook, which is a large flat hook of plastic, metal, or ivory. It should be flexible and easy to hold.

The reed is sleyed from the front of the loom. The reed can be in the batten or lying flat supported by two strips of wood that rest on the breast beam and batten or back beam.

To sley the reed:

1. Mark the width of the weaving in the center part of the reed by tying a fine piece of yarn around the dent at each edge of the measure. The reed can be sleyed from right to left, from left to right, or from the center out to each side. All warp ends *must* be in order through the heddles and the reed. They cannot be crossed over one another.
2. With one hand, release the slipknot from the first group of warp ends. With the other hand holding the reed hook, put it through a dent, hook onto a warp end, and pull it through a dent in the reed. After each group is through the reed, tie a slipknot again. (The warp ends can easily fall out of the reed.)
3. After all the warp ends are sleyed, replace the reed in the batten if it was lying flat for sleying.

The sett of the warp was determined when the weaving was planned. A weaver usually doesn't have a reed for every sett. The solution is *compound sleying:* dents can be skipped, or more than one warp end can be sleyed in a dent. It is necessary to work out a plan for sleying so the warp ends are evenly spaced. The accompanying table shows how to sley a specific dent-per-inch reed for a specific sett of warp, again per inch.

To use the table, find the number of dents in your reed by consulting the top row. Now move down to the number of warp ends to be used; then across to the left to determine the sleying order of the warp in the reed. For example, when using a 12-dent reed for 8 warp ends per inch, sley the reed in the following manner: leave an empty dent; sley a single warp end in each of the next two dents (as indicated by the 0–1–1 sequence on the table), and repeat.

Compound sleying will leave marks in the weaving. Sometimes the mark will disappear

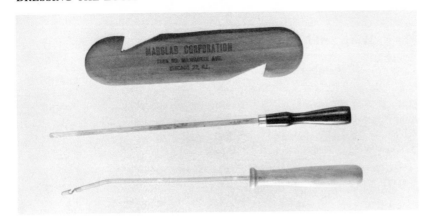

Reed hooks.

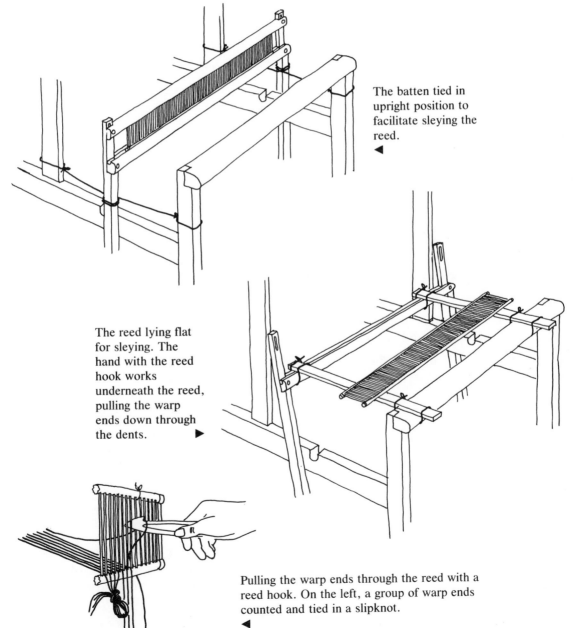

The batten tied in
upright position to
facilitate sleying the
reed.
◄

The reed lying flat
for sleying. The
hand with the reed
hook works
underneath the reed,
pulling the warp
ends down through
the dents.   ►

Pulling the warp ends through the reed with a
reed hook. On the left, a group of warp ends
counted and tied in a slipknot.
◄

Warp Sett for Compound Sleying

Number of Reed Dents

Sleying Order	5	6	8	10	12	15
			Warp Ends			
0–1			4	5	6	7½
0–1–1		4	5½	6½	8	10
1	5	6	8	10	12	15
1–1–2	5½	8	10½	13½	16	20
1–2	7½	9	12	15	18	22½
1–2–2	8½	10	13	17	20	25
2	10	12	16	20	24	30
2–2–3	11½	14	18½	23	27	35
2–3–3	13	16	21½	26½	32	40
3	15	18	24	30	36	45

when the weaving is removed from the loom, and at other times the mark can be used to advantage as part of the design.

A general rule when choosing a reed is that it is best to use a reed with fewer dents and sley double rather than single when fine yarns are used. There is less abrasion on the warp ends, and if there should be a knot in the warp it will more easily go through the reed because the space between the dents is wider.

TYING-ON

The next process in dressing the loom is tying the warp ends to the lash rod (or apron bar) attached to the cloth beam. The object is to attach all the warp ends securely, under even tension.

No additional equipment is needed for this process. The loom should have a sturdy wooden or metal bar attached either by ropes or by a canvas apron to the cloth beam. This bar must be parallel to the cloth beam.

First method:

1. Release the brake on the cloth beam so the apron can unroll. Bring the apron and rod up around the outside and over the top of the breast beam. The rod should be 4 to 6 inches (10–15 cm) beyond the breast beam. Secure the brake again on the cloth beam so it will not unroll.

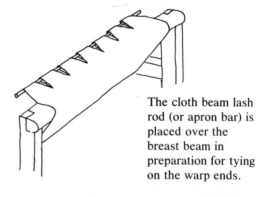

The cloth beam lash rod (or apron bar) is placed over the breast beam in preparation for tying on the warp ends.

2. Untie a group of warp ends from one side of the warp, take that group over the lash rod, split it, and bring up one half at the right, the other half at the left. Tie a single

knot on top. (Do not tie half-bowknot yet.) Do the same with the group on the opposite end, then the group in the middle, and lastly the groups in between. The single knot should be rather taut. If the warp ends are not long enough to tie a bowknot, release the brake on the warp beam and pull each group of warp ends gently forward. When they are long enough, make sure the warp beam will not unroll by securing the brake.

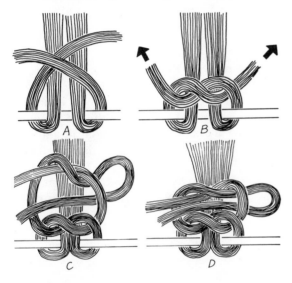

Method of tying warp ends to front apron:
 A. Take a group of warp ends, put over lash rod, separate underneath, and bring to the top.
 B. Tie ends in overhand knot. To tighten tension, pull ends forward.
 C. Tie half-bowknot.
 D. Tighten knot to finish.

3. Using both hands, take hold of the warp ends from each group and tighten. To do this, pull the ends forward, away from you; when all slack has been taken up, tighten the knot. Starting at one side, do this across the warp continuously.
4. Now be sure the tension is even across the entire warp. With the hand (palm down) parallel to the reed, gently touch the warp, moving across it, to check for even tension. The best place for testing tension is between the beater and the harnesses. The groups that feel spongy are loose and can be tightened by pulling

the ends toward the reed again. Any group that is too taut can be loosened by pushing down hard with the thumb on that group. If this doesn't loosen enough, make an adjustment at the knot.
5. When the tension is even, finish off the single knot with a half-bowknot.

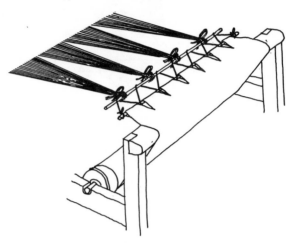

Warp tied to cloth beam lash rod.

Second method:

1. Follow step 1 in preceding method.
2. Untie the slipknot from each group and replace it with an overhand knot. By using small groups of warp in each knot, there is very little warp wasted.

Overhand knot in group of warp ends.

3. Take a strong piece of cord about three times as long as the width of the warp and fasten the end to the apron bar. Put the cord through the warp ends above the knot, around the bar, and on to the next

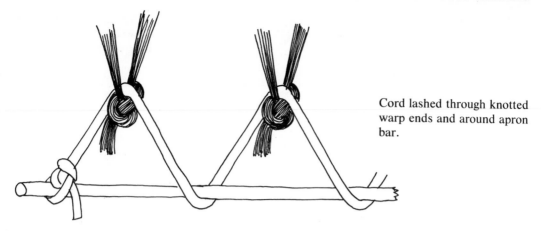

Cord lashed through knotted warp ends and around apron bar.

knot until all are fastened to the bar. Tie the other end of the cord to the apron bar.

4. Tighten the tension by turning the cloth beam. The cord will "give" or ease until all the groups of warp ends are under even tension. The knots will not necessarily be in a straight line.

Third method:

This method of tying on is used if the warp is made of yarns that slip easily and will not hold a knot. Tie each group to the lash rod with a single knot, as in the first method, then turn the cloth beam until the warp is tight. The shortest groups will slip and soon all groups will be at the same tension. Then finish off each group with the half-bowknot pulled very taut to prevent further slipping.

The first method described for tying on is best if you have to correct errors made in threading and sleying (mistakes will not show until you start to weave). The second method is much quicker, but it is more difficult to make corrections if there are threading or sleying errors.

Dressing the Loom from the Front Toward the Back

In this method, the processes previously described are done in the reverse order.

The warp should be cut at the porrey cross end. Take the warp to the front of the loom. Put the lease sticks through the cross

and securely tie the ends. So that the lease sticks will not teeter or fall out of the warp, tie them at each end to the breast beam. Leave a space about the width of a finger between the sticks and the beam to allow the warp ends to move freely through the sticks.

Sley the reed as before, but from front to back, taking the warp ends in order from the lease sticks. Next thread the heddles, working from the front to the back. Sleying the reed and threading the heddles can be done in one or two steps; that is, one warp end at a time can be sleyed in the reed and then threaded through the heddle, or all warp ends can be sleyed and then all threaded through the heddles.

The warp is still partially chained and hanging over the breast beam to the floor. It is not under tension at all. As each group of warp ends is threaded through the heddles, the ends are evened as much as possible and a slipknot tied. These groups of warp ends hang behind harness 4.

After threading is completed, remove the ties and spread the warp to its full width. You can stretch it out on the floor in front of the loom.

Take each group of warp ends and tie them with a knot to the rod in the warp beam apron. Now beam the warp exactly as described for dressing the loom from the back. Roll clean heavy brown paper, corrugated cardboard, or wooden sticks in with the warp. Check constantly to be sure the warp ends are not twisted around one another.

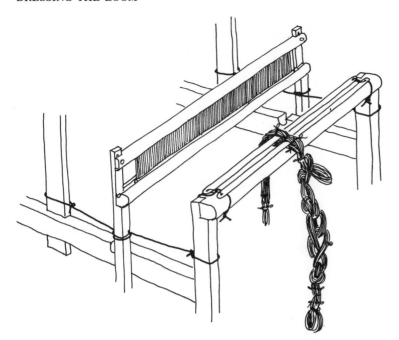

The warp at the front of the loom with the lease sticks tied together at the ends, then tied to the breast beam.

They must move uninterruptedly through the reed and heddles. If the warp was made with two strands or more at once—that is, when two warp ends go together over and under the lease sticks—then the lease sticks should be removed before winding the warp on the warp beam. The two ends will twist around each other, preventing them from sliding freely through the lease sticks. This puts undue stress on the yarn.

Stop beaming when the end of the warp meets the breast beam. Remove the lease sticks and tie on the warp in the same manner as when dressing the loom from the back.

Why dress the loom from the back?

1. There are no knots to interfere with tension on the warp beam.
2. The warp is not drawn through the heddles and reed twice (once in dressing the loom and once in weaving), which puts unnecessary wear on fine, delicate yarns.
3. More of the warp can be woven because it doesn't take additional length to tie to the warp beam lash rod.
4. A weaver can sit inside a large loom with a deep bed (distance from breast beam to heddles), making sleying and threading easy.

Why dress the loom from the front?

1. No raddle is needed.
2. It is easy to beam the warp because the reed keeps the warp ends evenly spaced and to the desired width.
3. A loom with a short bed (distance from breast beam to heddles) is more easily threaded from the front.

Joining New Warp to Old

The preceding section explains dressing an empty loom. There are times, however, when a weaver has a special threading on a loom and wants to continue weaving the same pattern, but the warp is used up. Dressing a loom is a slow process, so in this instance it is much quicker to tie a new warp onto the old one. To do this, there must be the same number of warp ends and the reed sley and heddle threading must be the same.

1. When no more weaving can be done on the old warp, grasp a bunch of warp ends in front of the reed and cut close to the weaving. Now tie a slipknot in the bunch of warp ends close to the reed. Continue in this manner across the warp and remove the weaving from the loom. Tie the

beater securely to the center part of the loom.

2. Prepare the new warp as usual and cut at the porrey cross end.

3. Take the warp to the front of the loom, insert the lease sticks, and securely tie their ends. Loosely tie the lease sticks to the breast beam. Don't forget to leave a space about the width of a finger between the sticks and the beam to allow the warp ends to move freely.

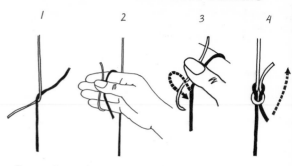

Square knot tied to join old and new warp ends:

1. Cross the warp ends, one under the other, as shown.

2. With one end coming from each direction, lay them over your hand.

3. Put one yarn over and through loop of other yarn. Pull each end in its own direction.

4. To undo, straighten one warp end; the other will slide off.

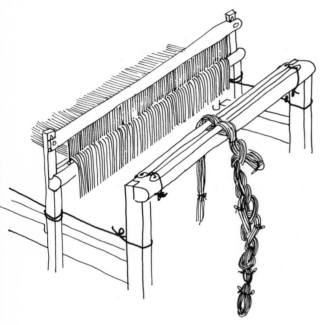

The new warp at the front of the loom ready to be tied to the ends of the old warp.

In this method the warp is put on from the front of the loom. The same results can be achieved working from the back, by cutting the old warp from the warp beam, beaming the new warp, tying the old and new warp ends together behind the harness frames, and pulling the old warp through to the front. Cut it off and tie the new warp to the cloth beam lash rod.

Much time can be saved in dressing a loom in this manner. After a little practice, you can tie the knots very quickly.

Spreading the Warp Ends

Before actual weaving can begin, the warp ends must be evenly spread across the loom. The triangular spaces made in the warp when it was grouped and tied to the lash rod must be closed. The warp ends should lie parallel to one another. This is called the *heading*.

The easiest method for weaving the heading is to use soft cotton roving (loosely spun yarn, about ½ inch [1.3 cm] in diameter), strips of knit fabric (1 inch [2.5 cm] in diameter), or bathroom tissue. Using a tabby shed, raise half the warp ends, put through the shed the material being used, beat it

4. Tie the new warp ends to the old warp ends in order. Use a square knot because it is distributed around the yarn and will slip easily through the reed dent; it is also easy to pull apart if a mistake is made. To pull apart, straighten either warp end and the other can be pulled off it.

5. When all new and old warp ends are tied, remove the lease sticks and start to wind the warp beam slowly. Gently ease the knots through the reed and heddles.

6. Cut off the old warp and tie the new one to the lash rod of the warp beam.

7. Beam the warp, then tie the warp ends to the cloth beam lash rod.

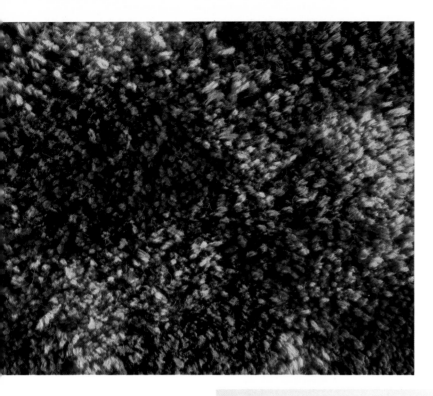

Pile weaves permit subtle grada-
tions of tones:

    1. (Above) Rug woven with
Ghiordes knots in a dense pile.

    2. (Right) Corduroy-weave
rug.

The effect of striped weaves:

3. (Right) A variety of belts woven on an inkle loom. It is the color sequence, usually in the warp, that gives the plain-weave article its pattern and distinction. *Photo by Allen Harrington.*

4. (Left) The white weft mutes and blends the warp of this throw woven with handspun wool yarn. After washing, the best way to dry a blanket such as this is to spread it on fresh grass in sunlight. The fibers brighten and soften, giving them a beautiful "hand." Woven by Valerie Creager.

5. (Below) A variation on this theme is this place mat woven with strips of fabric — a scaled-down "rag rug" by Marian Gooding.

6. Tapestry by Mary Nice in flat weave, demonstrating color blending technique.

7. A twill threading, woolen strips of fabric, and a fine color sense make a rag rug something special.

22

8. Eight-harness twill-variation threading and tie-up were used to weave "Birds" by Ros Weston.

9. *Left to right, top:* Cardinal, mockingbird, woodpecker, sparrow, bluejay.
Left to right, bottom: Hummingbird, purple finch, kinglet, wren, golden finch.

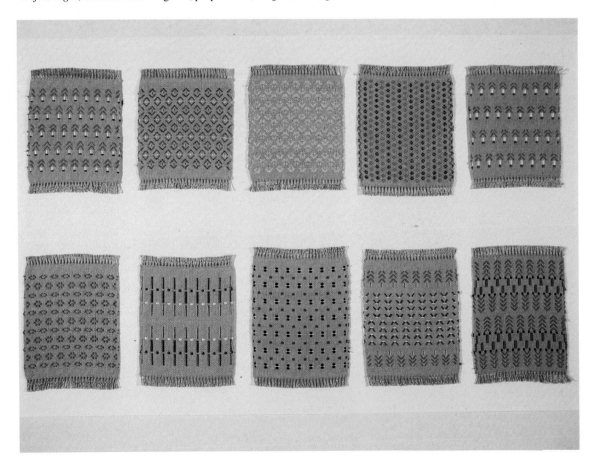

10. One of a series of pulpit frontals, each in a different color, representing the seasons of the Church calendar. This one is woven in twill.

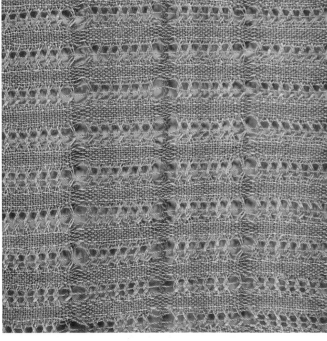

11. (Above) Hanging incorporating gauze weave, a two-harness technique. *Collection of Mr. and Mrs. Jeff Ankrom.*

12. (Left) Gauze weave is the essence of this piece.

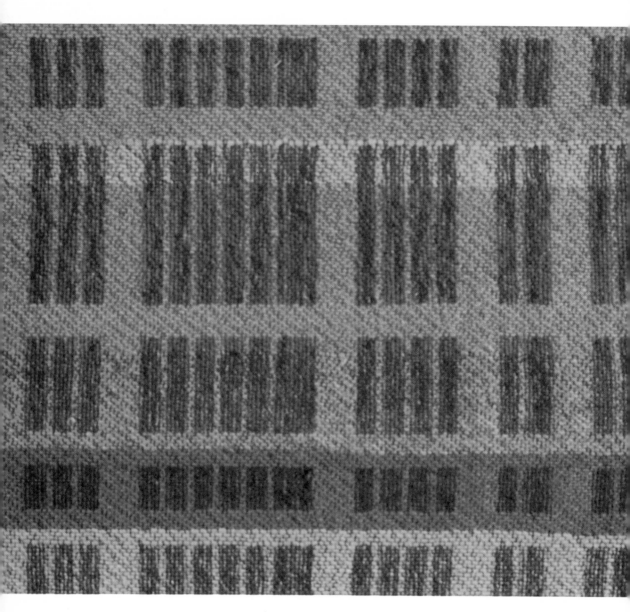

13. Quite a different example of the use of color: a ten-harness damask-weave fabric.

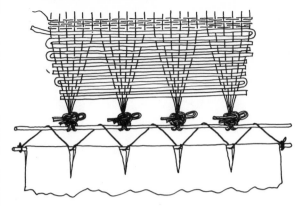

The heading, showing soft roving used to draw warp ends into line.

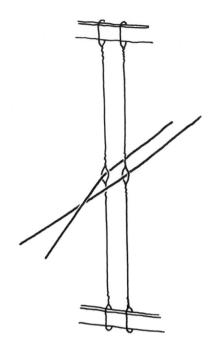

Warp ends twisted as they are taken from the heddles, ready to sley in the reed.

down, change the shed, and put through more material. (These weaving techniques are described in detail in Chapter 6.) Leave a 1-inch (2.5 cm) loop on the edge, being sure not to pull in the warp yarns. Continue in this manner until all the warp ends are parallel.

Another method is to use weft yarn similar to the warp. Open a tabby shed (half of the warp ends) and put the weft through, change the shed, and push the weft to a position halfway between the beater and breast beam. Put in another weft shot, leaving a 1-inch (2.5 cm) loop at the edge. Change the shed and push this shot to within ½ inch (1.3 cm) of the first. Put in about five shots in this manner. Now close the shed and beat all shots as close as possible to the tie-on knots. If the warp ends are not evenly spread, repeat this process.

Correcting Mistakes

Now that the warp ends are evenly spread, it is time to check for errors in threading and sleying.

Twisted or crossed warp ends occur easily and are just as easily corrected. They can become twisted or crossed as they are threaded in the harnesses or sleyed in the reed. When every other tabby shed is opened, these ends will be pulled up and stay in the middle of the shed. To correct this, simply untie the group from the lash

rod (apron bar), pull out the wrong warp ends, rethread or sley correctly, and retie to the lash rod, being sure to adjust the tension.

If a warp end does not weave at all, it probably is not in the eye of the heddle. Usually this is caused by missing the eye of the heddle while threading. It is easy to correct. Simply untie the group of warp ends from the lash rod, pull out the warp end and put it in the heddle, re-sley, and tie to the lash rod, adjusting the tension.

A mistake in the threading order can cause warp ends to appear in the weaving in parallel pairs or more. If there is no heddle where the correction is to be made, a repair heddle can be inserted. Use a ready-made one or tie in an extra heddle made of string. Simply take a length of sturdy string and hitch it to the lower heddle bar in the place where the heddle is missing. Make a granny knot at the same height as the lower end of the other heddle eyes and another knot at the top of the heddle eye. Then tie the string around the top heddle bar. It is important to have the eye at the same height (top and bottom) as the other heddle eyes. Now

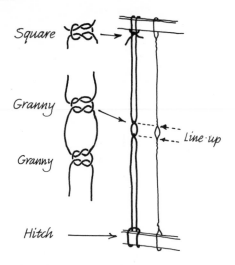

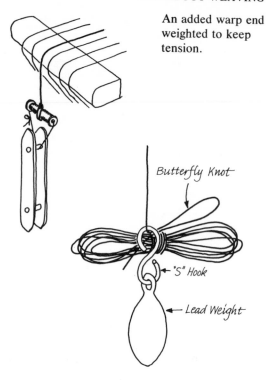

An added warp end weighted to keep tension.

Repair string heddle and granny knots used to tie eye of heddle. The granny knot is used as it will not release as easily as a square knot.

thread the warp end through this string heddle, through the reed, and tie on.

If one or more warp ends were completely missed in the threading order, it may be necessary to rethread the warp from the point of the mistake to the nearest edge. But if only one warp end was missed, it is often possible to add a warp end in the right place. Measure off the correct length of the warp and thread it through a repair heddle or string heddle. The reed must be re-sleyed from the point where the warp end was added to the nearest edge. This additional warp end can be weighted and hung over the back beam. During weaving, it should be checked often to maintain even tension.

Weave a little more tabby and examine the woven part for any irregularity. If the warp ends seem closer together in one area, there could be a mistake in sleying where two ends are in one dent and one in the next instead of one in each dent. Sometimes it is necessary to re-sley from the mistake to the edge. Always correct these errors before starting the actual project, otherwise the weaving will have an irregularity all the way through.

The edges of the weaving should be flat. If they are not but seem to pucker, put in one weft shot and carry the weft yarn around the apron rod. Enter another weft

For a long warp end, wind it in a butterfly and use a lead weight to hold tension.

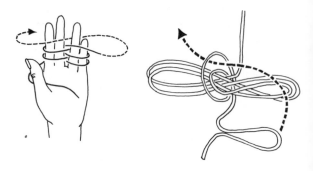

To wind the butterfly, wrap the yarn around your hand in a figure eight, remove from your fingers, wind the end around the center, and tuck it in. Release yarn from starting end.

shot and put the weft around the apron rod on the other side. By pulling the weft tight, you can make the weaving stretch and straighten out. Then continue weaving.

You should dress a loom in a manner that is most convenient for yourself, your loom, and available equipment. Whichever method is used, the basic principle of even tension on all warp ends must always be achieved.

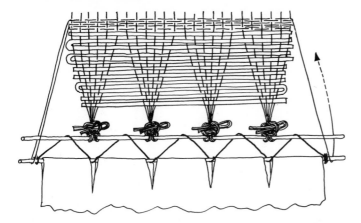

Method of straightening weaving when edges pucker. One weft shot is drawn around apron rod.

Gating the Loom

Each step in preparing the loom for weaving is vitally important, for the quality of the woven piece and the ease with which the weaving process can be performed are directly related to the attention given to preparation.

After the loom is dressed, the weaver must go over the loom and adjust necessary parts in order to get the best possible performance. This is called *gating the loom*.

The order of gating different parts of a loom depends on the loom's specific construction. Areas of possible adjustment are:

1. Harness frames should hang even and level. On counterbalanced and countermarche looms you may have to adjust the cords, and on jack looms be sure the frames sit squarely on or hang evenly from the jacks.

2. The height of the harness frames is important. The heddle eye center should be slightly lower than the tensioned warp when it is in a direct line from the breast beam to the back beam. The reason for this is that the lower shed should be tighter than the upper shed because the shuttle moves on the lower shed.

3. Adjust the battens or beater up or down so that the warp with the shed closed is close to the lower edge of the reed on a jack loom and is in the center of the reed on a counterbalanced and countermarche loom. When the warp is under tension

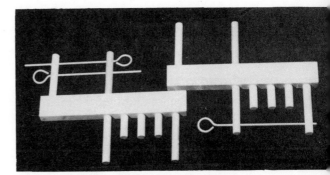

Harness stabilizers. This simple equipment is used to keep harness frames on counterbalanced looms at the same level and distance apart. Each harness frame is inserted between the five pegs and held in place with the metal pin. The two pegs support the lease sticks and hold the crossing at a convenient level. Harness stabilizers are useful when threading the heddles and gating the loom.

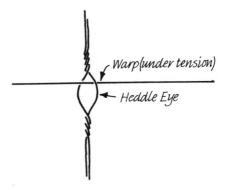

Position of warp in heddle eye is above the center when warp is under tension and shed closed.

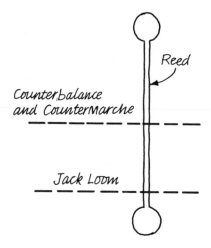

Reed

Counterbalance
and Countermarche

Jack Loom

Correct position of warp line in reed is in the center for a counterbalanced loom and much lower for a jack loom.

with the shed open, it should not rub on the top or bottom edge of the reed.

4. The warp must be centered, passing through the reed in line with the warp beam. The reed can be moved from side to side in the batten. The heddles can also move from side to side, to allow the warp to run straight, front to back.

5. If the loom has adjustable tie-up cords, they should be tied to produce a flat lower part of the shed when it is open.

6. Check for any loose bolts on the loom and place a drop of oil on any bearings. Also replace any frayed cords.

The lease sticks can now be removed. Sometimes, however, it is advisable to leave them in place, for example, if the warp is long and you might want to change the order of threading the heddles. To prevent the sticks from moving with the warp, tie them to the back beam. They cannot be allowed to move close to the heddle frames, as this prevents the opening of the shed. If the warp was put on the loom from the front, the lease sticks were removed when the warp was tied to the apron. They can be reinserted by opening the tabby sheds and putting them in the warp behind the harness frames.

When you are weaving with fine yarn, the lease sticks are very helpful. They prevent warp ends from twisting around one another

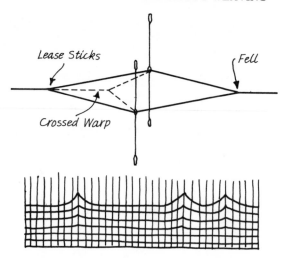

Lease Sticks   Fell

Crossed Warp

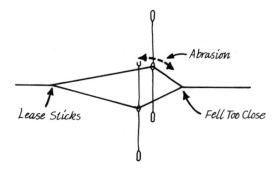

Top: Leave lease sticks in the warp while weaving to prevent warp ends from twisting around one another and causing uneven tension.
Bottom: If some warp ends are too tight, uneven weaving results.

Abrasion

Lease Sticks   Fell Too Close

Uneven shed in front or back of the heddles causes abrasion on the warp yarns. Here the fell is too close to the heddles. Lease sticks can be moved to equalize size of shed if necessary.

and therefore causing uneven tension when the shed is opened.

The size of the shed in the front and back of the heddles should be the same. This prevents the warp ends from sliding in the heddles and causing unnecessary wear; this is particularly important if the warp yarn is delicate. Placement of the lease sticks can determine the size of the shed behind the heddles.

With each of these points checked and adjusted, the loom is ready.

6

The Weaving Process

Seating Position at the Loom

Proper posture at the loom will eliminate fatigue. The correct seating height will increase comfort and efficiency and contribute to developing rhythm while weaving. This is an important factor in producing quality work.

1. Elbows should be at the same level as the warp when the arms are resting on the breast beam.
2. How close the weaver sits to the loom is determined by an easy reach for the batten without inclining the whole body forward; the knees should not touch the cloth beam.
3. When the feet are placed on the treadles, the thighs slope slightly down toward the knees.

4. A bench is more comfortable than a stool, since a weaver tends to move from side to side. The bench can also serve as a shelf for the tools while weaving. A bench that is not attached to the loom in any way is the most practical for adjustment of seating distance to the loom and when sitting down at and leaving the loom.

Lighting

The best light for weaving comes from one side rather than front or back. Natural light is ideal, but if artificial light is used it should be on a separate standard, not attached to the loom, as most looms tend to shake and an unstable light can be annoying to the eye.

Focus light on the loom between the

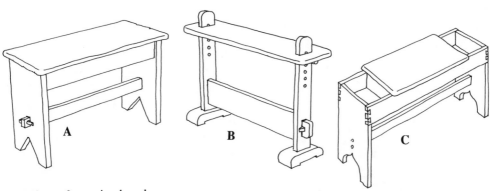

A variety of weaving benches:
  A. Sturdy bench for wide loom.
  B. Bench with adjustable height.
  C. Bench with open pockets on each side to hold accessories while weaving.

breast beam and harnesses for weaving. Adjust the light when warping, beaming, and threading.

If you use fluorescent light, be aware of its effect on yarn color.

Heating

Like any piece of furniture, the loom must not be placed over or close to the heat source in the room. The temperature should be even and as low as possible, but comfortable, with moderate humidity. Climatic changes do affect warp; when you are not working for a time, it is advisable to release the tension, as well as to cover the loom with a large cloth.

Accessibility to the Loom

Ideally, a loom should remain in the same place. There should be enough room in the back to sit when beaming and as much space in the front as possible. On the side of the loom where the crank for the warp beam is located, have enough room to work while beaming the warp. See Chapter 1 for further information on the ideal amount of space on all sides of the loom.

A loom tends to "walk" during the weaving process if it stands on a smooth floor. Beating makes the loom move toward the weaver. With rubber pads on the bottom of the loom or by having the loom stand on carpeting you can eliminate this sliding. If the loom must be used on a cement or hardwood floor, 2×4s may be used to prevent sliding. Place the lumber at the base of the

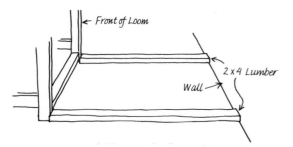

One method used to prevent the loom from sliding or "walking" on a smooth floor.

front post on each side of the loom and extend it to the wall. (The weaver is seated with back to the wall.)

Selecting the Proper Shuttle

A *shuttle* is a tool used to carry the weft yarns through the shed made in the warp yarns. There are basically two types—stick or poke shuttles and boat shuttles—and each is made in various styles.

The difference in the two types is how the yarn is released. The weaver must manually release the yarn from a stick shuttle, while the yarn unreels from a bobbin in the boat shuttle.

Stick shuttles can be from 6 inches (15 cm) to 36 inches (91 cm) in length and of different styles, depending on the yarn being used and the type of weaving. These shuttles are generally used for heavier yarn because they will accommodate larger quantities.

All shuttles must have a smooth finish so that they will slide over the warp easily. Ideally, a stick shuttle should be just a little wider than the warp so that you do not have to put your hand within the warp yarns when passing the shuttle through the shed, which tends to stretch or distort the yarn. Purchase (or make) several stick shuttles, to have the correct length on hand.

Stick shuttles have a notch at each end to hold the yarn. To put the yarn on, just fasten or hold it at one end and then continue winding end to end. So-called ski, rug, and rag shuttles are wound in a similar manner.

A flat stick shuttle, when wound from end to end, can become very thick through the middle and thus difficult to pass through the shed. To overcome this, the shuttle can be wound in a figure eight.

Boat shuttles are beautiful pieces of equipment, appropriately named, for they are gracefully shaped like a boat. They carry a bobbin or quill and have a smooth finish. A weaver finds pleasure in simply holding such a shuttle.

Many factors affect the kind of boat shuttle used. Over a period of time an individual weaver will develop specific preferences.

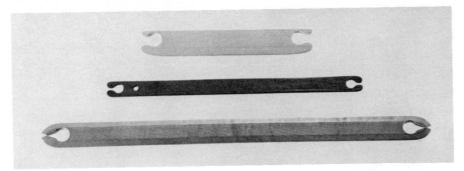

Stick or "poke" shuttles.

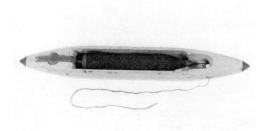

Commercial or industrial shuttle used on a fly-shuttle loom. Note metal tips.

A variety of rag or rug shuttles.

One factor to be considered is the weight of the shuttle. A 6-ounce (170 g) shuttle is recommended for warps up to 30 inches (76 cm) wide and an 8-ounce (227 g) for wider warps. The weight does not necessarily affect the shape or size of the shuttle. For the best results in weaving it is advantageous to have all shuttles the same shape, since the hand gets accustomed to a position of holding them. A shuttle should be light in weight at the center and heavy at the ends to stop it from veering from its path. A heavy shuttle travels straight and a light shuttle can be thrown faster.

Boat shuttles have a flat, straight bottom so that they will not roll or dip as they pass through the shed. The ends are raised higher than the center; this curve should be short. The pointed tips prevent the breaking of a warp end if the shuttle should strike it. The bobbin or quill carrying the weft yarn should

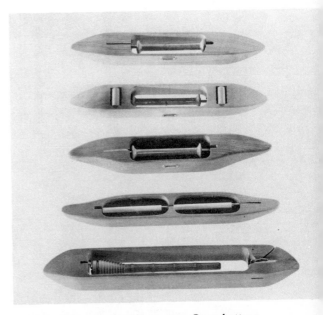

Styles of boat shuttle. *From top:* Open-bottom shuttle, shuttle with rollers, typical boat shuttle, two-bobbin shuttle, and shuttle with bobbin that unreels from the end.

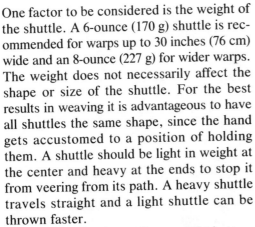

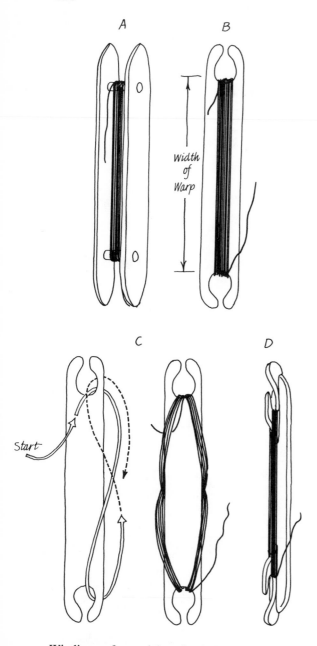

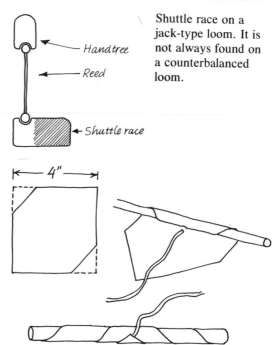

Shuttle race on a jack-type loom. It is not always found on a counterbalanced loom.

To make a paper quill, take a piece of stiff paper approximately 4 inches (10 cm) square. Cut off two corners and start winding it around the spindle of a bobbin winder. Just before the paper is completely wound, tuck in the end of the weft yarn and continue winding in the same direction as you wound the quill.

Winding weft on stick and rag shuttles:

A. Weft yarn on rag shuttle.

B. Weft yarn on stick shuttle.

C. To wind a stick shuttle in a figure eight: take the yarn from the top end of the shuttle, down the outside edge, crossing around the lower end, again along the outside edge, and crossing back over the top. This process is repeated about five times on one edge and then on the other edge. The yarn is built up along the edges of the shuttle, making it easy to pass through the shed.

D. Weft yarn on ski shuttle.

be hidden within the shuttle. It should never rub on the upper or lower part of the shed.

Some boat shuttles have an open bottom; these can be lighter, but again the bobbin or quill must not be wound so full that it extends beyond the bottom of the shuttle.

A shuttle with rollers on the bottom performs best if the loom is equipped with a shuttle race.

In a boat shuttle the weft yarn is carried on a bobbin or a quill. A *bobbin* can be made of wood or plastic and has ends formed so as to prevent the weft yarns from falling off. A *quill* is usually made of paper and can very easily be made by the weaver.

Properly wound bobbins are of utmost importance to quality weaving. The weft yarn should unroll easily from the bobbin and not jerk. A good selvage results from well-wound bobbins.

Bobbins can be wound by hand or on a

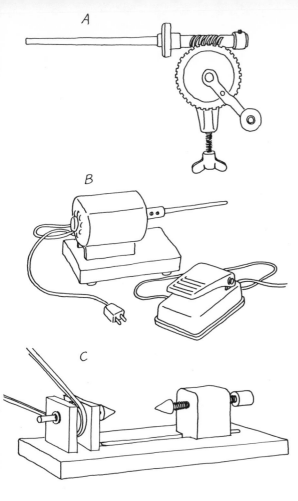

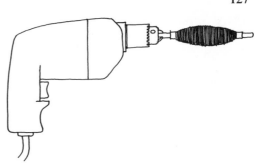

Improvised bobbin winder using an electric hand drill. Drill can be held in a vise if necessary.

Bobbin winders.

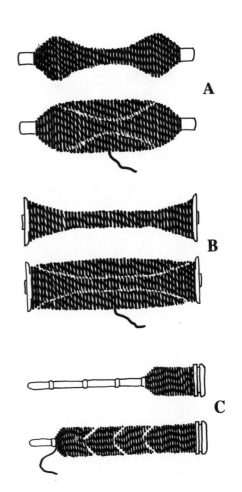

hand or electric winder. Place the bobbin on the spindle of a winder, as described in Chapter 4, "Warping Methods." Be sure it fits snugly and will not slip. Fasten the weft yarn and, without much tension on the yarn, start winding at one end, making a cone pointing toward the middle. Then do the same at the other end. Now, with greater tension on the yarn, fill the space between the cones but leave a depression in the center, which is filled in at the very end. While winding, crisscross the yarn so that, if the weft yarn breaks, it will not cut into the yarn on the bobbin.

To wind a quill, build up a hill at each end and build up the center as on a bobbin. Always be certain not to let the yarn go beyond the original "hill."

Boat shuttles have a spindle to carry the bobbin. The spindle can be attached at one end with a hinge and pulled out to slide the bobbin on. If the bobbin jams at the end,

Method of winding bobbins:

A. Cardboard quill.

B. Bobbin with ends.

C. Tapered bobbin that unwinds from one end.

place some washers or a wooden bead on the spindle at each end. If the bobbin unreels too fast, put a soft strand of yarn or a bit of tissue paper on the spindle under the bobbin to slow the speed at which it turns.

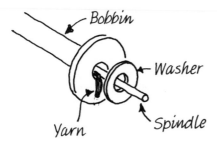

Put a washer on the spindle if bobbin jams at the end. Put a strand of yarn through the hole of the bobbin if it tends to unreel too fast.

The Doubling Stand

There are circumstances when you will want to use two or more strands of weft yarn at one time. Color and texture effects are the main reasons. There are also times when you have yarn of the right color and type for a project but it is too fine. By using multiple strands, you can obtain the correct size yarn.

To achieve correctly wound shuttles or bobbins in this case, the doubling stand is used. This is an uncomplicated piece of equipment that allows the yarns to wind around each other as they are drawn from tubes. It permits all the yarns to be of the same length, to avoid problems with the weft during weaving.

It is impossible to wind several yarns together successfully on a bobbin or stick shuttle simply by pulling them at the same time from spools, tubes, or cones. Yarns with different characteristics will not unwind at the same rate; as a result, loops can form on the edges during weaving, and if two colors are wound together, they will not always run parallel. A doubling stand will help to eliminate these problems.

Otherwise, two shuttles or a shuttle with two bobbins could be used, although the use of two shuttles is cumbersome during

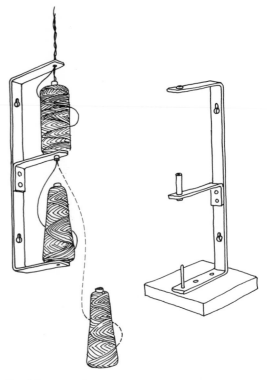

Doubling stands:
Left: Wall-mounted doubling stand shows position of spools. Any number of spools can be used below the stand. As all yarns unwind, the upper one slowly winds around the lower yarns. All yarns will be the same length.
Right: Floor or table model.

weaving. A two-bobbin shuttle is ideal for experimenting when combining two different yarns. One bobbin can be changed until the correct combination of yarns is achieved.

Starting to Weave

Actual weaving can begin when the loom is gated and the shuttles are prepared. The process of weaving can be described as the action of throwing and catching the shuttle, beating the weft yarn into place, and changing the shed. These actions are called the *rhythm of weaving*.

The first action—throwing and catching the shuttle—must be completely automatic. The procedures in using the different kinds of shuttle vary slightly. But with practice you will feel at ease using either a stick shuttle or a shuttle with a bobbin.

To use a stick or poke shuttle, simply push or poke it through the shed by taking hold of it by the outside end. When it reaches the outside of the shed on the opposite side, take hold of that end and pull it through the shed. Ideally, a stick shuttle should be about an inch or two (2.5–5 cm) longer than the width of the weaving. At each side, turn the shuttle one turn (end to end) to release enough yarn for the next weft shot. Do not unwind large amounts of yarn at one time, and do not put your hand within the warp ends—this could stretch the yarn and cause uneven tension. A rug, rag, or ski shuttle is used in a similar manner. These shuttles, however, are seldom wider than the warp, so you have to shove them through the shed, making every effort to keep your hands out of the shed.

A shuttle with a bobbin—a boat shuttle— is held by placing the thumb on top and the index finger at the end, the other three fingers acting as a balance on the bottom. When you start a new weft yarn, the end of the yarn is held by the little finger. The shuttle is thrown through the shed from a distance of about 12 inches (30 cm) out from the edge by a swing of the whole hand. The index finger guides the direction and is the last to leave the shuttle. If the loom has a shuttle race, the shuttle glides across it, close to the reed. At the opposite end of the shed the shuttle is caught by the thumb and middle finger of the other hand. The index finger is ready to find its position and to throw the shuttle back. Pull the shuttle out and away about 12 inches (30 cm) from the shed so that the weft yarn lies in a loose diagonal in the shed. The pick (or shot) of weft must never lie parallel to the fell, or former weft shot, before it is beaten. There must be enough ease in the weft to allow it to go over and under the warp yarns. If the bobbin is unreeling too fast, the thumb can move over and stop it, but there should be no tension on the weft yarn when it is beaten.

The body position when throwing the shuttle can best be described as having the

Position of the hand on the boat shuttle, ready to throw it through the shed.

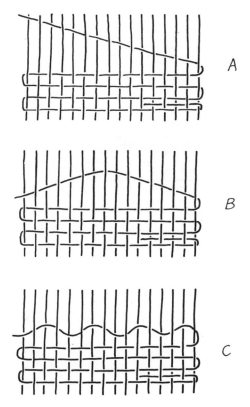

Method of putting ease or slack in weft shots:

A. Yarn in loose diagonal in shed just after shuttle is thrown.

B. Yarn pulled up in the middle. This is the ideal method for bound weaving.

C. Yarn in many half circles. Use this method for very wide warps.

arms extended with the hands in a position on the shuttle to move in a line parallel to the front of the body.

To beat the weft yarn in place, always grasp the batten, or beater, in the center. The hand that has just thrown the shuttle does the beating. Pulling the batten forward pushes the weft yarn down against the fell of the weaving. The beat of the batten should be quick but not hard. Do not force the beater into the weaving; let it do the work. The overhead beater will return to its original position after touching the fell. No effort need be made to push it away. You must always be aware of unnecessary motions that consume energy and time.

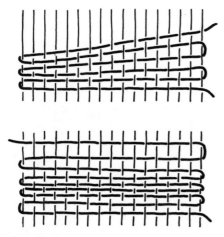

Uneven beating:
Top: Batten handtree pulled from one side; weaving builds up at an angle.
Bottom: Inconsistent beating results in tight and loose areas.

A well-woven piece will have consistent beating—the same force with each beat. When you are weaving at different times, personal feelings and tensions can affect the force with which you beat in the weft. Holding the completed piece of weaving up to the light will reveal any inconsistent beating.

Changing the shed or moving the harness frames up or down should be smooth and rhythmical. The feet are used alternately on the treadles. As one foot moves forward to push down a treadle, the other foot moves back. The shed is fully open only at the time the shuttle passes through, so there is sufficient time to change sheds.

As the batten strikes the fell, the shed is changed and the batten moves back. Normally the beat of the batten comes at the same time as changing the sheds. But note this helpful rule: beat just before changing the shed if the edges are to be tighter or drawn in, and beat just after changing the shed to spread the edges.

To avoid losing the rhythm while weaving, do not use the same foot twice in a row and don't watch the shuttle.

Generally, if more than one beat is necessary to put the weft shot in place, then the batten is too light and should be weighted. Two beats with the batten are, however, necessary when working with a warp that tends to stick together. The first beat is light and simply clears the shed; the next beat puts the weft yarn in place.

Rhythm can be achieved and quality weaving produced when weaving without stopping for several hours. It takes about a half hour to get into the rhythm of weaving; it can then be maintained for a length of time providing attention has been paid to all the details of getting the loom ready for weaving. Interruptions slow down the weaving and affect its quality. Quality weaving cannot be produced by irregular work methods. Weave with confidence at a regular speed.

Anyone can learn the theory of weaving; it is difficult to develop *skill*. If you analyze the movements of the parts of the loom and then execute each movement always in the same way and in exact sequence, rhythm will become natural.

THE WEAVING SEQUENCE

1. Open shed.
2. Throw shuttle and catch it.
3. Close shed as shuttle emerges from shed.
4. Beat.
5. As batten moves back, open shed for next weft shot.

The amount of weaving that can be done before moving the warp forward depends on the loom. Generally, weave for about 2 inches (5 cm) and then move the warp forward. An even beat can be achieved when the fell is always about the same distance from the harnesses. Rhythm cannot be achieved when the length of the batten stroke changes considerably.

To move the warp forward, release the brake on the warp beam and crank the cloth beam forward. The batten must strike only the weaving. If it strikes the breast beam, the warp has been moved too far forward: rewind the warp on the warp beam for a short distance.

If the loom is equipped with a friction brake, you don't have to move from the weaving position to move the warp forward. A lever at the front of the loom releases the warp beam brake, and the warp is moved forward by turning the cloth beam.

Tension on the warp during weaving should be tight—the yarn, weave, and type of loom all affect *how* tight. Warp on a counterbalanced loom can be tighter than on a jack-type loom. The shed on the counterbalanced loom separates as some warp ends move up while the others move down. All warp ends move the same distance each time the shed is opened. On the jack-type loom only the warp ends forming the upper shed move when the shed is opened, while the warp ends forming the lower shed remain stationary. These warp ends, therefore, must be able to be stretched. If the tension is too tight, either the upper shed

will not move or it will pull all the warp ends up, and an unsatisfactory shed is the result.

If the same yarn is used for warp and weft, remember that the warp is under greater tension than the weft. The warp relaxes and shrinkage occurs after the piece is finished and the tension is released. Experimenting will show how to balance the number of ends and picks per inch while weaving so the result will be a balanced weave, if that is what you want. This is a very important factor in checks and plaids. The easiest method is to weave a short distance, measure it, and then relax the tension, measure again, and calculate the shrinkage. If you are working with very stretchy yarn, relax the tension when the loom is not in use.

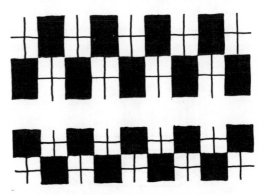

Check and plaid patterns require lighter beating when a stretchy warp is used.
Top: The pattern on the loom while the warp is under tension is not beaten square.
Bottom: After warp tension is released, the pattern assumes the correct shape.

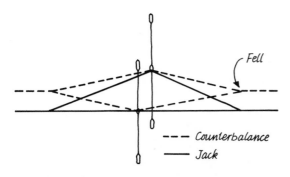

The manner in which the sheds open on counterbalanced and jack-type looms. Note the position of the fell.

Edges, or Selvages

A weaver achieves great satisfaction when the edges, or *selvages,* of the weaving are straight and without notches or loops. Many factors, such as warping, beaming, dressing the loom, preparing and throwing the shuttle, beating, and constant warp tension, affect the selvages. If careful attention is given to all these processes, the selvages will be straight and no special attention will have to be given to the edges while weaving.

Factors contributing to a good selvage are:

1. Warp at high tension.
2. Correctly wound bobbins.
3. Not touching selvages with your hands.
4. Beating and changing sheds at exactly the same time.
5. Fast weaving.
6. Plenty of ease or slack in weft pick.

Curving selvages are the result of not enough ease in the weft pick in each shed. A tight weft causes the edge warp ends to be pulled into a closer sett. The take-up in the warp is proportional to the sett, and where the warp ends are sett closer the take-up is greater. Therefore the edge warp ends get shorter and are consequently pulled into a curve.

A method of strengthening the edges of the weaving is to increase the size of the selvage yarns. This is done by doubling up

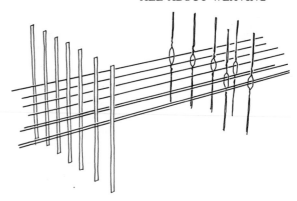

Selvage yarns are strengthened along the edge by using double warp ends in the heddles and reed.

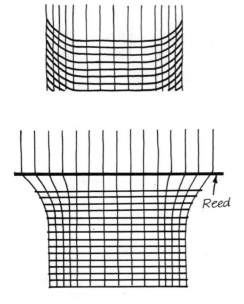

Problems in the weaving when not enough ease is put in each weft pick.
Top: Selvage edges curve because warp sett becomes closer on edges.
Bottom: The weaving becomes narrower than the warp as it was sett in the reed. When the weft is beaten, the warp is forced by the reed into a straight line. This stretches the edge warp ends and causes excess wear on them.

the warp in the heddles for a few ends on each edge. Setting the warp ends closer in the reed on the edge to make a good selvage is not a good idea. If the sett of the warp ends is closer on the edges, it will prevent an even beat in the middle of the weaving because the weft will not beat in as tight where the warp is close as it will where the spaces are wider.

Some weaves, notably twill, produce *floaters,* or *skips,* on the edge. This happens because the weft yarn doesn't go over or under the edge warp end each time it goes through the shed. If the selvage is a vital part of the finished product, there are remedies, but if the edge is to be cut or hemmed the best thing to do is ignore the floaters while weaving.

To "catch" the floater if it is continuous on one side, reverse the side from which the shuttle enters by cutting the weft yarn and starting the next weft shot from the opposite side. If a floater still appears on one side, rethread the end warp yarn on either side by moving it ahead one harness frame in the threading order, as long as you move it from odd- to even- or from even- to odd-numbered harness frame.

Two shuttles can also be used to eliminate the floaters. Each shuttle, with the same weft, is thrown alternately from side to side. Lay the shuttles down on the web (the woven part of the warp) in order as used, one behind the other.

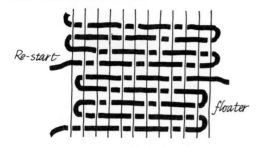

Floaters on edge of twill weave. By reversing the side from which the shuttle enters, sometimes you can catch the floater with the weft.

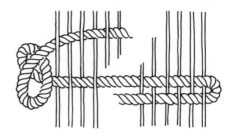

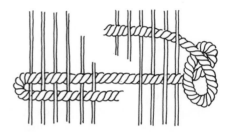

An exaggerated drawing of why one selvage is quite often better than the other.
Top: On the left-hand selvage, the direction of the weft yarn when it enters the shed opposes the natural lie of the Z-twist weft yarn, while on the right side the direction is the same as the twist of the yarn.
Bottom: With S-twist yarn, the left-hand selvage lies correctly while the right side lies in the opposite direction, causing extra twist in the yarn and an uneven edge.

Another method of picking up the floater is to pass the shuttle over the last warp end in the upper shed or under the last warp end in the lower shed, whichever is causing the floater. This is time-consuming, however, and interrupts rhythm.

A *catch cord* can be used on the edge of the weaving to aid in making a good selvage. It is an additional warp end used in a dent outside the selvage. It does not go through a heddle eye, so it is not raised or lowered with each shed. The shuttle is put around, either over or under, this cord as needed. This method is ideal when weaving basket weave or any weave in which more than one pick is put in a single shed. The shuttle is put around the catch cord each time it is put through the open shed.

Weavers frequently find that one edge of their weaving is better than the other. Naturally, one immediately attributes the cause to the weaver's being right- or left-handed, but this is not the reason. The variation is actually caused by the direction of the twist of the weft yarn. Whether S- or Z-twist yarn is used, there is one edge where the weft will form a loop because changing the direction of the shuttle slightly adds twist to or takes it out of the yarn.

The twist of the yarn is also affected by the manner in which the yarn is drawn from a spool or tube. The twist can increase or decrease, depending on which end of the spool is up or down. Set a spool or tube on the floor and watch how the yarn spirals as it is unwound, affecting the twist. Being aware of this factor can be an aid to the weaver. It is possible to slightly increase or decrease the yarn twist while winding bobbins or shuttles. The twist is unchanged when the yarn is drawn off a spool or tube on a rack.

Temple, Stretcher, or Tenterhook

Take-up in the weft—pulling in of edges— can be a serious problem on some weaving. The *temple,* or stretcher, is a piece of equipment used to help prevent this take-up.

A temple is two flat pieces of wood that either are hinged or slide on each other, making the length adjustable. Each end has a row of sharp needles, or *tenterhooks.* These needles are pressed into the weaving close to the edge. The temple is stretched to the desired width and locked in position.

The temple is most effectively used on

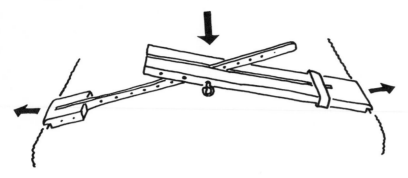

A temple or stretcher is an essential piece of equipment when weaving rag rugs. There are sharp needles on the ends, called tenterhooks—thus the expression "hanging by tenterhooks." These teeth are pushed into the edge of the weaving. When the center is pushed down, it is straightened out and locked in position.

very stretchy fibers or coarse fabrics. It does not excuse poor weaving technique. A temple should be used from the beginning of the web and not introduced in the middle after the weaving has pulled in. To be most effective, the temple should be moved often, to keep it close to the fell.

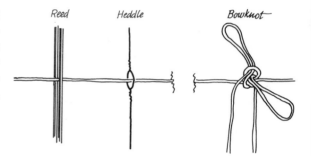

New warp end tied in bowknot near warp beam.

Broken Warp Ends

Occasionally a warp end will break. It should be repaired immediately and the cause determined to prevent future problems. Among the reasons for a warp end breaking are faulty yarn, jamming a warp end with the shuttle, poor adjustment of the loom, a repair heddle being too high or too low, and the use of inappropriate yarn for warp. The prime reason, however, is twisted warp yarns, which are caused by an improperly made cross during warping or by not selecting the warp ends in order when threading the heddles.

To repair a broken warp end, remove it from the heddle and take it back to the warp beam. Do not cut or break it off. Take yarn the same as the warp and about the same length as the remaining warp, pass it from the front through the reed and heddle eye, and tie it near the warp beam in a bowknot to the old warp end. In the front, adjust the tension of the new warp end and fasten it to the weaving by twisting it around a pin placed in the web. Continue weaving, and when the bowknot reaches the heddles, untie it and retie it again near the warp beam. (You should try to eliminate all knots in the warp and weft of the weaving.) After the

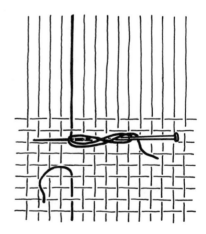

Other end of new warp end pinned to weaving to repair a broken end.

weaving is completed, the new warp end can be woven back in with a needle, overlapping the old warp end about 1 inch (2.5 cm).

Splicing Weft Yarn

If the weft yarn runs out during weaving, every effort should be made to join the new weft without the join showing in the weaving. If the yarn is plied, untwist the end of both pieces of weft for about 3 inches (7.5 cm). Place the old weft in the shed and bring one length of untwisted strand out between two top warp ends. Now bring in, from the opposite side, the new weft yarn with the end untwisted, overlap the split ends, and bring one untwisted strand out between two top warp ends as before. In this way the weft yarn is not doubled anywhere in the pick and the join doesn't show in the weaving. After the weaving is completed, trim off the ends from the surface of the weaving. Loosely spun single-ply yarn can be split in a similar way to plied yarn, but if the single ply is tightly spun, simply overlap the two ends in the shed where they are to be joined.

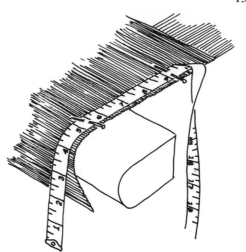

Method of measuring weaving without unrolling the web from the cloth beam.

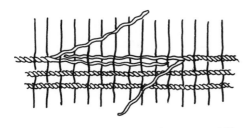

Method of splicing weft yarn by untwisting plied yarn.

Measuring the Web

The woven part, or web, is wound around the cloth beam. To keep an accurate measure of its length, pin a cloth tape measure along the edge of the weaving as it progresses. Never unpin the tape, but simply put an additional pin in every 4 or 5 inches (10–12.5 cm). The tension can be affected if the web is unwound from the cloth beam for measuring.

Cutting Off the Woven Piece

Sometimes it is necessary to cut off one piece of weaving before all the warp yarn is woven. If there is good tension on the warp and you don't want to waste warp retying onto the apron again, there is a simple method of cutting off the weaving and not wasting warp.

To do this, put four to six tabby shots of cotton yarn after the last shot of the completed piece. In the next shed put a piece of heavy wire several inches (centimeters) wider than the warp. Now weave in four to six more tabby shots of cotton yarn. Put white glue along the cotton weft shots adjoining the wire. When the glue is dry, remove the completed weaving from the loom by cutting at the edge of the weaving. Take a strong piece of cord and bind the wire to the lash rod. A new weaving can be started now; the tension was preserved and very

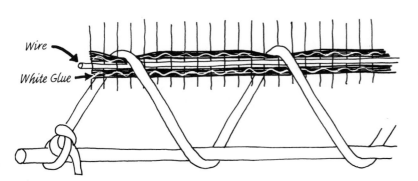

Method of attaching warp to the cloth beam lash rod with very little warp waste, after a piece of weaving has been removed from the loom.

little warp was wasted. To make the piece of wire easy to remove later, rub it with soap, candle wax, or petroleum jelly before you put it in the shed, to keep the glue from sticking to it.

Weaving can, of course, continue on the warp until the end comes over the back beam. The weaving stops when the lash rod comes close to the heddles and it is impossible to make a shed.

Before cutting the weaving from the loom, weave six or eight shots of a very fine yarn (it could be sewing thread). Beat it in very tight. This is a good way to end samples and is satisfactory for the finish on many decorative pieces. It prevents unraveling of the main weft yarns. Use an appropriate color that will not detract from the main part of the weaving.

Now release the tension and cut the warp ends from the warp beam lash rod. Pull the warp ends through the heddles and reed. The completed weaving can be unrolled from the cloth beam and untied or cut from the cloth beam lash rod.

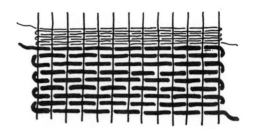

Method of ending a weaving. Fine weft yarns are beaten in solidly to prevent the weft from slipping out.

7

wwwwwwwwwwwwwwwwwwwwwwwwwwwwwwwwwwwwwwwwwwwwwwwwww

Drafting: The Language of Weaving

The weaving draft is the graphic expression of what is happening on the loom during weaving. A draft actually serves two purposes: it shows the weaver how to weave a specific design, and it also shows what the completed weave will look like. Sometimes drafts can also include written explanations of the yarns to use, how many warp ends, and the warp sett.

The Complete Draft

There are four parts to a complete draft:

1. **The threading order:** This part of the draft is most often shown in the upper left-hand corner of the complete draft. One harness frame is represented by the space between two horizontal lines. The

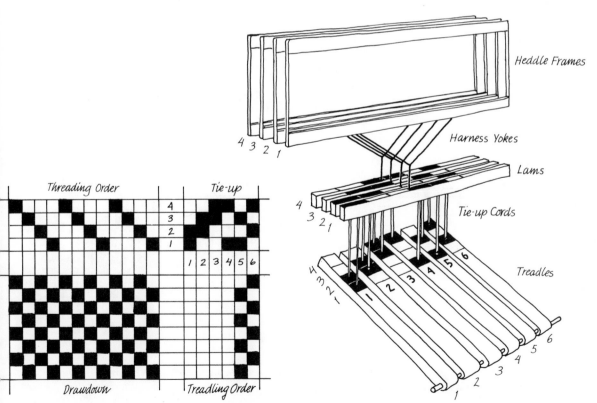

Example of a complete draft. The threading order is a straight draw or twill threading, the tie-up is standard, and it is a tabby treadling order. The drawdown shows a tabby weave.

Parts of the loom, showing the heddle frames attached each by a yoke to the lams. The lams are attached to the treadles with tie-up cords in a standard tie-up.

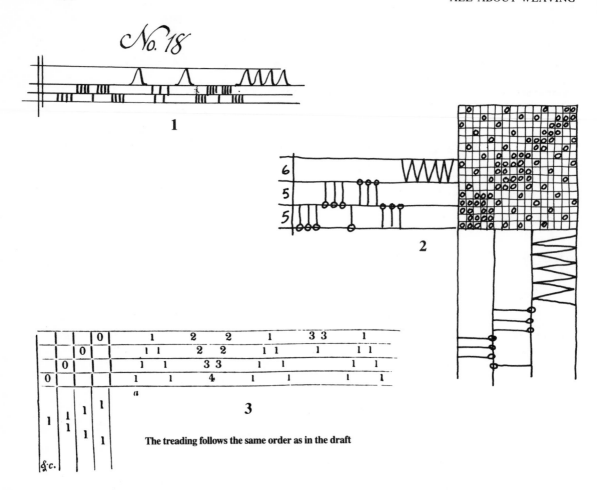

No. 18

1

2

3

The treading follows the same order as in the draft

4

5

Weaving drafts are as individual as handwriting. Each of these facsimiles conveys its message to a weaver in its own distinctive style.

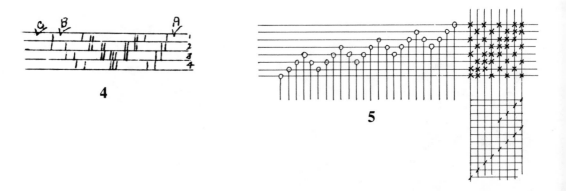

1. An eighteenth-century draft.
2. Early-eighteenth-century multiple-harness draft.
3. John Murphy draft, Scotland, ca. 1820.
4. American draft, ca. 1920.
5. Draft from a Norwegian handbook, ca. 1950.

6. Early-nineteenth-century draft.
7. Swedish draft, ca. 1950.
8. English draft, ca. 1910.
9. French Canadian draft, ca. 1940.
10. American draft, ca. 1930.

6

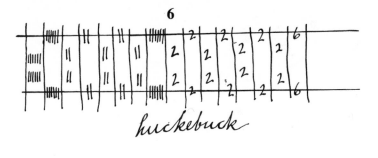

huckeback

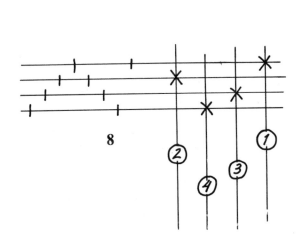

8

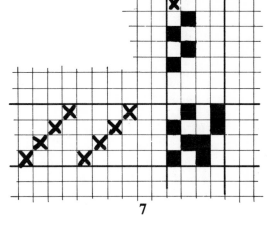

7

9

Overshot Border   **10**

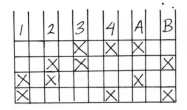

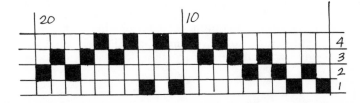

| | | | | | | | | | | | | | | | | | | | | | | | | 4 |
| 3 |
| 2 |
| 1 |

24 23 22 21 20 19 18 17 16 15 14 13 12 11 10 9 8 7 6 5 4 3 2 1

Threading order. The first warp end is threaded in a heddle on harness 2; the second warp end, in a heddle on harness 3; the third, on harness 4; the fourth, on harness 3, and so forth.

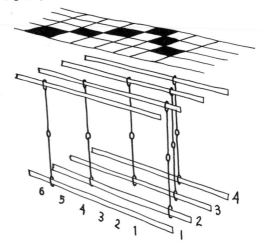

The threading order in relation to the heddles. Each mark on the draft designates one heddle.

harness frames are numbered from the bottom up. Number 1 is closest to the weaver. The threading order is generally read from the right to the left. Each mark for a heddle designates that a warp end is threaded in a heddle on that harness frame.

2. **The tie-up:** This part of the draft is shown beside the threading order, usually in the upper right-hand corner of the complete draft. One treadle is represented by the space between two vertical lines. The tie-up draft must be in line with the threading order, since the horizontal spaces still designate harnesses. Each mark shows which harness frames are tied to each treadle. On most looms the harness frames are attached to lams, which are parallel beneath the frames. It is then the lams that are tied to the treadles.

3. **The treadling order:** This part of the draft is placed just below the tie-up and must be in line with the treadles in the tie-up. Each shot of weft is shown by a mark between vertical lines that mark off spaces corresponding to the treadles. This part of the draft is read from the top down. A mark in a vertical space means that the treadle just above it is used to open the shed for the weft shot.

4. **The drawdown:** This part of the draft shows what the weave will look like—in other words, it gives the interlacement of the warp and weft yarns. It shows the construction of the weave but does not give instructions on how to set up the loom or how to weave the fabric. This part of the draft can be done by the

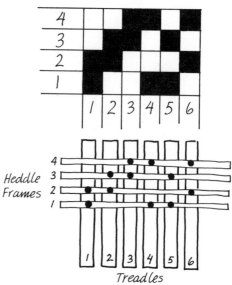

Top: Standard tie-up as shown in a complete draft. A standard tie-up consists of two harness frames tied to each treadle. With four harnesses there are six combinations. They are harnesses 1–2, 2–3, 3–4, 1–4, 1–3, and 2–4. These combinations make up the standard tie-up; however, they are not always in the order shown here.

Bottom: The position of the harness frames in relation to the treadles. Each mark designates which harness frames are tied to each treadle.

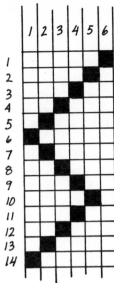

Left: Direct tie-up for four-harness looms with four treadles. While weaving, two and sometimes three treadles are used. This is compound treadling.

Right: Skeleton tie-up for four-harness looms with six treadles. This tie-up is used so the weaver can get as many harness combinations as possible. One or two treadles are used simultaneously for the necessary harness combinations.

This treadling order shows that the first weft shot goes in a shed opened by using treadle 6; treadle 5 is used for the second shot, and so forth.

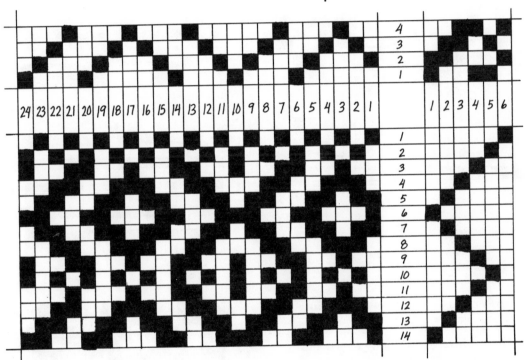

The complete draft showing the threading order, standard tie-up, treadling order, and drawdown. Harnesses, heddles, treadles, and weft shots are numbered to show how to make a drawdown. These numbers are not usually shown on a draft. The first mark (1) in the treadling order is under treadle 6. In the tie-up it shows that treadle 6 is tied to harnesses 2 and 4. If the loom has a sinking shed and treadle 6 is pressed, harnesses 2 and 4 will go down and all the warp ends in heddles on these harnesses will form the bottom part of the shed and be covered by the weft yarn. Now, in the first line of the drawdown, a mark is put below each warp end that is threaded on harnesses 2 and 4 (1, 3, 5, 7, 9, 11, 13, 15, 17, 19, 21, and 23). *Thus each mark shows weft and each blank space is warp.* The second weft shot is below treadle 5, which is tied to harnesses 1 and 3. All warp ends in heddles on these harnesses will be covered by weft. So in the second line of the drawdown each square below warp ends 2, 4, 6, 8, 10, 12, 14, 16, 18, 20, 22, and 24 will be marked. Succeeding rows in the drawdown are marked until at least two repeats of the treadling order are made. This will give a clear picture of the weave construction.

weaver before actually starting a project, and will show the fabric design. The drawdown is a result of the threading order, tie-up, and treadling order and therefore must be in line with all these parts of the draft.

Of course, the actual fabric has three dimensions, while a draft is two-dimensional.

It is important to understand how the different parts of the draft relate to each other. Once you do this, a drawdown becomes very simple.

There is no one universal way of writing or recording drafts, but basically the idea is always the same. The country of origin and the mechanical means for recording a draft account for the main differences. Some drafts show the drawdown and treadling order at the top and the threading order and tie-up at the bottom. Other times the tie-up and treadling order are on the left instead of the right.

A typewriter can be used to record a draft, in which case it would not be necessary to use graph paper.

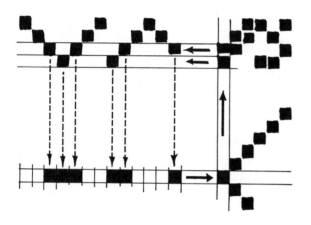

Steps in making a drawdown: start at bottom left.

Basic rules to follow when making a drawdown:

1. In the line of the drawdown being marked, move horizontally to the treadling order.
2. Move vertically from the treadling mark to the treadle in the tie-up draft.
3. From the marks on the treadle move horizontally to the threading draft and the warp ends threaded in heddles on the harness frames tied to this treadle.
4. Move from these warp ends down to the drawdown line and put the marks.

The easiest method of recording weaving drafts is to put them on graph paper. This makes it easy to keep each part in line with the others.

A: How actual yarn appears when woven, forming the weave construction, and, *below,* warp and weft as they appear in a drawdown. Weft is dark and warp is light. This is line 5 of the larger area shown below in C.

B. The weaving as it is seen on the loom. The first weft shot is at the bottom, closest to the weaver.

C. In a drawdown the first weft shot is actually shown at the *top.*

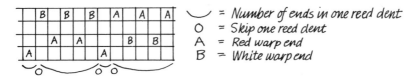

= Number of ends in one reed dent
O = Skip one reed dent
A = Red warp end
B = White warp end

Threading draft, showing special instructions for setting the warp in the reed.

When recording a draft on graph paper, it is easiest to use an X for the threading order, tie-up, and treadling order, but for the drawdown it is easier to see the weave construction if the graph paper block is fully shaded.

Different letters used in the threading and treadling order could designate color. Remember, basically one mark between two lines of the graph paper designates a harness frame, a treadle, a warp end, or a weft shot. Certain marks will appear below the threading order if special spacing is used in the warp sett.

Drafts do not always tell you whether the tie-up is for a rising- or sinking-shed loom. To convert a tie-up for a sinking-shed loom for use on a rising-shed loom (or vice versa), tie the treadles to the opposite harnesses to those shown in the tie-up. It really doesn't matter if you do not know which type of shed the draft is for; the weave construction will be the same on either type, but on the loom the top side of the weaving on one type of shed will be the underside on the other. When a draft produces a weaving that has a pile, it is advantageous to use a tie-up that makes the pile on the top side when the weaving is on the loom. If you do not know if the tie-up is for your particular loom, just weave a few shots to find out and then change the tie-up if necessary.

If there is a photograph of the weave and the piece you are weaving does not resemble it, be sure to look at the underside before

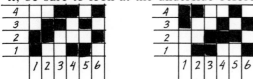

Left: A tie-up for a sinking-shed loom.
Right: The same tie-up converted for use on a rising-shed loom.

you decide you are doing something wrong. The tie-up may be for the opposite type of shed to the one you are using.

There are many fine books written in other languages that show drafts. With an understanding of a few basic words of the language, it is possible to use any of these drafts (see Appendix, "Some Common Foreign Weaving Terms"). Even though the full text may not be translatable, the draft can be understood and used. Refer to the many styles of drafts illustrated at the beginning of this section.

Short or Profile Drafts

The reason for writing a threading draft is to record the order of all the warp ends in a specific pattern. In some instances the number of warp ends involved in one pattern is so high that it becomes impractical to write the draft in its entirety. A method of abbreviating the draft becomes necessary. There are several ways of writing a shortened draft. The method used depends on the weave, since different weave classifications have specific units of threading that occur in the same number and order throughout the draft.

A few ways of shortening drafts are:

1. **Repeats:**   The easiest way to show a threading draft shortened is to give only one repeat and designate how many times that repeat is used.

2. **Twill short drafts:**   A twill threading draft is made up of descending or ascending groups of warp ends. This draft can be shortened by showing continuous lines on the draft instead of a mark for each warp end. A draft like this must have horizontal lines showing the harness frames, or else the weaver would not know which heddle is the turning

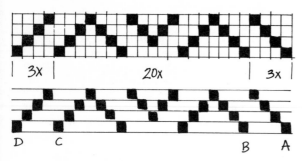

Top: Threading draft showing number of times to repeat each unit.
Bottom: Written instructions tell the weaver how many times to repeat the units of warp ends between the letters. *Example:* Repeat A to B three times, B to C twenty times, and C to D three times.

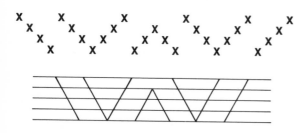

Top: A twill threading draft.
Bottom: Twill threading draft shortened by using continuous lines to show the warp ends.

point when the order reverses in the middle.

3. **Overshot short drafts:** The threading order for overshot weave cannot be shortened any further except by a method that cannot be applied to other weaves.

Overshot is a pattern weave that uses floats or overshots (where the weft crosses two or more warp ends) of different length to make a pattern. The length of these floats and their relative position produce the pattern. Four combinations of harness frames make the floats: 1–2, 2–3, 3–4, and 4–1. The *position* of these floats refers to these combinations, and the *length* means the number of warp ends skipped in a float. The full draft is:

To shorten this draft, designate one row or line of the threading draft for each combination, such as:

Harness 4	1–4
Harness 3	3–4
Harness 2	2–3
Harness 1	1–2

Circling groups of warp ends on two adjoining harness frames makes it easy to see the length of floats.

In overshot weave, the groups will overlap one another by one warp end. Overshot weaves have an even number of warp ends in a float when the blocks follow a diagonal and an odd number when the diagonal changes direction.

When the numbers showing the warp ends in each group are placed beside the harness frame combinations, the draft is considerably shortened; this is a *numerical short draft*.

4. **Spot weave short drafts:** A shortened draft for spot weave is easy, because half the warp ends are carried on one harness frame and the blocks of pattern use the combinations 1–2, 1–3, and 1–4.

To shorten this draft, a solid line can be used for harness 1 and only the number of heddles on the pattern harnesses are shown by marks. To further shorten it, numbers can be used for the heddles on each pattern harness.

5. **Profile drafts:** There are many weaves that have *units* in the threading draft, units being groups of warp ends that are always used in the same order and number. These units are repeated and combined in a variety of ways to make a pattern in a specific weave. For a shortened draft, one unit or group is represented by one square or mark on the draft. A shortened draft with units of threading is therefore called a *profile draft*. There are as many units as there are blocks of pattern in a specific weave.

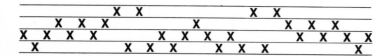

An overshot draft.

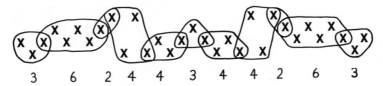

3   6   2   4   4   3   4   4   2   6   3

An overshot draft with groups of warp ends on adjoining harness frames circled. The number designates the number of warp ends in each combination.

4	1-4
3	3-4
2	2-3
1	1-2

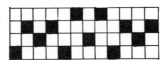

Shortened overshot draft. Each row of the threading draft designates one combination of harness frames that makes a float. Each number in the threading order is the number of warp ends in that combination, showing the length of the float.

Left: Summer and Winter threading order. Note that every other warp end is on harness 1 or 2. Right: Profile draft of the same Summer and Winter threading order.

The Summer and Winter pattern has two units on a four-harness draft.

To use profile drafts, you must be familiar with the units of specific weaves. In Summer and Winter, once you know that every other warp end alternates on two harnesses, it is not necessary to show these warp ends on a profile draft. The important information is the length of the units or blocks, which the profile does show.

Crackle weave has four units, plus the connecting, or incidental, warp end.

Each unit can be represented by one harness frame in a profile draft.

A profile would show which unit and the number of repeats. The weaver knows the incidental heddle is included in the full crackle weave draft.

Any other weave with units in the threading draft can be shown in a profile draft. Many of the lace weaves have units and can be shortened in this way.

A numerical short draft shortens the draft still further and is ideal for very long drafts. The weaver assigns one unit of a draft to one row of the draft, and then the number of times the unit is repeated is shown instead

Threading order for spot weave. Note that every other warp end is on harness 1.

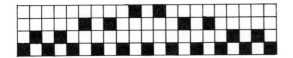

Spot weave short drafts. Left: A solid line represents harness 1 and marks show the number of warp ends on each harness frame. Right: Numerical short draft; the numbers show the number of warp ends on each harness frame. Written instructions should describe the weave represented in the short draft.

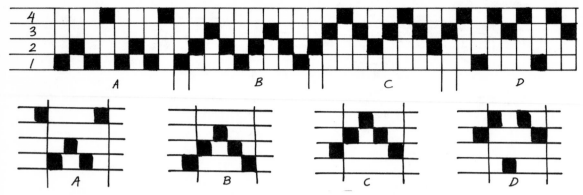

Top: Crackle weave threading order. *Bottom:* The four units of four warp ends each that make up a crackle weave. The one warp end beside each unit is the incidental heddle used in the threading order between different units but not in repeats of the same units.

Left: Profile draft of the same crackle weave shows each row of the threading draft represented by each unit. Marks show how many times each unit is repeated. *Right:* Numerical short draft of the same crackle weave.

A numerical short draft.

of there being one mark for each unit, as in the profile draft.

A profile, short draft, or numerical short draft must have written information for the weaver on which weave the draft represents. If this information is not given, it is a draft of a pattern and not a specific threading draft. A weaver can take a profile draft and produce from it several different weaves, all according to the units of the specific weave. Do not worry about which units to assign to which rows in a profile draft, because the pattern will not be affected as long as the units and sequence are correct.

Borders and Selvages in Draft Writing

A threading draft usually has two or three parts. The main part has the necessary *repeats* for the weave or complete pattern. The second part is the *borders*, which are used only with overall pattern weaves, to give a finish to the design. The third part is the *selvages*, consisting of up to eight warp ends on each side. They are intended to give firm, uniform edges to the weaving.

These parts of the draft must all work together so that they do not appear as separate units in the overall design.

It is necessary to make sure there is a continuation of design from the main part to the border. Also, the tabby order must be maintained; that is, there cannot be two warp ends together on the same harness frame, nor can there be a skip in the threading from harness 1 to 3 or 2 to 4.

Treadling Order

A weaver must be given the threading draft or no draft in fact exists. Many times, however, the treadling order is not given. It is easy to write the treadling order because for each threading order there are any number of ways of treadling to achieve a satisfactory pattern. Here are two using a standard tie-up.

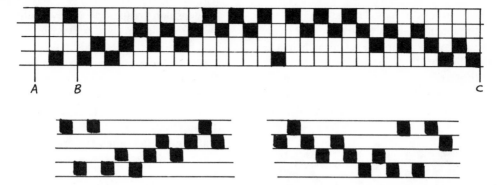

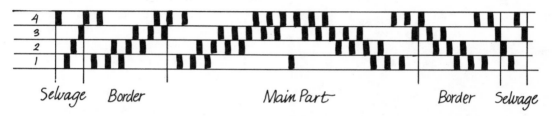

Selvage   Border   Main Part   Border   Selvage

Top: The main part of the draft must be balanced. Start at A, repeat A to C as many times as necessary and then add to the end A to B.
Center: The borders are a smaller, simplified pattern similar to the main part.
Bottom: A complete threading draft. The selvages are simply the edge of the fabric and are usually a straight draw or twill threading. The main part and borders can be repeated as many times as desired.

Top: An overshot draft with overlapping pairs of warp ends circled.
Lower left: Tie-up and treadling order for weaving the above draft as-drawn-in.
Lower right: Tie-up and treadling order for weaving the above draft rose fashion. Note that tabby treadles (5 and 6) are not written in the treadling order and are not shown in the tie-up. ▶

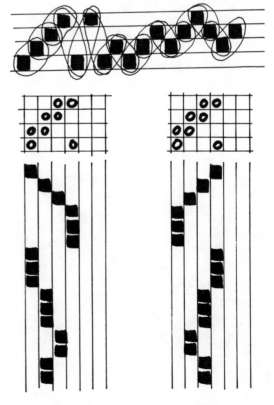

1. **Woven-as-drawn-in:** This is an old term meaning "treadled the same as threaded." This method of treadling applies to overshot weave because the object is to produce a pattern that is square and symmetrical.

   To weave as-drawn-in (sometimes termed *tromp-as-writ),* circle overlapping pairs of warp ends in the threading draft. From this you can write the treadling order. Each circled pair designates which harness frames are used, and you can put the mark in line with the treadle tied to those harness frames. Overshot is woven with alternate shots of tabby; however, the tabby shots are never shown in the treadling order.

In patterns woven-as-drawn-in, a diagonal is produced. If the pattern is symmetrical, diagonals will run in both directions.

An overshot draft woven-as-drawn-in. This pattern is square and symmetrical. Note the diagonal line in both directions.

Reverse side of same weaving.

2. **Rose-fashion treadling:** Many traditional overshot patterns are woven in what is called *rose fashion*. This also produces a symmetrical pattern. To find the treadling order for weaving rose fashion, first work out the basic treadling draft, or woven-as-drawn-in. Then simply write the mirror image of the basic treadling draft and it becomes the treadling draft for weaving rose fashion.

These are but a few of the methods of recording threading and treadling orders for a weaving draft. With a basic understanding of how a draft is written, you can read and use all drafts no matter what form they are written in. Weaving is a creative process, and all weavers must have the confidence to write their own drafts for the patterns they wish to weave. A knowledge of the units comprising basic weave structures is all that is needed to write drafts for any weave. If only the threading draft is available, be creative and try a variety of treadling orders to arrive at a satisfactory pattern that can be exclusively your own.

Pattern Analysis

The drawdown part of the draft shows the weave construction, or what a fabric will be like if the threading and treadling orders are followed. The whole process can, however, be reversed, a *drawdown or pattern graph* being made from a piece of fabric, from which graph the threading order, tie-up, and treadling order can be written, enabling you to reproduce the fabric on a handloom. This process is called *pattern or fabric analysis*. You can derive great satisfaction from being able to do a fabric analysis because it demonstrates that you have a full understanding of the structure and classification of weaves.

Equipment needed for fabric analysis: the piece of fabric with at least one complete pattern repeat (it is easier with two), graph paper, straight pins, soft pencil, and magnifying glass or thread counter.

The first time, choose a fabric with coarse yarn, preferably with one color for the warp and another for the weft. Determine which

An overshot pattern woven rose fashion. This piece is woven in four colors. Note the border.

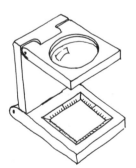

A magnifying thread counter to use when analyzing a piece of fabric. The viewing aperture is about ½ inch (1.3 cm) square.

A lupe or magnifying glass for close-up viewing of an area about 2 inches (5 cm) in diameter.

is which. If there are selvages, this is easy, but if not, generally the warp yarns are sett closer and will be the stronger, while the weft will be the novelty yarn. Place the fabric so that the warp yarns run vertically and the weft horizontally.

Choose an area of the fabric that has at least one complete repeat of the pattern. Pin the fabric to a pillow or other surface so that

the area to be analyzed is in a convenient working position.

Find the warp yarn at the outer right-hand side of the area to be analyzed. Mark it with pins: this is the *warp guide yarn*. In the same manner, mark the *weft guide yarn* that is at the base of the area to be analyzed.

The fabric should be analyzed from right to left. Starting at the lower right-hand corner, follow the weft guide yarn. Mark on graph paper wherever the weft goes over the warp (the unmarked squares are where the

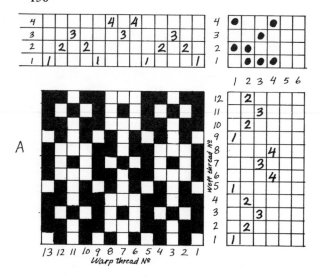

A

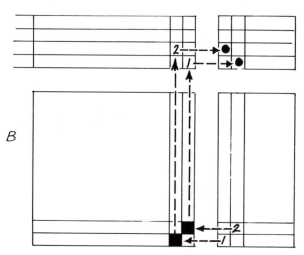

B

A. The pattern graph *(lower left)* was made by analyzing a piece of fabric. The threading order, tie-up, and treadling order were made from this graph. Note the numbers on the warp columns and weft rows. These numbers indicate the repeat warp ends and weft shots or rows.

B. Steps in finding the threading order, tie-up, and treadling order from the pattern graph. Put a mark in the treadling draft beside the first weft row. From the first mark in that weft row, move vertically to the threading draft and put a mark on the harness frame. Then move horizontally to the right to the tie-up and place a mark. Beside the second weft row put a mark under treadle 2 and follow the same procedure. Continue to do this for each weft row until the threading order, tie-up, and treadling order are complete for one pattern repeat. The tie-up and treadling draft on the upper right show the tie-up on the analysis draft converted to a standard tie-up.

warp goes over the weft). Proceed across the row until the marked area is complete. Do the same for the next weft row, being sure to mark every weft yarn and to include tabby when it is used between pattern shots. Continue to mark all the rows until one pattern repeat is represented on the graph paper. This is the pattern graph.

The next step is to find the threading order for this graph-paper drawing of the pattern. Starting at the lower right with number 1, number each warp column of the pattern.

Each column designates one harness frame. Number 1 will be harness 1; mark it in the threading order just above column 1. Look at the second column; if it is different, assign it to harness 2 and mark it in the threading order draft. Continue across the columns, and assign each column that is unlike any previous one to another harness frame. Identical columns are assigned to the same harness frame.

Next, number the weft shots on the graph pattern. Start with number 1 in the lower right-hand corner. Also number the treadles in the tie-up draft. In the treadling order draft place a mark or number beside weft shot 1 under treadle 1. Starting with the mark in the treadling order, draw a line horizontally to the left across the first weft shot. Where this line crosses a marked square in the graph pattern, draw a vertical line to the heddle in the threading draft. Then make a horizontal line to the right to treadle 1 in the tie-up and place a mark. Do the same for each mark in the pattern graph in weft row 1. This row will show one weft shot and the harnesses tied to treadle 1. Do the same for weft row 2; it will show the tie-up for treadle 2. Continue marking all the weft rows in the pattern; watch for repeat rows and mark them on the same treadle.

The draft is now complete, providing that a complete pattern was analyzed. The directions here for fabric analysis are very basic. If you understand and follow an analysis of a small basic pattern you will have no difficulty in analyzing more complicated patterns.

There are ways of making the analysis systematic; follow or devise one that you find convenient. For instance, for a multiple-harness pattern, each warp column can be marked on the edge of a strip of graph paper. This makes comparing repeats much easier. Also, if two people work together in making the pattern graph, there is less chance of error when moving from the fabric to mark the graph paper. Or you can use a tape recorder.

Pattern analysis can be fun, especially when you are making your own designs.

8

mmmmmmmmmmmmmmmmmmmmmmmmmmmmmmmmmmmmmmmmmmmmmm

Two-Harness Technique

Basic Methods of Weaving

Many effects in weaving can be achieved by using the simplest or most basic weave, which is **tabby**, or **plain weave**. Any number of harnesses can be used for tabby; it is, however, *the* weave used in two-harness weaving.

Tabby can be defined as a weave that repeats on two warp ends and two weft picks. One end passes over one pick and under the next pick. The next end reverses this action. To weave tabby, pass weft yarn successively over and under each warp yarn and alternate each row.

Tabby is a plain weave, but it does not have to be a balanced weave, which has an equal number of warp ends and weft picks in a given area.

Fabric woven in tabby is strong but stiff. These characteristics must be remembered when weaving fabric for a specific purpose. Tabby fabric is not easy to weave. It requires that there be absolutely no variation in beating, and the same warp tension must be achieved or unevenness will show in the weave. Tabby can be woven on two harnesses, but if the loom has more it is advisable to use them because, as the sheds change, the friction on the warp ends is reduced.

The direction of twist of the yarn used in a tabby weave can determine how smooth the fabric surface will be. If you want a smooth surface, the best results are obtained by using yarn with one twist for the warp

Tabby weave showing direction of twist (S or Z) in warp and weft yarn:
Left: Warp and weft yarn with same twist. Where yarns cross each other, fibers are parallel and tend to lock, causing a rough surface.
Right: Warp and weft yarn with opposite twist. Where the yarns cross, the direction of the fibers is reversed and they tend to slide on each other, making a smooth surface.

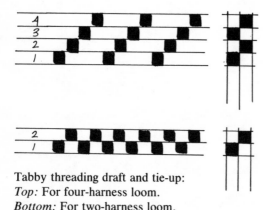

Tabby threading draft and tie-up:
Top: For four-harness loom.
Bottom: For two-harness loom.

and the opposite twist for the weft. It does not, however, matter which twist—S or Z—is used for which. For a rough or crepe-like surface, use yarn with the same twist for warp and weft.

Many threading drafts for pattern weaves will also give a tabby weave. This is important because on a long warp there is more versatility. On the same warp, you can use a pattern weave for one piece of weaving and then use techniques described in this chapter that require a tabby weave for another piece. Or in the same piece you can combine techniques: a tabby weave with a pattern weave. Some threading drafts will not give a tabby weave, and it is valuable to know this before starting a project.

It is easy to find out if the threading will give a tabby weave. Put the threading draft on graph paper, and just below it mark two rows of tabby weave. Now check the heddles that will make the first line of tabby and mark the tie-up. Do the same for the second line. If any harness frame is tied to both treadles, that threading draft will not weave tabby.

The patterns or designs that can be achieved with tabby weave are endless. Color need not be uniform in tabby. You can weave stripes, either vertical or horizontal; plaid effects; two-block patterns; and free patterns such as tapestry. Novelty yarns will give a textural effect.

The following techniques serve as an introduction to what can be woven in tabby weave. Use a frame loom, rigid-heddle loom, or a loom that has two (or more) harnesses to make a shed.

Using color in tabby weave is the easiest way to make a pattern. Putting color stripes in the warp and weaving with a single color creates horizontal stripes, but by also using stripes of color in the weft you can weave checks and plaids.

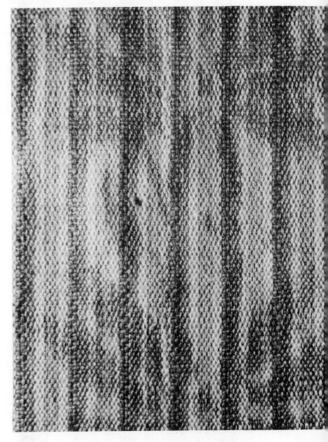

Striped warp in tabby weave with single-color weft. Warp also has design painted on it.

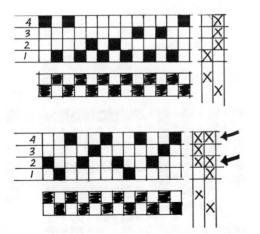

Method of finding out if a draft will weave tabby:
Top: This draft will weave tabby; no harness is tied to both treadles.
Bottom: This draft will not weave tabby; harnesses 2 and 4 are tied to both treadles.

When changing color in the weft it is important to end one color and start the next color in an unobtrusive manner. The basic rule is never to mix colors in the same shed. When ending one color, put the end of the

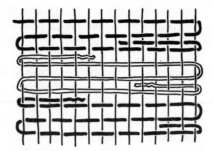

Method of starting and ending colors in weft. Note that colors are never mixed in the same shed.

yarn in the same shed as the last shot. Manually put the weft around the end warp yarn to catch it. When starting a new color, you can put the end of the yarn in the next shed. Alternate sides of the warp where colors are ended and started. The weft is double at these places, and if they were all on one side the weaving would build up more on that side.

Do not forget that the warp is under tension. A square block will appear rectangular while you are weaving; when the tension is released, it should be square.

Rep weave. *Rep* is the term used to describe weaving that produces a rib in either the warp or the weft. *Warp-faced weave*—where the warp is sett very close and covers the weft—produces a horizontal rib. *Weft-faced weave*—when the warp is sett wide and is covered by the weft—produces a vertical rib.

Warp-faced weave is most commonly known as the rep weave. By the alternation of colors in the warp and of heavy and fine

yarn in the weft, ribs (or cords, as they are sometimes called) are formed. This makes a fabric that is predominantly one color on one side and another color on the opposite side.

If the position of the colors in the warp is changed, color blocks will form in the pattern. When one shed is opened, it will not be all one color, as is the case when one color is all on one harness and the opposite color all on the other harness. Weave in the same manner, alternating heavy and fine yarn. Rep weave with blocks is appropriately called *Log Cabin Weave*. Rep weave can be woven on two, four, or more harnesses.

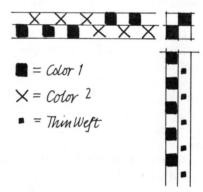

Rep weave threading order, tie-up, and treadling order. This draft produces color blocks in the design.

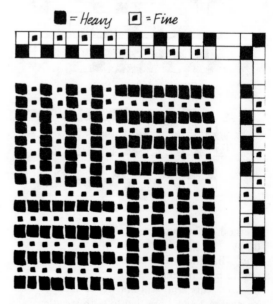

Complete draft of rep weave with fine and heavy yarn in warp and weft. This is called Log Cabin Weave.

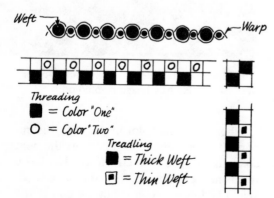

Top: Cross section of weft yarn in rep weave. *Bottom:* Threading and treadling order for a rep weave.

Tapestry. Tapestry is the most commonly known of the weft-faced weaves. Although not truly rep, weft-faced weaves do produce a vertical rib in the weaving. The design is made by the placement of the weft yarn color in specific areas.

To weave tapestry, the warp must be strong. It can be plied cotton or linen yarn with a tight twist. Linen warp yarn will give the piece more body than will cotton yarn.

The loom for weaving tapestry can be a frame loom without a beater, referred to as a *high-warp loom;* or a *low-warp loom,* which has a beater and a means of making the sheds. The threading is a straight draw or twill threading, and the warp is sett in the reed so that the spaces between the warp ends are wider than the size of the weft yarn. This enables the weft yarns to be beaten down and to completely cover the warp. Always put sufficient slack in the weft so the warp ends will be covered and the edges will not pull in.

Traditionally, tapestries were woven wrong, or back, side up and sideways. When the piece was completed and removed from the loom and the design was in the correct position, the warp was horizontal. When planning a design for a tapestry to be hung in this manner, remember that the back side is up and the design as it is seen during weaving is a mirror image of what it should be.

Tapestries can, however, be woven in any number of ways. They do not have to be woven wrong side up or hung so that the warp is horizontal. In some instances, color in the warp could be an important part of the design and therefore would not be totally covered by the weft.

In weaving a tapestry, specific color areas are built up. The weft is carried on bobbins or wound in butterflies. It is not shot, or thrown, across the loom, so the beater is not used. It is customary to put the weft yarn in place with a tapestry comb or fork. Tapestry weaving is a slow process, but with an understanding of the basic techniques used for joining colors, the weaver can execute any desired design.

There are limitless possibilities in weft-faced weaving: horizontal and vertical stripes, checks, and geometric and irregular shapes. Some shapes may present a challenge, for the principle of pictorial tapestry weaving is the gradual buildup of an area, with its background field, in such a way that no shed is closed to subsequent weft shots.

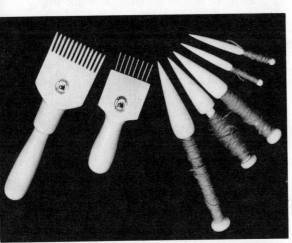

Tapestry forks and bobbins. *Left:* Weighted fork for heavy beating.
Middle: Fork with smooth metal teeth is ideal for any warp sett.
Right: Various sizes of tapestry bobbin for different weights of yarn. *Photo courtesy Nilus Leclerc, Inc.*

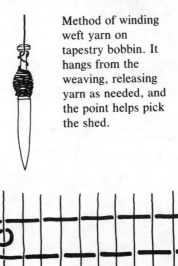

Method of winding weft yarn on tapestry bobbin. It hangs from the weaving, releasing yarn as needed, and the point helps pick the shed.

For weft-faced weaves, loop the weft once around the outer warp end to make a solid edge.

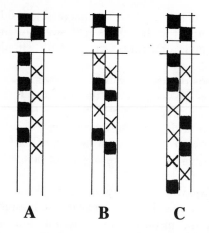

A   B   C

Tie-up and treadling order for weft-faced weaving:

A, vertical stripes; B, horizontal stripes; C, checks.

Horizontal stripes are made by weaving two or more shots of weft of one color, then two or more shots of weft of another color. There must be at least two shots of a color to make a solid line of color. Change shed after each shot.

Vertical stripes are alternate shots of color in the weft. The stripe width can vary by putting the weft over and under a different number of warp ends. EXAMPLE: One shot is put over three warp ends, under one warp end; the next shot with alternate color would be under three, over one.

To make *checks,* have alternate shots of color in the weft for three or four shots, then two shots of the same color; alternate color shots three or four times again, and then put in two shots of the same color. Repeat.

There are a number of *slit techniques* (see the illustrations), to determine how one color area changes into another. Most simply, weave the two different-colored wefts in the same shed from opposite directions and bring both out of the warp between the same two warp ends. Change the shed and weave the weft yarns back to the sides where they started.

1. A straight slit (A) can be made any length. It makes a clean, straight line where colors meet. When the tapestry is finished, the slit can be hand-sewn together on the reverse side with fine thread.
2. A diagonal line (B) in the design can be made when the slits are moved to the right or the left at regular intervals.
3. Irregular slits (C–F) can be made in the design simply by varying the point where the colors meet. This is one technique used to suggest shaded areas.

You can also *interlock* two areas of color. Interlocking does not make as straight or sharp a line where the colors join as do the slit techniques.

1. Weft interlock: weft yarns are joined by linking them around each other between two warp ends (A). This interlock is

◄

Weft-faced rug using two-color techniques for vertical and horizontal stripes and checks.

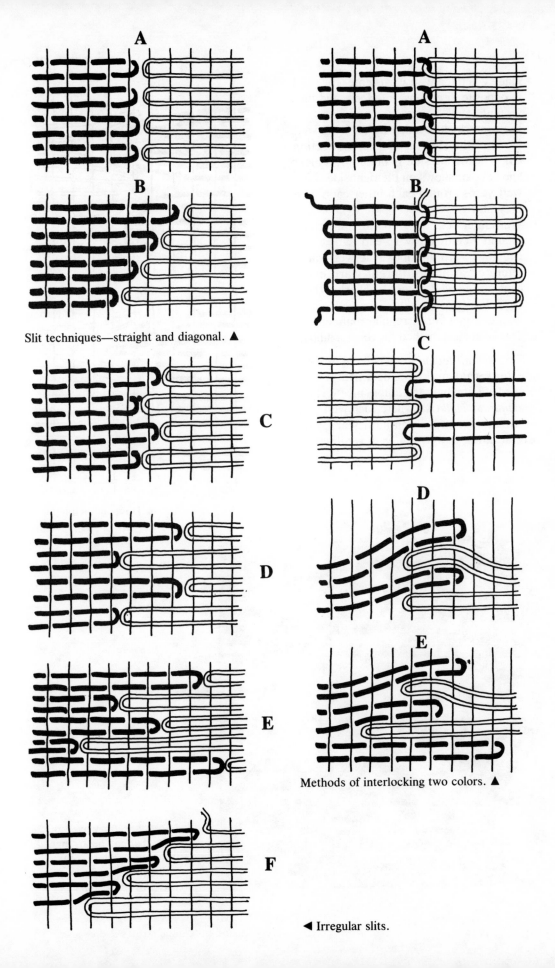

Slit techniques—straight and diagonal. ▲

Methods of interlocking two colors. ▲

◀ Irregular slits.

made when the weft yarns enter the shed in opposite directions, interlock, and turn around.

2. Weft interlock is made by entering weft yarns in the shed in the same direction (B). The wrong side is pictured; a clear line of color shows on the right side. Link weft yarns around each other each time they meet.

3. Warp interlock: the weft yarns interlock around a common warp end (C).

4. Irregular warp interlock: the weft yarns interlock around different warp ends, causing the weft colors to overlap (D).

5. Irregular warp interlock: the weft yarns interlock in a very irregular manner (E). This is an ideal method for color shading.

The *dovetail technique* is a form of warp interlock that makes a definitely saw-toothed effect where the colors meet. There is *regular dovetail* (A), where each weft yarn interlocks around a common warp yarn several times, and *irregular dovetail* (B).

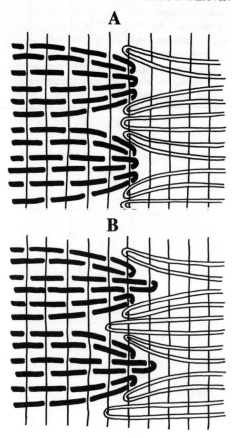

▲ Dovetail technique.

Large tapestry woven in units that can be arranged in various patterns. In brilliant blue and red, it was woven by Mary Nice.

Tapestry designed by sculptor David Black and professionally woven. Much practice and control are needed to achieve this symmetry of semicircles.

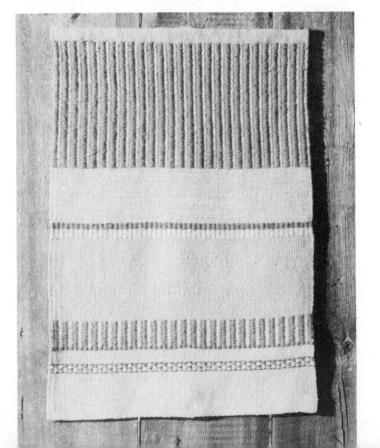

Small tapestry with vertical and horizontal stripes of yellow and gold. *Photo by Charles Vorhees.*

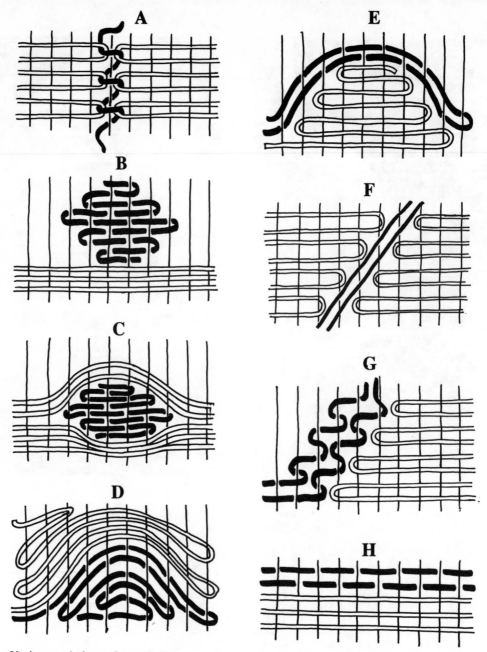

Various techniques for outlining.

An *outline* defines a particular area. In tapestry weaving, outlines can be made by means of many techniques.

1. A *vertical outline* is made by using two weft yarns and a third to interlock them (A).
2. A *curved outline* is made by weaving a specific color area and then weaving completely around the area with another color (B and C).
3. Another method of weaving a *curved outline* is shown (D and E).
4. A *diagonal outline* is made by building up one color area on the diagonal (F and G). Two shots of another color are put in and then the third area is built up to join the outline. The third area can be the same color as the first or an additional color.
5. A *horizontal outline* (H) is sometimes needed: a straight solid line can be made by weaving two shots of one color.

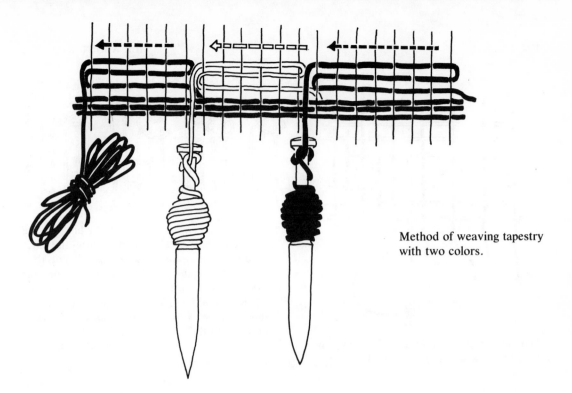

Method of weaving tapestry with two colors.

When weaving any tapestry technique using more than two colors, always lay the colors in the weaving from the same direction. Here all colors are put in from the right. The next shed will have them all going from left to right. Weft yarns are released from the bobbins or butterflies as needed.

There are many different ways of finishing the edge of a tapestry. Most often the warp is not left as a fringe, but all warp ends are woven back into the web or fastened to the back.

The finished tapestry may not be as straight and flat as desired, but never iron it. Spread it on a flat surface and fasten it down with rustproof pins. Put a wet cloth over it and then several dry towels. Then put a heavy weight on top. After twenty-four hours the weight and cloths can be removed and the weaving allowed to dry thoroughly before being moved.

Embroidery or laid-in weaving. Using tapestry techniques, you can make a small pattern on a fabric that is itself woven with shuttles thrown across the entire width. Yarns of different color and weight from the warp and weft are laid in specific areas during the weaving to create the pattern. The effect resembles embroidery.

There are several names for this type of weave. Each has a complete background web, but the weaver places the design on each in a slightly different manner. Some of the names used are *Brocade,* which is French embroidery; *Dukagang,* Swedish; and *Calabrian,* Italian. But *laid-in* is probably the most common term and best describes the technique.

It is most often used on a tabby background. (Actually, the pattern can be laid in in any number of ways and on a variety of the threading orders, such as twill and overshot, that are explained in Chapter 9.)

Draw the design on graph paper. Choose warp and background weft yarns of the same weight and color. Use a softer, heavier yarn of a different color for the laid-in design.

It is easier to weave with the wrong side up (remember that the design you see while weaving is a mirror image). Change of color and ends of the pattern yarn can be controlled better on the surface, and when the pattern yarn changes direction the small loops can be kept uniform. The pattern yarn can be laid in on every shed for a more solid color area, or it can be laid in on every other shed. Semitransparent or translucent hangings can be woven by using fine yarn for the background warp and weft and heavier pat-

FINISHING TECHNIQUES FOR TAPESTRIES.

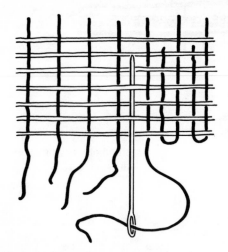

Method of weaving warp ends back into the tapestry for a straight, smooth edge, like a selvage.

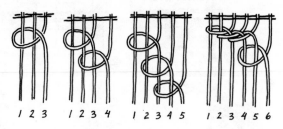

A firm, solid edge can be made by hitching the warp ends around one another. From the left, hold two warp ends in the left hand. With the right hand, hitch the third warp end around the first two. Drop warp end 1; hold 2 and 3 in the left hand and hitch 4 around them. Continue in this way across the weaving. Pull the hitches up close to the edge of the weaving. This produces a chainlike effect along the edge.

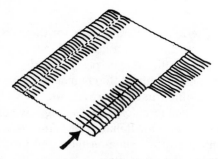

If the warp color complements the color of the woven tapestry, the warp ends can be left to hang down straight. If no fringe is desired, fold the warp ends to the back and sew them with fine thread to the tapestry, being sure the stitches do not show on the surface.

Another way to finish a tapestry with a firm edge is to hitch warp ends around a lead cord. The cord is anchored securely by pinning the end down, and then each warp end is hitched to the cord. This makes a "beaded" edge. Pull each knot up tightly and place close to the edge of the weaving.
Left: Warp hitched on lead cord.
Middle: Front, showing "beads."
Right: Reverse side of hitch.

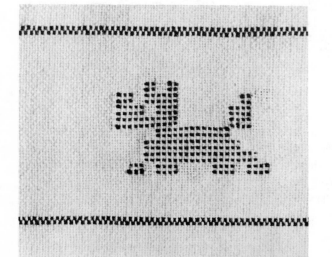

Border pattern using laid-in technique.

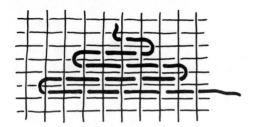

Method of placing pattern weft yarn for laid-in weaving. This is the wrong side.

Translucent hanging using heavy alpaca yarn ▲ in laid-in technique. *Collection of Peter Crosby; photo by Charles Vorhees.*

◄

Partly transparent hanging using laid-in technique. Woven by Mary Nice.

tern yarn laid in every shed for a solid pattern area.

To weave, work with a shuttle with weft yarn the same as the warp. Open one shed, throw the shuttle across the warp, and in the same shed place the pattern yarn only in the desired pattern area. This yarn can be carried in a butterfly or on a tapestry bobbin. Change the shed and throw the shuttle across the warp again. Put the pat-

tern yarn again in the desired area in the same shed, or skip that shed and put it in the next. Continue in this manner until the design is completed. Finish weaving the piece with the shuttle with background weft yarn.

The use of heavy yarn for warp and background weft requires a geometric design, but with fine background yarn the design lines can be more gently curved.

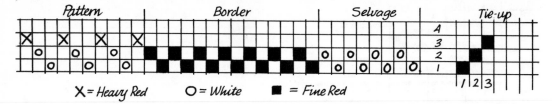

X = Heavy Red   O = White   ■ = Fine Red

Threading draft and tie-up for a pickup weave. Note the two colors in pattern area, one for the tabby background and the other for the pattern.

Pickup weave. On a tabby threading a very intricate design can be made by picking up the required warp ends by hand to make the design. Pickup is usually a warp-faced weave with a two-color warp. The warp ends for the pattern are threaded on a different harness (harness 3 in the draft). On a two-harness loom they would not be threaded on any harness. They are not woven with the tabby background. The warp ends used for the pattern or design are held on a pickup stick above the tabby warp ends during weaving. The pattern warp ends not used in the design lie underneath the tabby sheds, creating the reverse design on the opposite side of the weaving. The design consists of warp floats. The pattern warp ends are woven only in the shed when they move from the top to the underside and vice versa. If the design is drawn on graph paper it is very easy to follow.

Basket weave. A derivative of tabby, basket weave is characterized by having two or more ends and picks used at the same time. Each warp end for basket weave should, however, be threaded in an individual heddle and in separate dents of the reed. This permits them to lie flat in the weaving. Likewise, each weft pick should be on a separate shuttle so the yarns do not twist around each other. Put a catch cord (see page 133) on each edge of the warp to pass the shuttles around to make a firm edge.

Texture weaves. Texture can be achieved in two ways in weaving: use yarn that is not smooth, or use an irregular threading or sleying order. A weaving can have too many different textures, each competing for attention, and the result is

A primitive piece in pickup weave. The design is in soft-twist red yarn. Warp floats appear on the surface where the design is picked up.

Draft for basket weave:
Top: Threading draft and tie-up for two-harness loom.
Bottom: Threading draft and tie-up for four-harness loom.

Fabric woven in basket weave, and treadling ▲ order for two- or four-harness loom.

Looped mohair yarn used for a texture weave. ▼

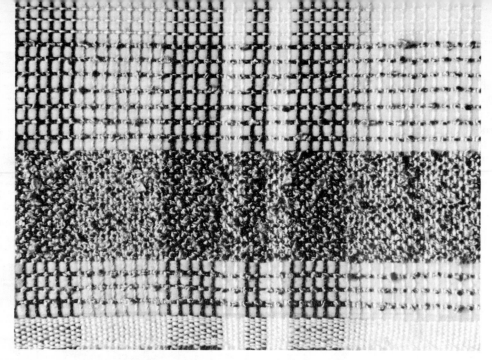

A balance of color and texture for a lightweight blanket in tabby.

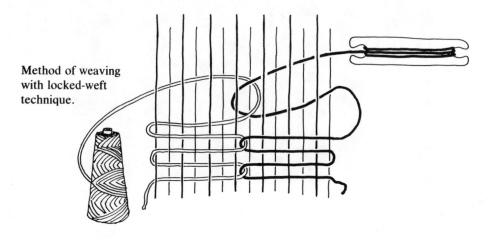

Method of weaving with locked-weft technique.

confusion. If very textured yarn is used, stay with tabby weave. Limit texture yarn to either warp or weft, not both. Keep to just a few colors within a close range. Pattern threadings can produce very interesting texture when woven in one color and with smooth yarn. Try many combinations, but *always set limits* when weaving texture.

Locked wefts. This weaving technique makes patterns as two weft yarns interlock. Its limitation is that only two colors can be used horizontally at one time. Use a tabby weave and prepare a shuttle of one color to be used in your right hand. On your left side place a spool of yarn of a different color. Open the shed, throw the shuttle from the right, catch it on the left, and interlock it by passing it around the yarn on the spool at the left. Without changing the shed, throw the shuttle back to the right. The wefts are interlocked, and by pulling the shuttle you can place the point of interlock—where the color changes—anywhere in the shed. Now beat and change the shed. The weft yarn is double in each shed. The weaving is rather fast.

Shuttles and spools with different-color

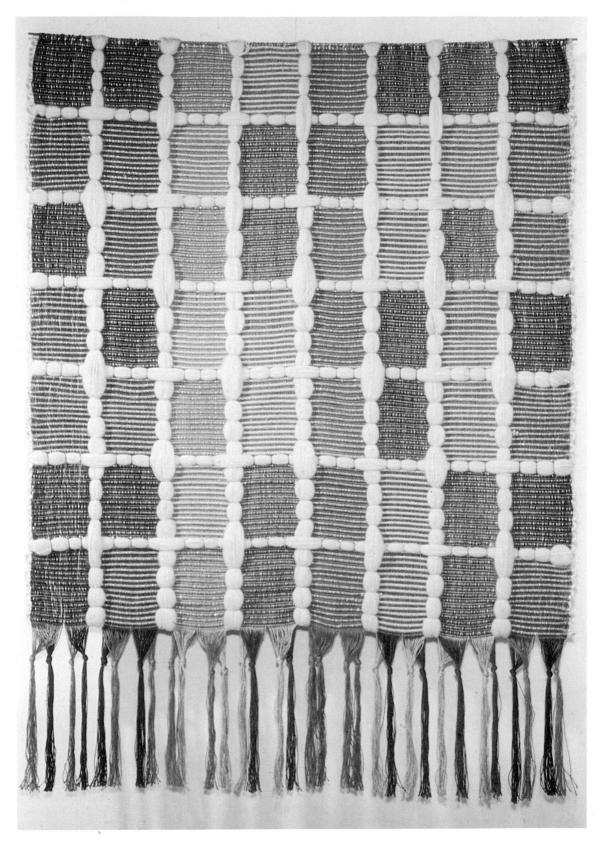

14. Wall hanging using jute rope and linen warp, woven in Log Cabin weave on twelve harnesses. A combination of two different colors was used on every two harnesses.

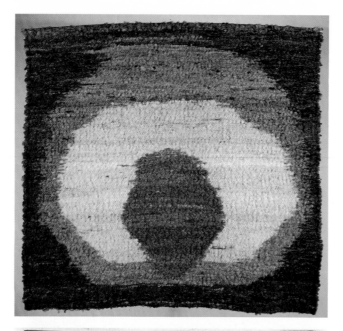

Three examples of double weave:

15. Wall hanging in stitched double weave.

16. Also stitched double weave. *Collection of Attorneys Murphy, Young and Smith.*

17. "Daybreak," woven with unspun wool in double weave.

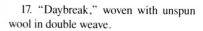

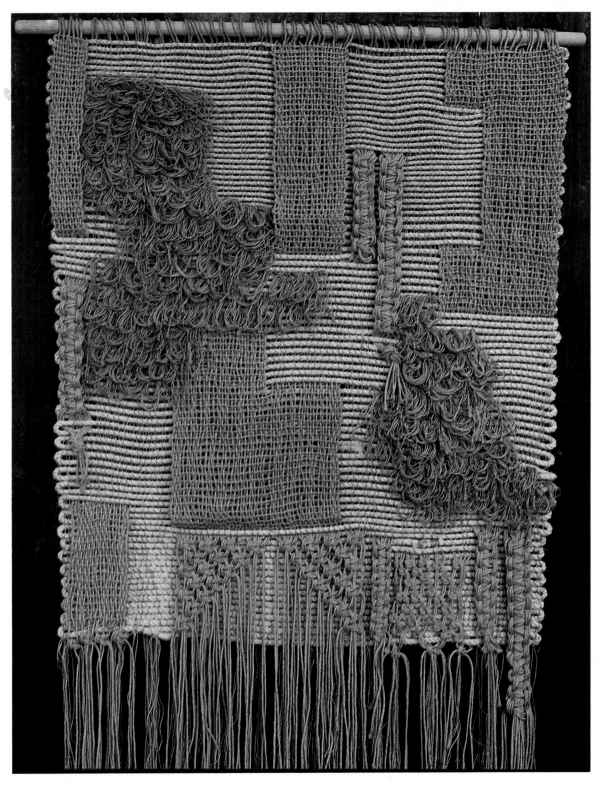

18. Wall hanging in double weave, using linen yarn and jute rope. *Collection of Massillon Museum, Ohio.*

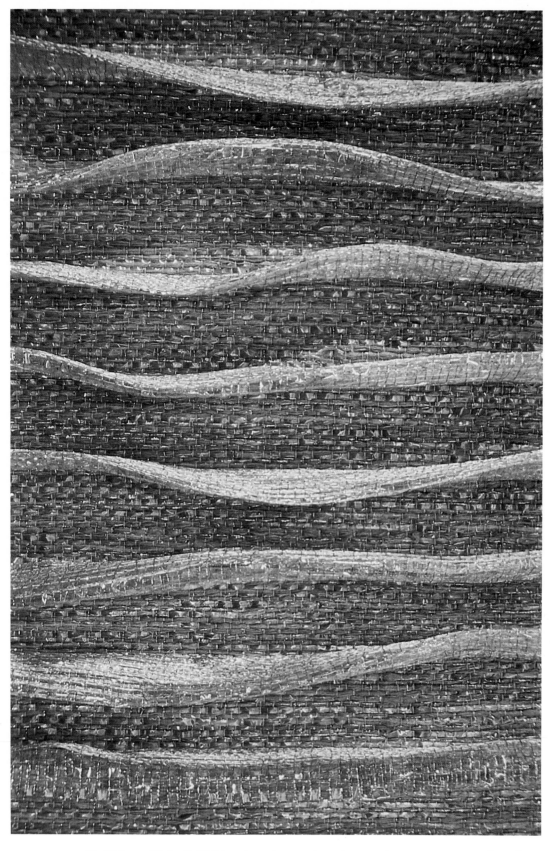

19. "Saharan I," detail. Wall hanging using a variety of yarns, pleated on the loom; 44″ x 60″, by Nancy Guay. *Photo by Greg Heins.*

20. "Sunshine Biscuits" — favorite woven samples in boxes.

21. Wall hanging by Kevin Regan, woven with strips of fabric and then painted.

22. (Left) ''The Changing of the Guard'' — light-reflective panels of wool, rayon, and metallic thread, by Nancy Guay. *Photo courtesy of the artist.*

23. (Below) "Doric Eclipse," wool and rayon; 48″ x 26″, by Nancy Guay. *Photo by Greg Heins.*

25. (Above) Large tapestry woven in units that can be rearranged to create new patterns. Woven by Mary Nice.

26. (Below) "Ticonderoga," multiple panels woven separately but hung together, using a variety of yarns in plain weave.

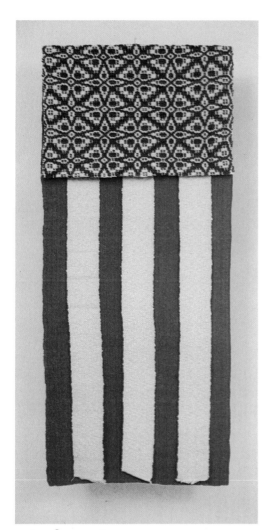

24. (Above) Woven hanging in overshot. Treadling order as-drawn-in and a variation. Woven in one piece, but folded over rod to hang in panels. *Photo by Charles Vorhees.*

27. (Above) Osage orange fruit and wood chips with various mordants used to dye spun and unspun wool.

Top: The fruit with (first row): chrome; alum; dyebath fermented, then alum; (second row): tin; iron; blue vitriol.

Bottom: Wood chips with (first row): chrome; alum; alum mordant and dyed, then iron mordant only; (second row): tin; iron; blue vitriol.

28. (Right) Sampler using various hues of handdyed yarn.

Fabric woven with locked-weft technique. Warp was tie-dyed.

yarn can be used, but only two colors (one from the shuttle and one from the spool) can be used in each shed. Large patterns with diagonal lines are most effective in this technique.

Seersucker. Many interesting textures resembling seersucker can be achieved in handweaving. *Seersucker* can be described as a fabric with woven crinkle stripes in the warp direction. It is woven while sections of the warp are under normal tension but the crinkle warp ends are slack.

Use yarn for the warp that has different stretching qualities, or put sections of the warp under different tension (see "Double-Tension Warp," in Chapter 12). Combining yarns of different fibers in the warp will also create a seersucker effect, especially if the woven piece is washed and some of the fibers shrink.

This is a technique not often used, but it offers the weaver many possibilities. Work with familiar yarns and try something that hasn't been done before. You will probably achieve pleasing results.

Large hanging, woven on frame loom using torn strips of fabric, by Linda Fowler.

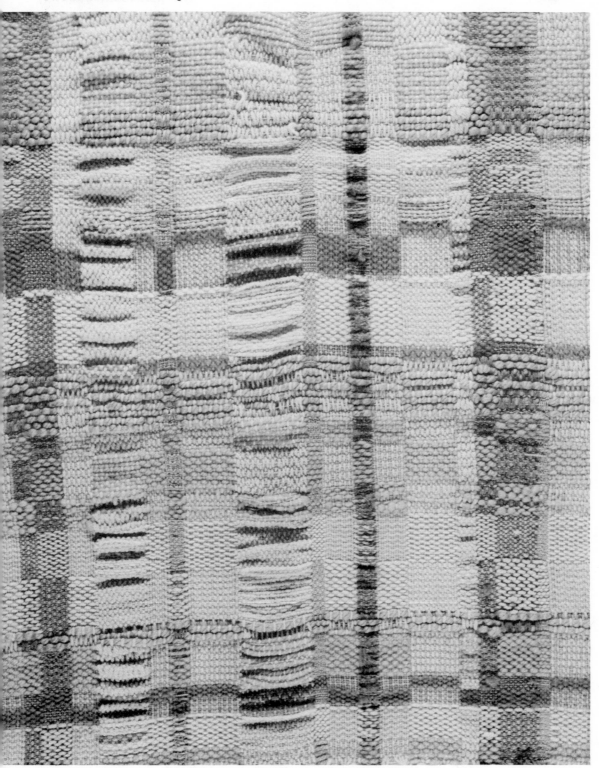

Fabric woven in seersucker technique by student Mary Alice Wurster.

Weaving with Strips of Fabric

In addition to the rag rugs that naturally come to mind, many interesting pieces can be woven using fabric strips. A plain, or tabby, weave is satisfactory. The actual weaving, using such thick weft, goes quickly. The most time-consuming part is preparing the strips. The finished product is only as good as the materials that have gone into making it.

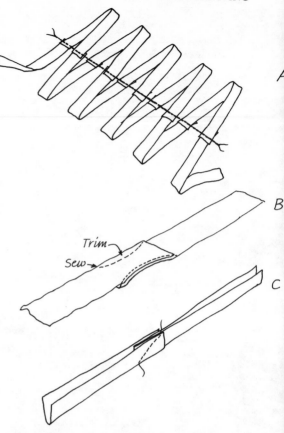

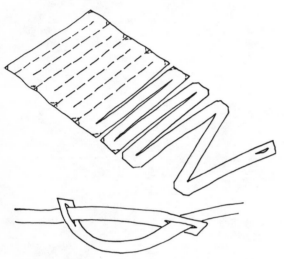

Method of cutting and joining strips of fabric for weaving: To make one long strip, cut a piece of fabric first from one side and then from the other. To join fabric strips, make a slit in each end and pull the end of the next piece through each slit.

Methods of sewing fabric strips together:

A. Fold ends over and machine-stitch in one continuous piece. Snip stitching between pieces to make one long joined strip.

B. Overlap ends and stitch; trim out curved part to lessen thickness in overlapped area.

C. Fold each piece and stitch on the diagonal.

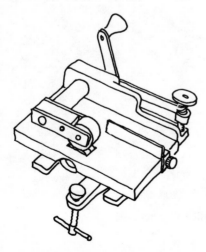

A cloth-cutting machine can be used.

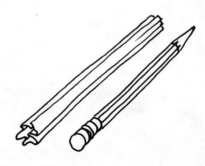

The fabric strip for weaving rag rugs should be about the size of a pencil when it is folded or twisted. The width of each cut strip depends on the weight of the fabric being used.

If you are using fabric from old clothing, tear the items completely apart at the seams, thoroughly machine-wash the pieces in hot water, and dry in the clothes dryer. Wool will felt or shrink, making it ideal for rugs. Tear or cut the fabric in strips and join the strips in the most convenient method. Wind the strips on a rag or rug shuttle for weaving.

Alternate knit and woven fabrics when joining the strips. Knit fabric needs the woven fabric to maintain firmness, thickness, and good edges on a rug. To estimate the amount of fabric needed, allow 1½ to 2 pounds (0.68–0.91 kg) of fabric for each square yard (0.82 m²) of rug. The weight of the fabric being used is the variable when you are estimating the amount of fabric required for a given project.

Use a strong warp and sett it for a weave that allows the weft to almost cover it. Remember a rug must be beaten so it is solid. Generally the pattern in rag rugs comes from the color. We always associate hit-or-miss patterns or horizontal stripes with rag rugs—but why not try tapestry techniques! Use interlocking techniques to achieve specific design areas, therefore eliminating horizontal stripes. Also, if you use several different colors randomly placed in the warp, the striped effect of the weft will be minimized.

Finger-manipulated Lace Weaves

These are in a class by themselves but are most always done in a tabby weave. Even though they may seem complex, they can be done on a loom with only two or with more harnesses. Finger-manipulated lace weaves are different from loom-controlled lace weaves (see Chapter 9). They bear no resemblance to each other and are differ-

Hanging using gauze weave. *Collection of Mr. and Mrs. Jeff Ankrom; photo by Charles Vorhees.*

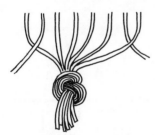

To finish rag rugs and mats, tie the warp ends in an overhand knot. Cross the warp ends on the edge of each grouping to prevent the last weft shot from sliding down. This knot is the easiest finish for any woven piece.

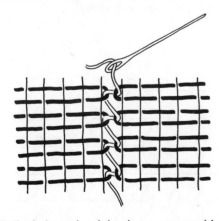

Ball stitch used to join pieces woven with strips of fabric.

ently constructed. They are both called lace weaves simply because they have an open, lace-like effect. True lace is not woven.

Warp yarns under tension on a loom can be twisted around one another, tied, wrapped, and grouped to form open spaces or dense areas. There are basic principles to follow with finger-manipulated lace weaves, but then the variations are endless.

Yarns for finger-manipulated lace weaves depend on the intended use of the woven piece. All fibers and sizes of yarn can be used. However, most of these weaves impose some limitations of color and texture when you are choosing yarn for warp and weft. The weave itself is intricate, and too many colors or textures can visually complicate a weaving.

Gauze weave. This is the most common finger-manipulated lace weave. To weave gauze, use a pickup stick and a narrow stick shuttle. Work in an open shed or a closed one (all harnesses in the rest position). The result of each is slightly different. Start *all* the finger-manipulated lace techniques by putting in a tabby heading.

To weave gauze weave with a CLOSED shed:

1. Starting at the right edge of the warp, with your fingers put the first warp end over the second. Put the pickup stick through the two warp ends where they cross. The second warp end will be on top of the pickup stick. Continue twisting the ends and putting in the pickup stick in this manner across the warp.
2. Turn the pickup stick on its edge. Put the shuttle carrying the weft pick through this opening.
3. Remove the pickup stick and lightly beat in the pick. It will not beat down right next to the last tabby shot.

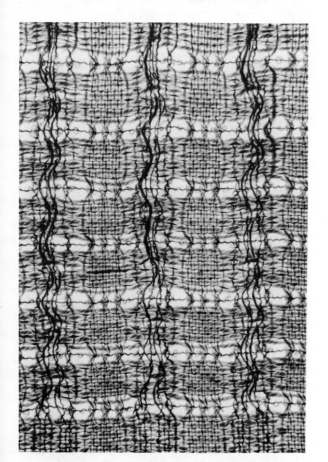

Gauze weave with novelty yarn and a spaced warp.

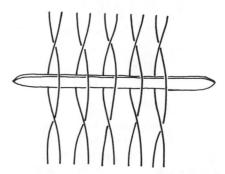

Gauze weave in a closed shed, showing pickup stick holding crossed warp ends.

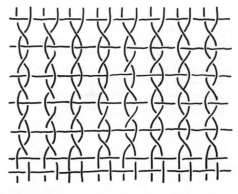

Gauze weave in a closed shed using two warp ends for twist.

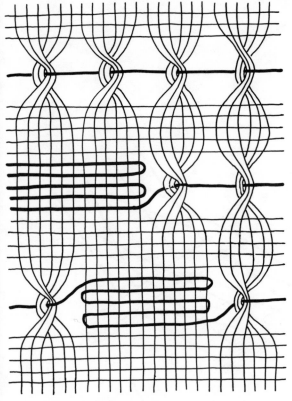

Method of using gauze weave in combination with solid tabby areas.

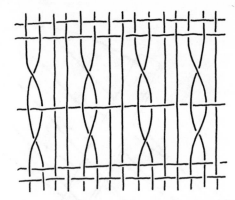

Gauze weave with an open shed when the first warp end is in the top shed—shows straight warp ends between twisted warp ends.

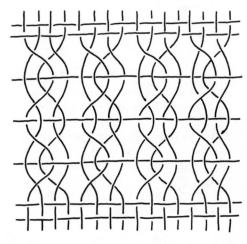

Gauze weave with an open shed when the first warp end is in the bottom shed.

Now put in several rows of tabby, or put in another row of lace using the same procedure as above, but going from left to right. Twist the same two warp ends around each other again, or split the warp groups *this* time, to make a net-type design.

To weave gauze weave with an OPEN shed:

1. Open the tabby shed that puts on the top the first warp end at the right selvage.
2. At the right side and from the top put the pickup stick between the third and fifth warp ends. Pick up the second and fourth warp ends, which are in the bottom shed, and bring them to the top.
3. Continue in this manner across the warp.
4. Turn the pickup stick on its edge and put in the weft pick in the same way as when working in a closed shed.

By opening the shed so that the first warp end is in the top shed, you obtain two straight warp ends in between each twist, and there is a twist above and below the pick.

If you open the shed the opposite way, with the first warp end in the bottom shed, all the warp ends will twist and the result is more like working with a closed shed. The second pick, which is put in on the opposite shed, is just the reverse twist and does not have to be picked up. Pick up only when

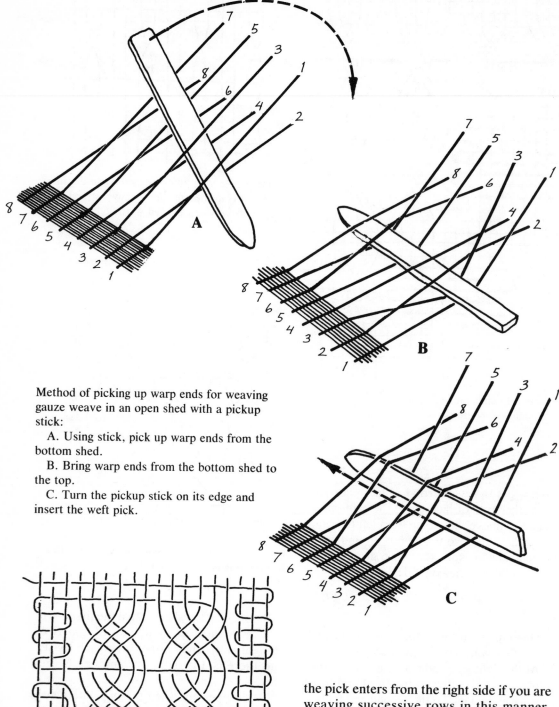

Method of picking up warp ends for weaving
gauze weave in an open shed with a pickup
stick:

A. Using stick, pick up warp ends from the
bottom shed.

B. Bring warp ends from the bottom shed to
the top.

C. Turn the pickup stick on its edge and
insert the weft pick.

To make straight edges with a gauze weave,
use a narrow border of tabby weave.

the pick enters from the right side if you are
weaving successive rows in this manner.
Change the shed after each pick.

All gauze weave techniques can be varied
by twisting two or more warp ends around
one another. You can also weave several
rows of tabby after each row or after two,
three, or more rows of gauze weave.

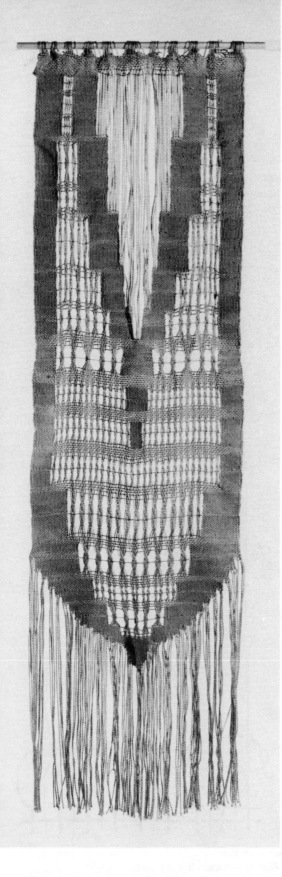

Hanging of gauze weave with tabby borders.
Woven by student Holly Kahle.

Spanish Open Weave. Openings in a tabby ground are made with this lace weave. There are a few basic steps to follow, but variations are endless. Best results are achieved when the weft yarn is heavier than the warp yarn and when the weft is not beaten in too tight.

1. After weaving a tabby heading, start at the right side and weave tabby in a group of warp ends. The number of warp ends used depends on the desired effect. If the "open" area is intended to be small and fine yarn is used, group just a few warp ends. But for a strong dramatic effect with heavier yarn, group as many warp ends as you wish. Weave an odd number of shots. Pull the weft yarn a bit tighter than usual, and use a comb or fork to beat the weft picks.
2. Carry the weft to the next group of warp ends and weave as in step 1.
3. Repeat these two steps as often as desired.

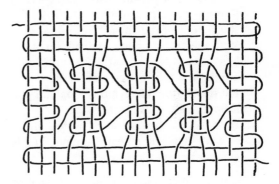

Spanish open weave.

Spanish open weave variation.

The weft yarn that connects each individual group is part of the design. Variations are the result of weaving one row in one direction and the next row in the opposite direction; splitting the groups of warp ends from row to row; and changing the number of warp ends in each group.

Weave tabby after each row or after several rows. The number of shots and how close the warp ends are pulled together in each group affect the design.

Danish Medallion. Its oval or circular design is most effective when both a heavy and a fine yarn are used in the weft.

A crochet hook and two shuttles are needed for this technique: one shuttle is for the fine yarn, one for the heavy.

1. With fine yarn, weave a tabby heading.
2. From the left, put one shot of heavy yarn in the next shed.
3. With the fine yarn, weave at least 1 inch (2.5 cm) of tabby.
4. In the next shed, with heavy yarn, weave through a group of warp ends. Bring the shuttle out of the shed.
5. With the crochet hook, pull a loop of the heavy yarn underneath the tabby and around the first heavy weft shot.
6. Put the shuttle through this loop and pull it up as tight as desired.
7. In the same shed, weave another group of warp ends and repeat. Continue in this manner across the warp.

You can make the medallions as large or as small as desired. Rows of medallions are more effective if tabby is woven between each row, and their size can vary in each row. Take into consideration the effect that is to be achieved and the yarn being used.

Brooks Bouquet. The easiest of all the finger-manipulated lace techniques, it is done in an open shed. The warp ends are grouped and tied. Tie all warp ends in the group, or group and tie only the ends in the top shed.

1. Weave a tabby heading.
2. In the next shed, put the shuttle through the first group of warp ends.
3. Bring the shuttle to the top and completely encircle the group of warp ends.
4. Put the shuttle through the loop made when the weft was taken out of the shed.
5. Pull this knot up tight. Go to the next group, and repeat this process for as long as desired.

Follow the same steps when grouping and tying only the top warp ends. This leaves

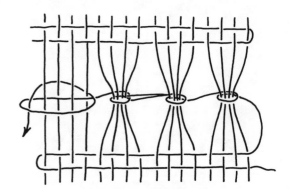

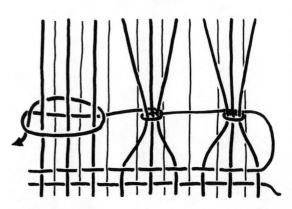

Brooks Bouquet:
Top: Grouping all warp ends.
Bottom: Grouping only warp ends in the top shed.

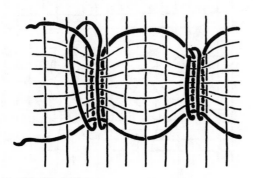

Danish Medallion.

warp ends that are untied between each
group.

Try variations of all these finger-manipulated lace weaves and try combining several in one weaving. They complement each
other and work well together.

A variation of Danish Medallion combined
with gauze weave.

9

‍‌‍‌‍‌‌‌‍‍‌‍‍‌‌‍‌‍‍‌‌‍‌‍‍‌‌‍‌‍‍‌‌‍‌‍

Pattern or Loom-Controlled Weaves

Patterns or designs are made in weaving by the order in which the warp ends are threaded in the heddles and the order and combination of harnesses that are used in the treadling. The weaves that create these patterns or designs are generally termed *pattern weaves* and/or *loom-* or *harness-controlled weaves,* to distinguish them completely from finger-manipulated weaves.

Loom-controlled weaves use both color and texture in the pattern. These weaves are classified according to weave construction. Each type has a different structure and appearance and countless variations.

Most pattern weaves are associated with traditional weaving. This is because drafts for patterns have been handed down for centuries. Yet, through their variations, pattern weaves offer handweavers another means of experimenting to find just the right way of expressing themselves. Typical of pattern weaves is symmetry; whether this is an advantage or disadvantage must be a personal decision.

One area of traditional pattern weaving that many people are familiar with is colonial coverlets. Many of the coverlets were woven on four-harness looms that operated mechanically in the same way as present-day looms. A study of coverlets will reveal that they were named by sentimental association after flowers, feelings, and events. This demonstrates beautiful personal expression by their weavers.

The pattern weaves are classified according to structure, and each class has units. Units are groups of warp ends that are always used in the same order and number. It is these units that weavers must be familiar with in order to create their own patterns. The manipulation of the units, the interlacing, any change of direction, and the spacing and lengths of floats create variety within the weave structure. There are books that give drafts for many weaves. Use them to be aware of variations, but try to learn the units of specific weaves and write your own drafts.

Following are weave classifications and the units that make up each weave. From these units write the draft you want for a specific project. Have confidence in your own resources and do not be concerned about whether or not your specific threading order has been used before; make it your own.

The first group of weaves here is the *twill weaves.* Twill is a basic weave, but it also offers many threading orders. When woven, they make patterns similar to other pattern weaves.

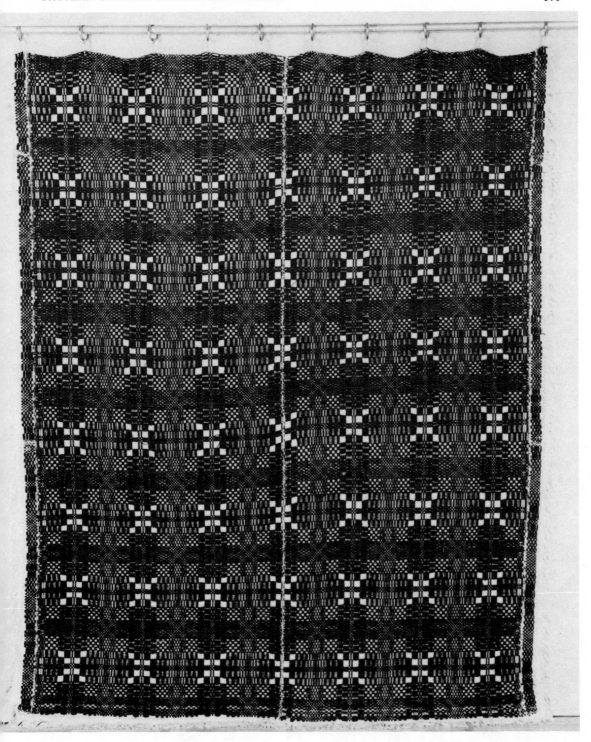

A four-harness blue and white "coverlid," as it was called, woven about 1824 in Jericho, Vermont. *Photo courtesy the Shelburne Museum, Shelburne, Vermont.*

Twill Weave

The distinguishing feature of twill is a diagonal line in texture. Twill is a derivative of basket weave. It has floats, sometimes of the same length as in basket weave, but they are staggered, producing the diagonal line. If the diagonal line is visible, it denotes a *bias twill;* if it is concealed, you have a *broken twill*. A twill weave is stronger than basket weave and makes a softer fabric than tabby.

A *float* is the result of a warp or weft yarn crossing over other yarns without forming a tie. A float is measured by the number of yarn ends it crosses over—at least two and usually no more than sixteen.

A twill weave is described by two numbers designating the length of the floats on each side of the weaving. A 2:2 twill means that the floats skip over two warp ends on each side. It is woven with two harnesses up and two down. A 3:1 twill has floats over three warp ends on one side and over one on the reverse. It is woven with one harness up and three down or just the opposite. The sum of the two numbers tells how many harnesses are needed to produce that twill weave.

The diagonal line of a twill weave shows to best advantage when it is at a 45-degree angle to the weft. The angle can, however, be more or less than 45 degrees; it can change direction; and at times it can be almost invisible because it changed direction so often.

The number of twill variations is unlimited. In fact, twill can be woven on many drafts. Since twill is defined as a weave showing a diagonal on one side, then almost all drafts can weave twill with the exception of two-harness drafts and those that make long floats.

A straight draw or twill threading produces a diagonal in one direction. If the direction of the threading or the treadling order changes, patterns such as diamonds are made; all, however, are variations on the diagonal.

One of the best-known diamond twills is Bird's-Eye or Goose Eye, sometimes called Rose Path. This twill produces a small pattern and is a very firm weave. No floats are more than three warp ends long, making it ideal for many purposes. There are many ways of treadling Bird's-Eye:

1. Woven-as-drawn-in.
2. With a binder. Put an alternating tabby shot after each pattern shot or the opposite shed of twill. (A binder is shots of weft used to strengthen the fabric.)
3. On opposites. Treadle harnesses 1–2 and 3–4 or 2–3 and 1–4. The position of the harness frames is reversed with each weft shot. This is a weft-faced weave, and sometimes called Bound Weave.
4. In any of the above, color will make a clear pattern and lack of color highlights texture.

For multiple-harness looms, expand the twill threading. On a straight draw or twill threading, endless patterns can be woven by varying the tie-up and/or treadling order.

A weaver could spend a lifetime weaving twill. It is the perfect weave for fine clothing fabric, especially with wool yarn. Subtle images are evident when color is used, or with one color subtle texture results. Twill weave is not limited to fine or heavy, dull or shiny yarn. It can be used for any weaving, no matter what its intended purpose. I hope you will experiment endlessly with twill weave.

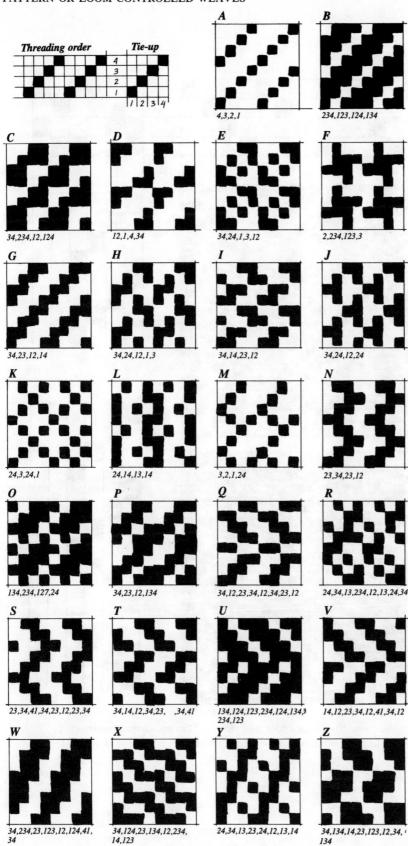

Threading order   **Tie-up**

A
4,3,2,1

B
234,123,124,134

C
34,234,12,124

D
12,1,4,34

E
34,24,1,3,12

F
2,234,123,3

G
34,23,12,14

H
34,24,12,1,3

I
34,14,23,12

J
34,24,12,24

K
24,3,24,1

L
24,14,13,14

M
3,2,1,24

N
23,34,23,12

O
134,234,127,24

P
34,23,12,134

Q
34,12,23,34,12,34,23,12

R
24,34,13,234,12,13,24,34

S
23,34,41,34,23,12,23,34

T
34,14,12,34,23, ,34,41

U
134,124,123,234,124,134,3
234,123

V
14,12,23,34,12,41,34,12

W
34,234,23,123,12,124,41,
34

X
34,124,23,134,12,234,
14,123

Y
24,34,13,23,24,12,13,14

Z
34,134,14,23,123,12,34,
134

Twills, A to Z.
Drawdown and
treadling order
(shown below each
draft) for twenty-six
patterns on a basic
twill threading order
and tie-up.

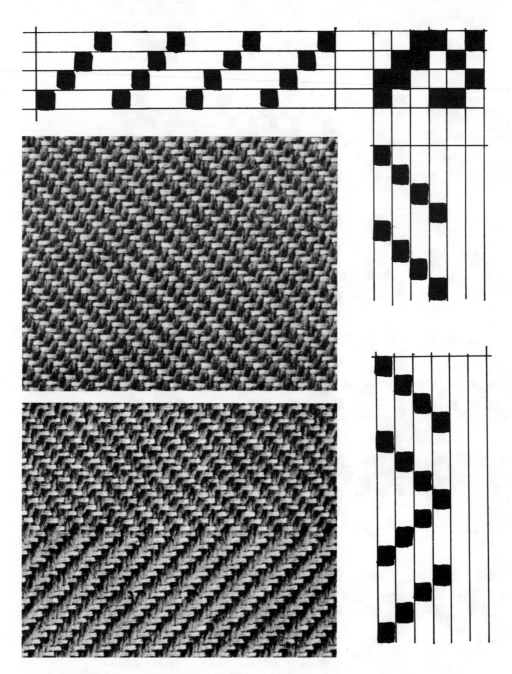

A 2:2 twill with the basic threading order and standard tie-up: woven as-drawn-in produces a diagonal in one direction; when the treadling reverses, the diagonal line reverses direction.

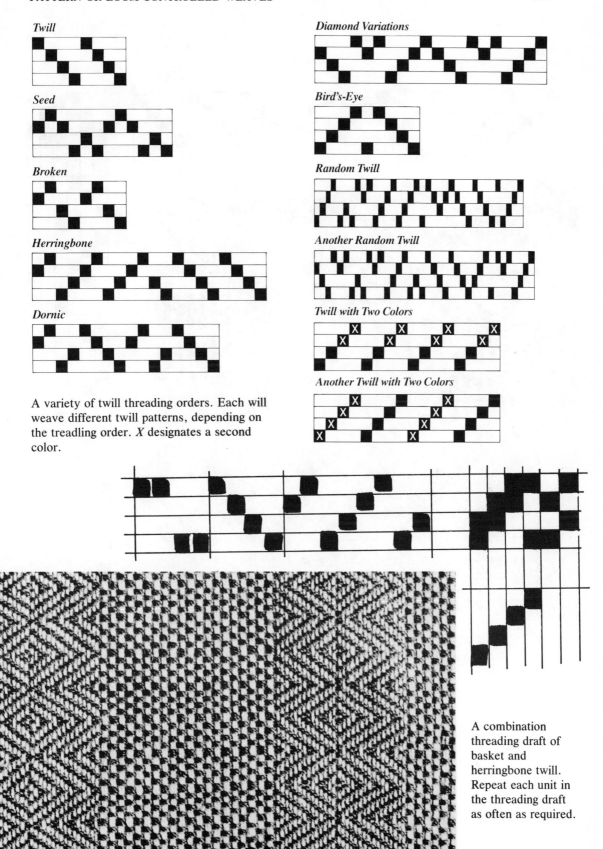

Twill

Seed

Broken

Herringbone

Dornic

Diamond Variations

Bird's-Eye

Random Twill

Another Random Twill

Twill with Two Colors

Another Twill with Two Colors

A variety of twill threading orders. Each will weave different twill patterns, depending on the treadling order. *X* designates a second color.

A combination threading draft of basket and herringbone twill. Repeat each unit in the threading draft as often as required.

Twill weave variation. A change in the
direction of the threading and treadling order
produces diamonds.

Bird's-Eye twill threading draft:

A. Border patterns using a variety of treadling orders with tabby binder.

B. Bound weave using color in weft for pattern.

C. Woven on opposites (see page 191).

D. Woven with tabby binder. Pattern makes large diamond shape on one side and is reversed on the opposite side. Both sides have interesting texture.

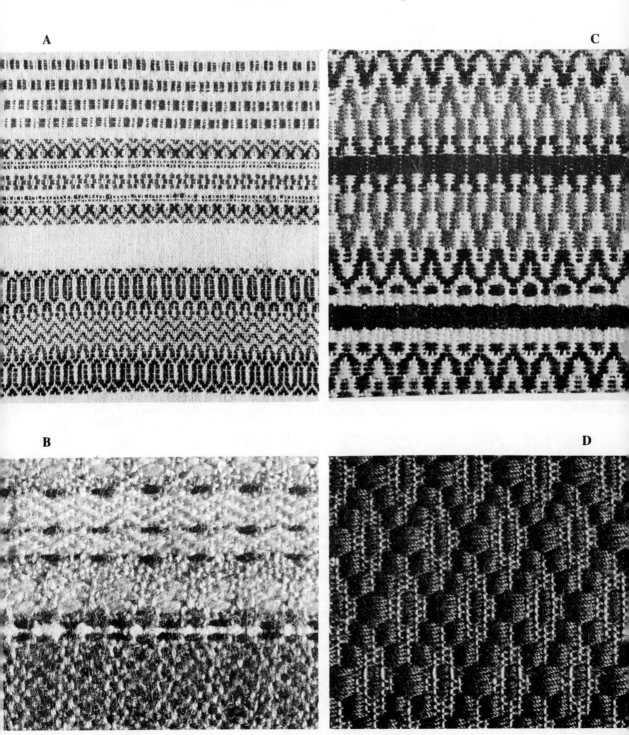

A

C

B

D

First "Rose"
12-2x, 14-2x, 12-2x, 14-2x, 12-2x
Second "Rose"
23-2x, 34-2x, 23-2x, 34-2x, 23-2x

Small twill threading draft:

A. Woven with tabby binder. Color on selected weft shots produces a small ''rose'' design. Both sides are shown.

B. Same threading woven in bound weave.

A

B

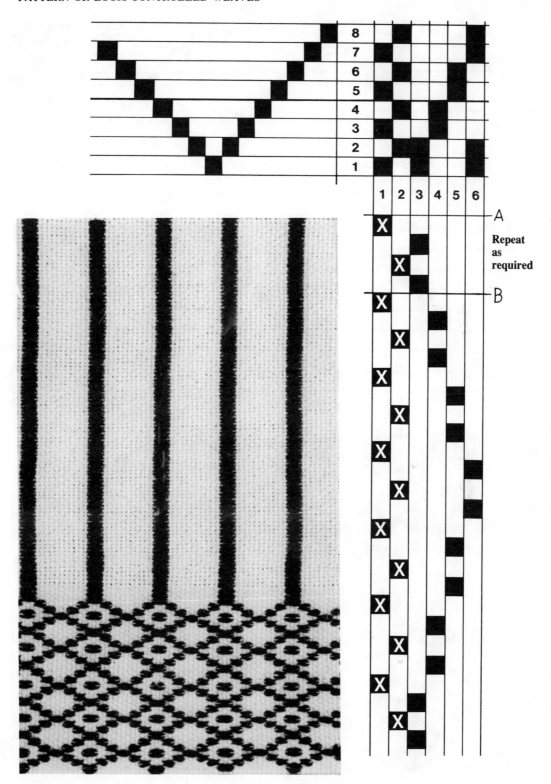

Eight-harness reverse twill woven in two colors. Treadling order produces diamonds and columns. A to B is column repeat.

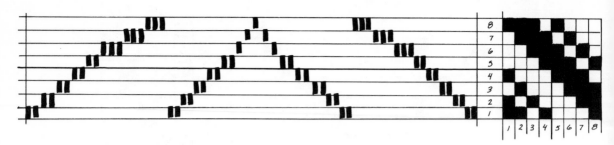

Eight-harness undulating twill weave with a laurel leaf design. Try it in one color with dull warp and shiny weft yarn.

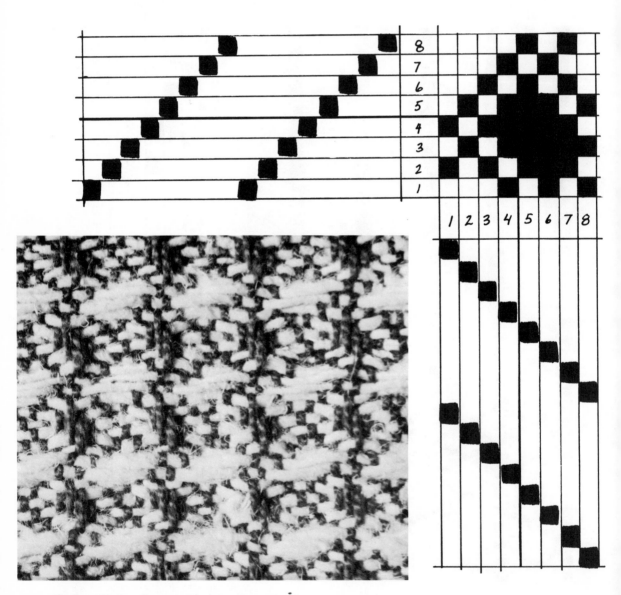

Basic twill threading on eight harnesses. The tie-up and treadling order produce a weave similar to waffle weave.

A wool fabric in a herringbone twill threading ▲
order.

Rag rug woven on a twill threading. ▼

Overshot

This is the weave most commonly associated with colonial weaving, and it is still very popular, probably because it is easy to weave in many different ways and produces a great variety of patterns. The pattern is made by floats in the weft on a tabby ground called the binder.

Overshot is a three-thread construction—one for warp, one for pattern, and one for tabby binder. The yarn for warp and tabby binder are usually the same color and weight. The pattern yarn is of another color and heavier. This rule can vary, but this is the way overshot was traditionally woven.

One of the most distinguishing characteristics of overshot is its three-tone effect. The pattern formed by the floats stands out. In the background there are blocks of tabby weave and blocks combining tabby weave with the pattern color. (The term *block* refers to a group of threads arranged together to produce a pattern element.) The pattern is different on each side of the fabric; tabby on one side is pattern on the other side.

There are four blocks of pattern in overshot, each being formed by a group of threads on two adjacent harnesses. The groups form a twill—overshot is a twill derivative.

When weaving overshot, follow each pattern shot with a shot of tabby. The tabby order must be preserved. To remember the order, always put the pick in the shed made by raising harnesses 2 and 4 when the shuttle enters from the left side, and put the pick in the shed made by raising harnesses 1 and 3 when the shuttle enters from the right. The tabby shot is not shown in the treadling draft.

The standard tie-up is normally used for overshot. Traditionally, the treadling order was as-drawn-in (treadled as it was threaded). However, many different treadling combinations can be used and completely different effects achieved with the same threading draft.

To make an overshot draft, it is necessary to work out the combination of heddles, the order they are to be used, and the number of warp ends in each combination. A *combination* is a group of two or more heddles on two or more harnesses to form a pattern block.

Overshot combinations are 1–2, 2–3, 3–4, and 1–4.

In an overshot draft, the combinations overlap. If the first combination chosen is 1–2, it should be followed by a combination that has either 1 or 2, such as 1–4 or 2–3. The two heddles may be repeated as many times as desired, but more than sixteen is impractical.

Border, flower, and *table* are the design components of most overshot drafts.

There are three different borders:

1. **Block:** Use two combinations only; they do not have to overlap. The number in each combination can vary, but the combinations must be repeated in the same order with the same number of heddles.
2. **Zigzag:** Use all combinations (1–2, 2–3, 3–4, 1–4), repeated in the same order and number. To vary the number of heddles in each combination, always keep every other one the same. For example, 1–2 and 3–4 will have four heddles, and then 2–3 and 1–4 will have six heddles. Repeat the combinations in the same order. Reverse the order of the combinations on the opposite border to contain the design.
3. **Diamond:** Use three or four different combinations. Do not repeat them in the same order, but after all combinations are used, reverse the order. This makes a diamond. Repeat the order as many times as desired.

The *flower* can be two, three, or four combinations. Work to a center, then reverse from the center out. A *table* may be the center unit. The design depends on the order of the combinations and the number of heddles in each. Combinations should overlap—for example, 2–3 followed by 3–4 or 1–2. (See page 194 for examples.)

The table design uses the same combinations as the block border repeated at least five times.

Plan the selvages when making an overshot draft. Use four to eight warp ends, and for the right-hand selvage use the 1–2, 3–4 combination, with the 1–4, 2–3 combination for the left, or the reverse. The joining of the selvage combinations with the design combinations is important. The combinations must overlap in the same way as in a pattern block.

The Honeysuckle pattern (see illustration on page 195) is probably the best-known overshot threading. It has short floats and is practical for many projects.

An overshot draft can be woven in a number of different ways. Each produces quite different effects.

Weaving on opposites uses two alternating colors for weft, with no tabby shot, and covers the warp. *Opposites* means that the position of the harness frames is reversed with each weft shot. (See below.)

Bound weaving is another term used for weaving on opposite sheds.

Write your own overshot draft, weave it in any number of different ways, and use favorite colors. Overshot is easy to weave and the most versatile draft in handweaving.

Opposite Sheds on a Four-Harness Loom

Pattern shed:	1–2,	2–3,	3–4,	1–4	1–2–3,	1–2–4,	1–3–4,	2–3–4	1,	2,	3,	4
Opposite shed:	3–4,	1–4,	1–2,	2–3	4,	3,	2,	1	2–3–4,	1–3–4,	1–2–4,	1–2–3

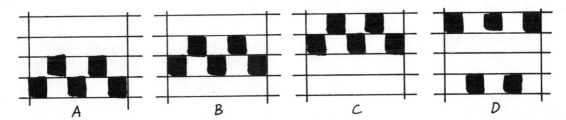

A   B   C   D

The four blocks of pattern in overshot:
  A. First block, with yarns threaded on harnesses 1 and 2.
  B. Second block, with yarns on harnesses 2 and 3.
  C. Third block, with yarns on harnesses 3 and 4.
  D. Fourth block, with yarns on harnesses 1 and 4.

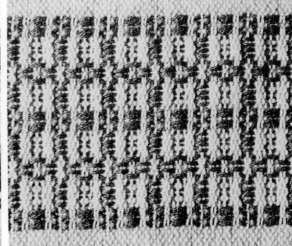

Small border designs in overshot weave.

"St. Anne's Reel," a personalized weaving by Daron Douglas. A fiddle tune made into a weaving draft by assigning two notes to each harness. Some changes are made to work out the tabby. The woven piece is the threading from the tune, and the mirror image, then the entire sequence repeated.

A. Music notes for the fiddle tune.

B. Music notes assigned to each harness frame; each note then becomes a warp end.

C. Weaving draft derived from the tune.

D. Tie-up and treadling order for St. Anne's Reel.

Overshot weaves (left is top side; right, reverse):

A. Circle and flowers.

B. Butterflies.

C. Daybreak.

D. Gregson Springs.

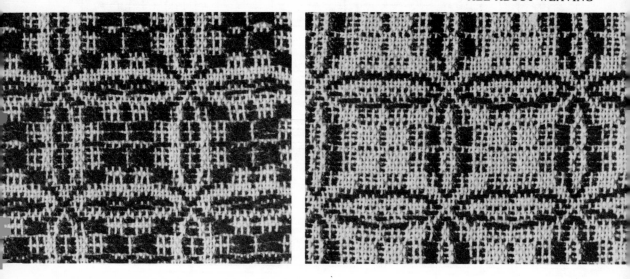

Front and back of the "flower" element in an overshot draft.

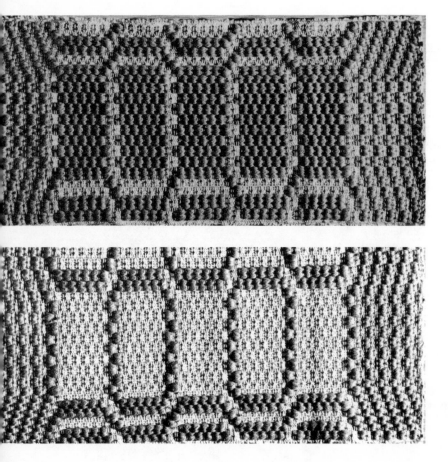

Front and back of
the "table" element
in an overshot draft.

Overshot draft, Honeysuckle pattern. ▲

Overblouse woven in overshot, Honeysuckle pattern, with striped warp, by Micki Johns. ▶

Overshot draft in Honeysuckle pattern with variation in treadling order within a shot, by student Gina Petruziello. ▼

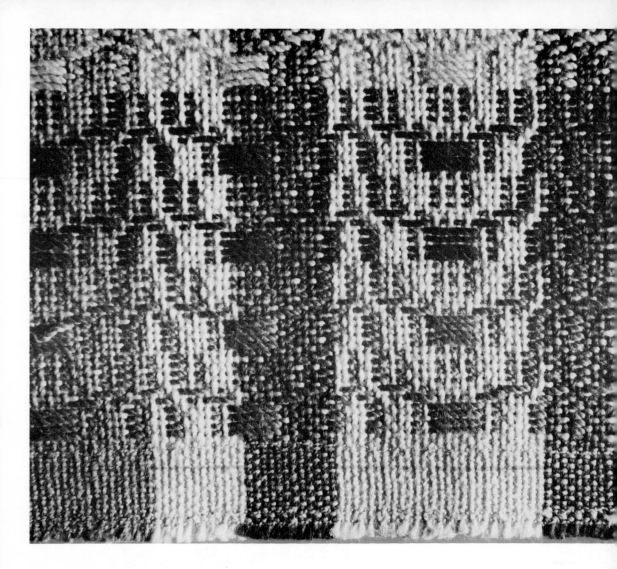

Border design on overshot draft in
Honeysuckle pattern on striped warp.

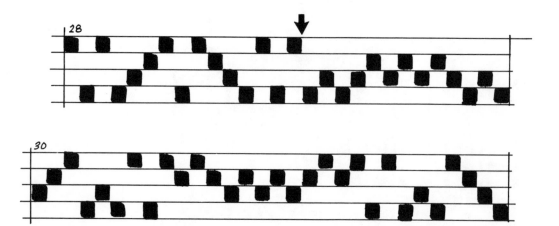

Short overshot drafts ideal for weft-faced and bound weaving.
Top: Repeat as desired, and then thread to arrow to balance the threading order.
Bottom: Repeat as desired.

Summer and Winter

This weave produces blocks in the pattern. The woven fabric is reversible, with the same texture on both sides but the colors reversed. One side will be light in color, the other dark—perhaps the reason for the name.

This is a two-tone weave: pattern and background. It is a three-thread construction: warp, tabby, and pattern.

The pattern is formed by blocks; their size is set in the threading and can be woven any size in treadling. The blocks have small overshots, but no floats are longer than three warp ends. The overshots build up like bricks—a distinguishing characteristic of Summer and Winter weave.

On a four-harness loom, you can weave a two-block pattern in Summer and Winter. Two harnesses are for the background or tabby weave, with one harness for each block of pattern. On six harnesses, there can be four blocks of pattern; on eight harnesses, six blocks.

There are two ways of writing a Summer and Winter draft: short draft and expanded draft. (See Chapter 7, "Drafting.")

The short draft does not show the tabby ends, but only the length of the blocks. In an expanded draft, a tabby end alternates with each end shown in the short draft. A short draft is easier to follow when threading. When designing the pattern, you will find it easier to see the size of the blocks in a short draft.

When weaving Summer and Winter, alternate pattern shots with tabby shots. Tabby sheds are made by using harnesses 1–2, then 3–4.

A variety of sizes of blocks can be threaded and woven in Summer and Winter. The regular structure makes it excellent for use in table linens, upholstery fabrics, and rugs.

When the blocks are warped and woven in different colors, the fabric takes on a new dimension. Traditionally, Summer and Winter is woven by alternating two pattern

sheds. It can, however, be woven in several ways; for instance, use only one pattern shed alternating with tabby, or make it weft-faced with no tabby. Try different ways of weaving Summer and Winter, but just be sure the structure of the weave meets the requirements for the project.

Sampler of weft-faced weaves on an overshot draft. Different color combinations make variety in the design, woven by Russ Kunst.

Weft-faced, no-tabby weave on an overshot draft. Four colors woven twill fashion (1–2, 2–3, 3–4, 1–4) and reversed. Colors alternate in each block. EXAMPLE: Color A is in shed 1–2 in first block, shed 1–4 in second block, shed 3–4 in third block, and shed 2–3 in fourth block. Woven by Russ Kunst.

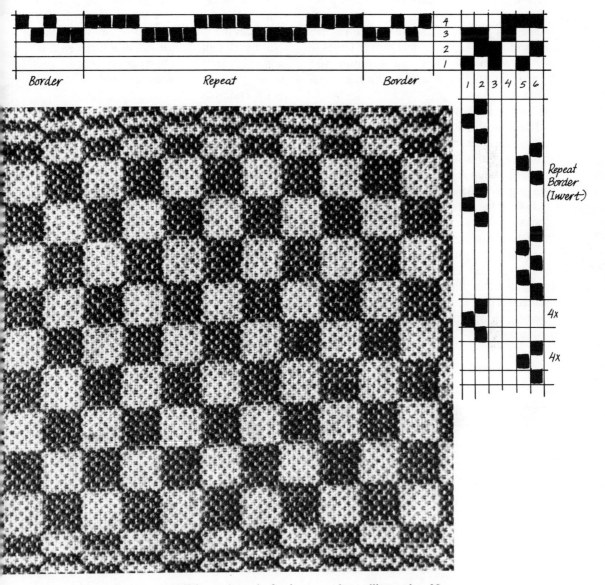

Four-harness Summer and Winter short draft, tie-up, and treadling order. Note weave structure: floats are never over more than three warp ends. Tabby is treadles 3 and 4. Tabby shots alternate in weaving but are not shown in treadling order.

Crackle Weave

This weave is distinguished by the narrow crack or opening that appears in its texture. Crackle is another weave with a three-thread construction: single warp, pattern weft, and tabby weft. The weave produces a two-tone effect of pattern and background. The pattern weft goes over three warp ends and under one to form the pattern. It simply reverses for the background.

The structure of Crackle weave is firm and uniform. The characteristics of Crackle fall between overshot and Summer and Winter, but its appearance is different from either.

Crackle is woven on a standard tie-up and, like overshot, has four pattern blocks. Pattern shots alternate with tabby shots. The structure of this weave is the same on both sides, but what is pattern on one side of the weaving is background on the other.

On four harnesses, there are four pattern blocks; each block is four warp ends of a three-harness point twill. A *point twill* is when the direction of the twill diagonal line reverses, either in the warp or in the weft. In the instance illustrated below, the diagonal line reverses in the warp. When designing a draft, you may repeat each block as desired.

The blocks overlap in the pattern, or, rather, they do not join at the corner. They combine, making a diagonal line as in twill (Crackle is a twill derivative).

To maintain the basic twill nature of this weave, the blocks must be adjacent to one another. The twill combinations of 1–2, 2–3, 3–4, and 1–4 must be the same in threading and weaving.

Each block ends on the same harness on which the next block starts. In order to maintain the tabby succession, an additional warp end, called an *incidental warp end,* is added between each two pattern blocks. The point twill is balanced by this incidental warp end.

To weave Crackle, repeat one pattern treadle as many times as desired, following each pattern shot with one tabby binder. This is one pattern block. Or alternate two pattern treadles, again following each pattern shot with a tabby shot. This produces two pattern blocks.

The blocks in the vertical rows build up in a columnar effect. Each vertical row contains only one block. The horizontal rows are a combination of two pattern blocks.

In designing a Crackle weave, the choice of yarns is important. Yarns of similar color value are best for pattern and background, as texture is more important than pattern.

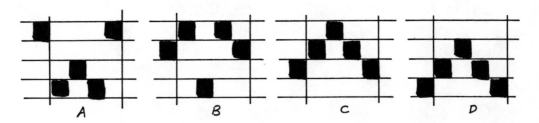

The four pattern blocks in a Crackle weave. The heddle outside each group of four warp ends is the incidental heddle, necessary when changing blocks in the threading order.

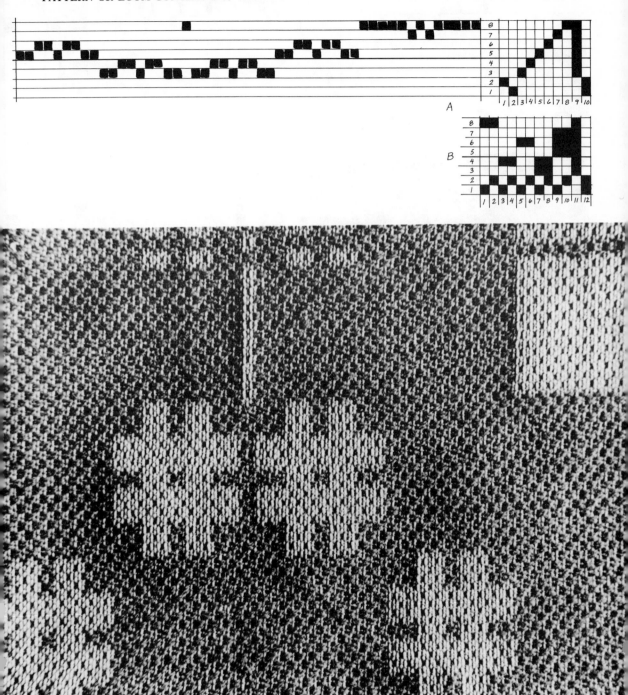

Eight-harness Summer and Winter short draft. An eight-harness loom generally does not have enough treadles for all the harness combinations needed for this weave. An alternative method is to use a skeleton tie-up (A), then use treadle 1 or 2 as required and insert a pickup stick under the raised warp ends. Both feet then can be used to treadle the required harness combination. Tabby is treadles 9 and 10 in tie-up A and treadles 11 and 12 in tie-up B.

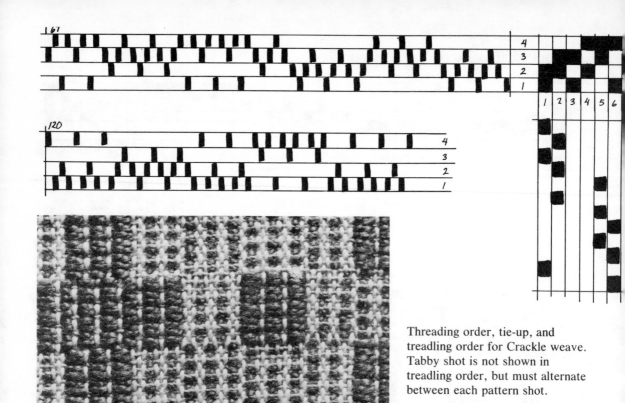

Threading order, tie-up, and treadling order for Crackle weave. Tabby shot is not shown in treadling order, but must alternate between each pattern shot.

Crackle weave variation. The vertical zigzag lines are made by threading 1, 2, 3, 4; the horizontal zigzag lines, by treadling 1–2, 2–3, 3–4, 1–4.

M's and O's Weave

Where this weave gets its name is unknown. It is also a twill derivative. It should be woven with a soft yarn, whether heavy or fine, such as a single-ply.

A two-thread construction, M's and O's is woven with one shuttle. The warp and weft yarns are the same size but can be of different colors. Pattern blocks have small alternating overshots of weft that enclose warp ends, forming a cord. The area next to the corded pattern blocks is tabby background. Pattern on one row becomes tabby on the next row when the treadling is changed.

The woven fabric is the same on either side. On an M's and O's threading, you cannot weave a true tabby from selvage to selvage.

A basic M's and O's draft is given here, but this weave can be woven on any draft by alternating opposite sheds for several shots and then changing to another pair of opposite sheds.

Try weaving in opposite sheds on any draft. Some will produce a fabric with a satisfactory structure and others will be sleazy and unsatisfactory for practical or decorative purposes.

M's and O's threading order, tie-up, and treadling order:
  A. A variety of treadling orders using different colors in the weft.
  B. A traditional M's and O's fabric using the same color in warp and weft. ▼

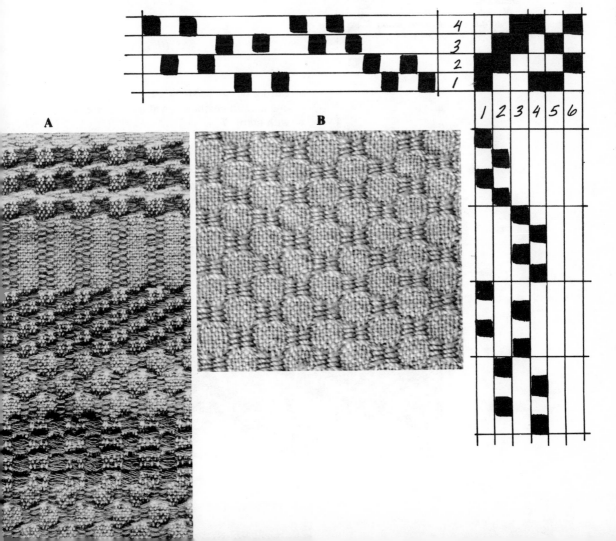

Monk's Belt

This is a pattern weave very similar to overshot. The difference is that Monk's Belt is only a two-block pattern, so the design possibilities are limited. Typical of some European weaving, it makes nice border designs in addition to overall patterns.

Monk's Belt is a three-thread construction: warp, tabby, and pattern yarn. It is woven with alternating shots of tabby binder.

It can be woven by using one pattern combination alternating with tabby as many times as desired, or with two pattern combinations, also alternating with tabby.

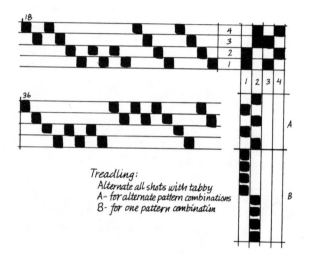

Treadling:
Alternate all shots with tabby
A- for alternate pattern combinations
B- for one pattern combination

Monk's Belt threading order, tie-up, and treadling order:

A. Treadling order for weaving with both pattern combinations.

B. Treadling order using one pattern combination.
◄

Border design in Monk's Belt. Woven with one pattern combination at a time, alternating with tabby.▼

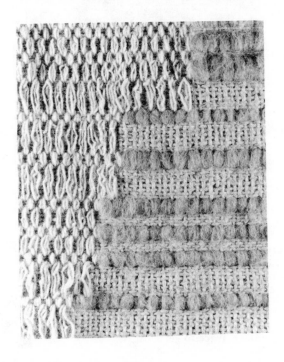

Wall hanging woven on a Monk's Belt
threading. This piece is hung sideways from
the way it was woven. It uses alternating
pattern shots with tabby. The close-up shows
the reverse side.

Lace Weaves

Loom-controlled lace weaves produce a fabric that is an imitation of real lace. Some of the names used for these weaves are Bronson Lace, Swedish Lace, and Spot Lace. They all have similar effects but use slightly different threading orders. The weaving has blocks giving the effect of lace combined with blocks of tabby background.

Lace weaves are a two-thread construction—one warp and one weft. The weft yarn can be the same as the warp or a bit softer in texture. To give the lace effect, the sley should be rather open and the beat light. There should be as many warp ends as weft picks per inch.

Small parallel overshots produce the pattern, which has a tabby background. The pattern and tabby areas change from one row to the next. The overshots are warp on one side and weft on the opposite side of the fabric.

Any fiber yarn can be used for lace weaves, to produce practical or decorative fabrics, but plied yarns give the best results.

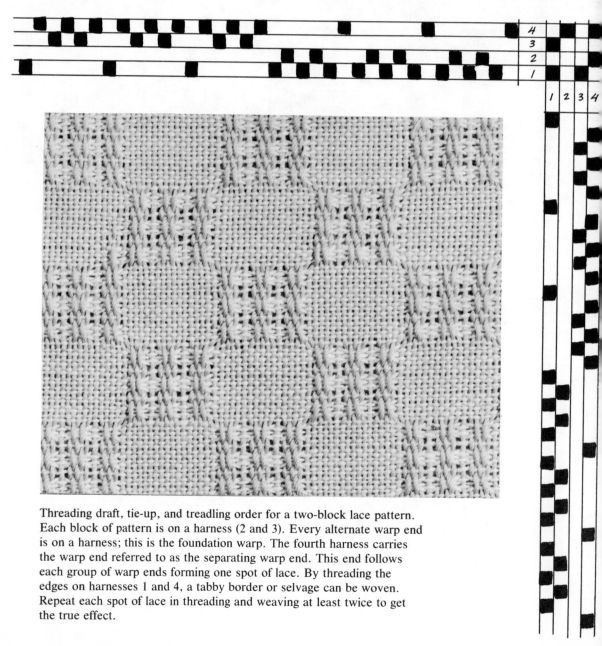

Threading draft, tie-up, and treadling order for a two-block lace pattern. Each block of pattern is on a harness (2 and 3). Every alternate warp end is on a harness; this is the foundation warp. The fourth harness carries the warp end referred to as the separating warp end. This end follows each group of warp ends forming one spot of lace. By threading the edges on harnesses 1 and 4, a tabby border or selvage can be woven. Repeat each spot of lace in threading and weaving at least twice to get the true effect.

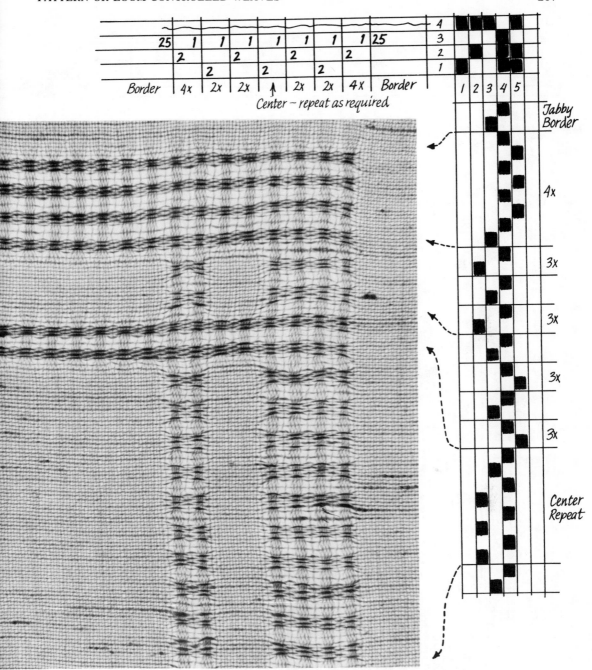

Threading draft, tie-up, and treadling order for a border design in lace weave. In the threading draft, every alternate warp end is on one harness (harness 4). Each remaining harness carries the warp end for a single pattern spot. On four harnesses, three blocks of pattern can be woven. The order of treadling follows the order of threading. Every alternate pick is a multiple-harness tabby shot.

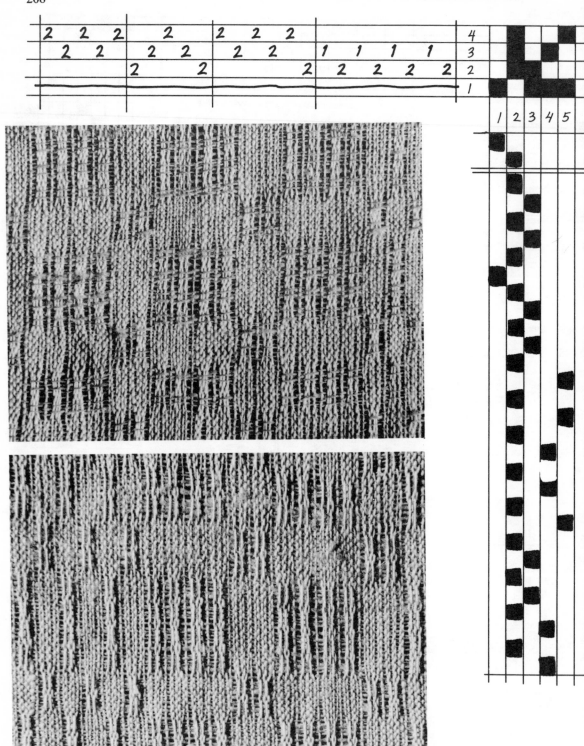

Threading draft, tie-up, and treadling order for an all-over lace weave.
Top photo: One side of the weaving shows weft overshot. *Bottom photo:*
The side of the weaving, showing warp overshot.

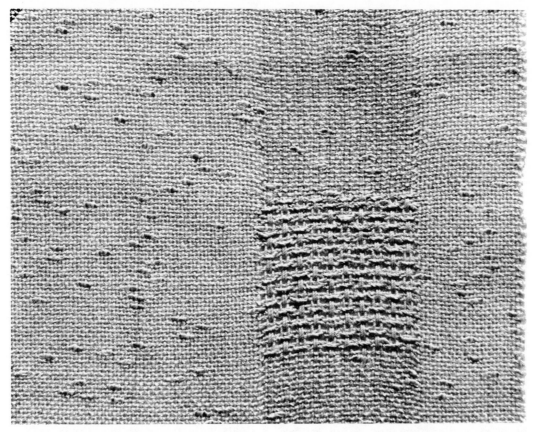

A spot of lace can be placed anywhere in a ▲ weaving. This piece also uses novelty yarn.

Overshot weave with warp patterns. The warp has two colors in some areas, creating a striped effect in the weaving. ▼

Turned or Warp Pattern Weaves

It is most common in loom-controlled weaves to have the pattern made by the weft yarns. However, any pattern that can be woven in the weft can also be woven in the warp.

Any four-harness draft that can be woven as a weft-faced weave can be "turned." Weft-faced weaves are the bound weaves, that is, those woven on opposite sheds (1–2 and 3–4, or 1–4 and 2–3) and woven without a tabby binder.

The reason for turning a weave is to make the weaving process faster. The color is put in the warp and one shuttle is used while weaving. If a long warp is made, the weaving time can be cut considerably. This method is ideal for production weaving.

To change a draft from a weft-faced to a warp-faced weave, just turn the draft 90 degrees. The treadling now becomes the threading, and the threading becomes the treadling order. Be sure to mark the color shots in the treadling order so that when it becomes the threading order it will be easy to follow.

Consider the yarn being used; remember the yarn used for a weft-faced weave would not necessarily be satisfactory for a warp. The warp is also sett closer than usual, more than double the sett for weft-faced weave.

To turn a four-harness overshot draft is a bit different because the tabby shots in the treadling must be also included in the

threading draft. To turn a four-harness weave with tabby binder, two additional harnesses are needed.

Assign each block combination to one harness, such as:

```
1–2—harness 3
2–3—harness 4
3–4—harness 5
1–4—harness 6
```

On harnesses 1 and 2, alternate warp ends for tabby weave between each combination of warp ends from the original draft.

When preparing the warp, use color on pattern shots as desired.

The tie-up is made by the combinations in the new draft. The type of loom (rising or sinking shed) being used will determine whether the right side appears on the top or bottom as the pattern is woven. The weave construction is the same either way.

A weave can be turned by changing the tie-up. The sinking shed becomes a rising shed, and vice versa. The reverse side of the weaving then becomes the top. In spot weave and huckaback weave, the horizontal floats will become vertical floats, or vice versa. The tie-up change can occur during the weaving of a single piece.

Monk's Belt is a pattern weave with two blocks or combinations. It can be turned and woven on four harnesses. Assign 1–2 to harness 4 and 3–4 to harness 3. Harnesses 1 and 2 will alternate for plain weave between each pair of warp ends from the original draft.

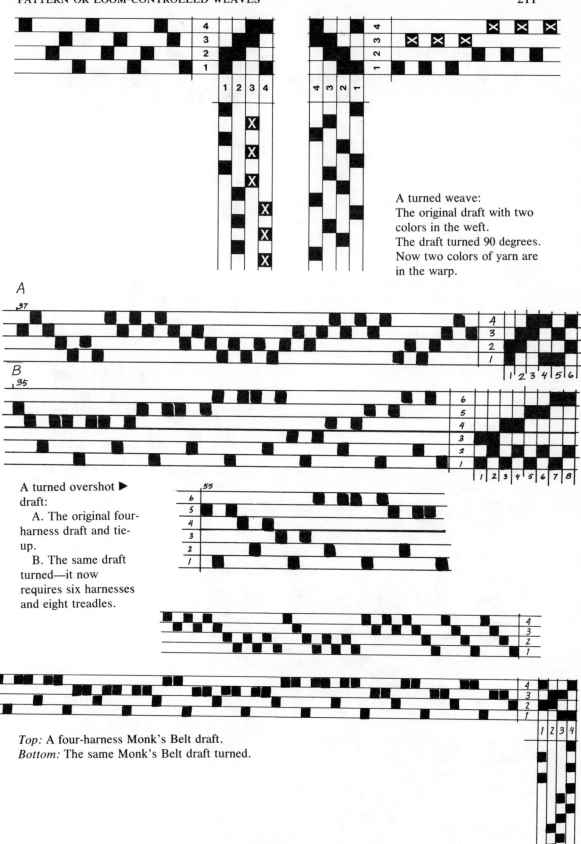

A turned weave:
The original draft with two
colors in the weft.
The draft turned 90 degrees.
Now two colors of yarn are
in the warp.

A turned overshot ▶
draft:
    A. The original four-
harness draft and tie-
up.
    B. The same draft
turned—it now
requires six harnesses
and eight treadles.

Top: A four-harness Monk's Belt draft.
Bottom: The same Monk's Belt draft turned.

Huckaback Weave

Huck is a typical woven-as-drawn-in weave. Repeats in threading and treadling are identical in length and order. One side of the fabric is the same as the other after it is turned 90 degrees. Sometimes huck is classified as a lace weave. Repeats can have 6, 10, or 14 yarns in both directions (warp and weft). In huckaback it is written 6×6, 10×10, or 14×14. Threading drafts can be written in several ways, but how you write them does not affect the fabric. When weaving huck, to get tabby borders thread the edges 1, 4, 1, 4.

A true huck threading can be woven in many different ways. By using the treadling order of other weaves, many interesting weave structures can be achieved. Some are attractive and practical weaves; others are not. Experiment with many treadling orders.

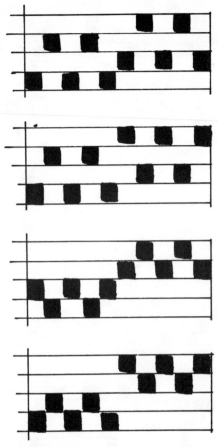

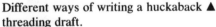

Fabric woven in huckaback using yarn soft in both color and texture. ▼

Different ways of writing a huckaback ▲ threading draft.

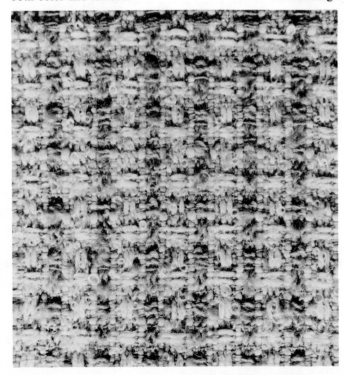

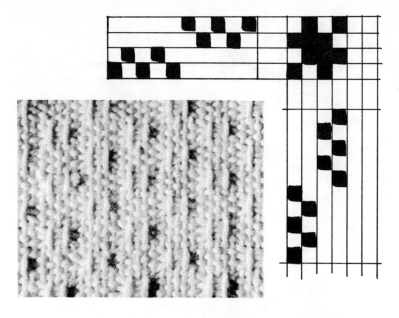

True huckaback. This is a 10 × 10 huck weave. It has a very peculiar texture, which can be seen when the woven piece is looked at against the light. There are tiny slits that run on a diagonal in both directions.

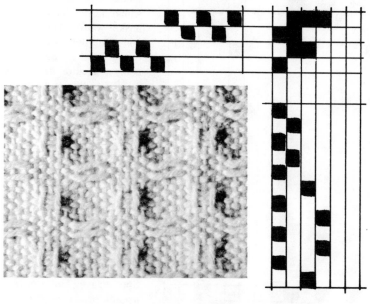

Turned huckaback. True huck has floats running in one direction on one side of the woven piece and in the other direction on the opposite side. In turned huckaback the floats run in both directions on one side. The repeat in treadling is longer than in the threading, so beat harder to square it off.

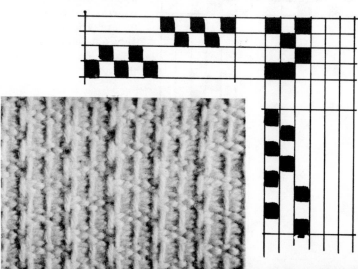

M's and O's. Use only the principle of M's and O's in treadling (see the illustration for M's and O's, on page 203). The result looks like huck on one side and M's and O's on the opposite side. The texture here is softer than in true huck.

Turned M's and O's. Similar to turned true huckaback; the floats are longer (7 instead of 5) and form squares on one side. The repeat is longer in treadling. Beat harder to make square.

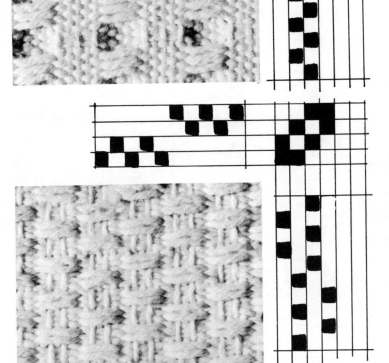

Huckaback lace. This is sometimes called a false basket weave. The floats will stand out on the background if a darker color is used on harnesses 2 and 3 in threading, and on treadles 1 and 4 in weaving.

Spot weave. This weave usually produces involved patterns, but in huck only texture. The weaving is very soft and is effective if four colors are used in the weft.

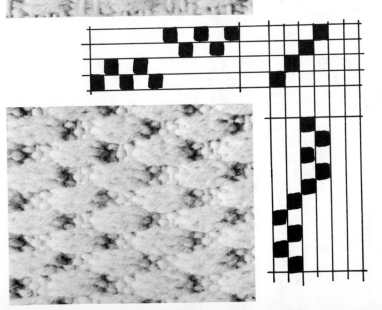

Overshot. This is not a pattern weave like true overshot. It is a texture based on overshot principles. Weave with one shuttle. The number of pattern shots depends on the size of yarn used for the weft. The weaving should be square.

Bound overshot. Woven on opposite sheds, the huck draft makes floats all the same length. The weaving is heavy, the warp will be partly visible; beat normally and use the usual sett for warp.

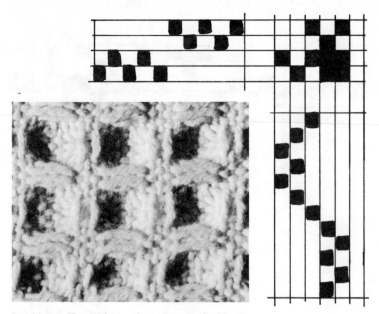

Double waffle. This produces a practical and
attractive weave. There are two floats around
each square instead of one, as in plain waffle
weave. This is a firm weave and is reversible,
since both sides are identical. The weaving
should be square.

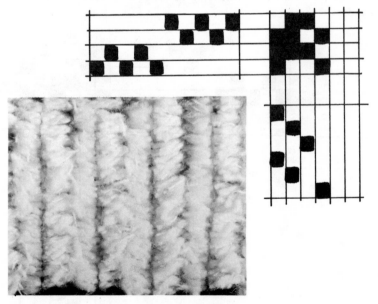

Corduroy. The easiest weft-pile fabric to
make. Corduroy can be woven on many
different threadings. Use a soft wool yarn on
treadles 3 and 4, and a strong thin yarn on
treadles 1 and 2. Use one color for warp and
weft. Pile is made by cutting the floats while
the fabric is still on the loom, or later. For
interesting surface patterns, try not cutting all
the floats.

Shadow Weave

This weave makes a pattern in the weaving if you always use at least two colors alternating in warp and weft. The yarns can be dark and light, shiny and dull, rough and smooth, or thick and thin.

Four-harness drafts produce patterns that are geometric; but with eight or more harnesses, curved and wavy lines add another element of design.

Weave the shadow weave draft as-drawn-in, then try variations. It can be woven on opposites; two different blocks can be made by alternating the colors in each shed in the two blocks. EXAMPLE: In one block use one color in sheds 1 and 2; then use the same color in sheds 3 and 4 in the next block.

Shadow weave is in a classification by itself. The weave structure is similar to Log Cabin weave, various twills, rib weave, and some double weaves.

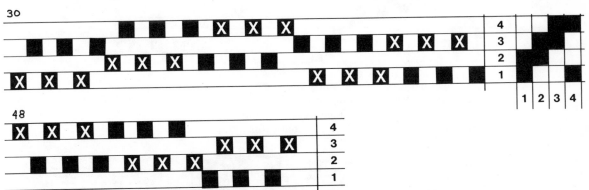

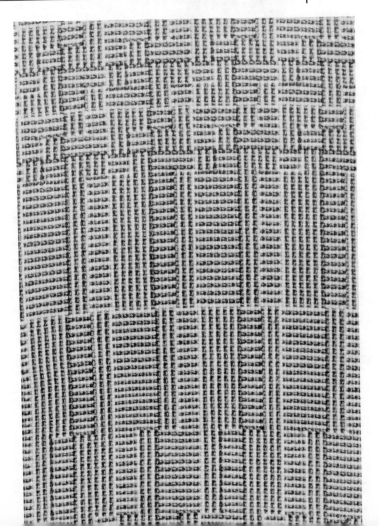

A four-harness shadow weave threading draft and tie-up. The photo shows various blocks made by weaving on opposites and alternating colors in each block.

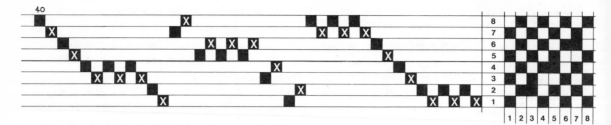

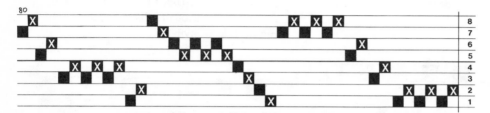

An eight-harness shadow weave threading
draft and tie-up. Pattern in the weaving is
made by alternating adjoining treadles in the
tie-up. This piece uses thick and thin yarns.

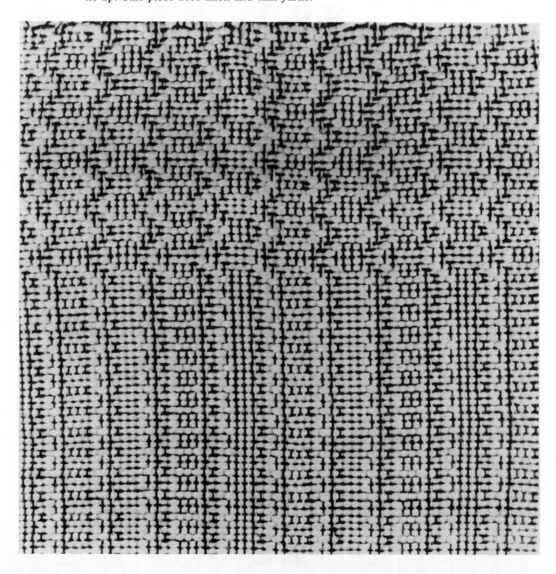

Damask Weave

This weave was traditionally used for fine table linens. Shiny and dull fine yarns were combined, and reflected light made the pattern visible.

Colored yarns and yarns of different size can be used for damask weave; it offers many design possibilities. The most practical damask weave is woven on ten harnesses. It is a two-block pattern. Additional harnesses are needed for more blocks.

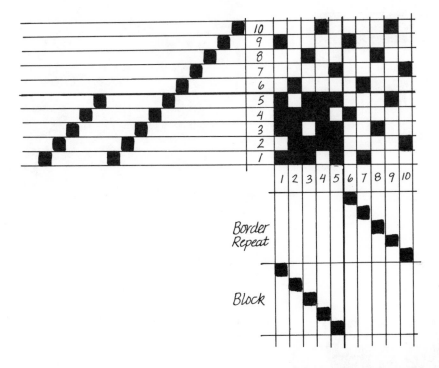

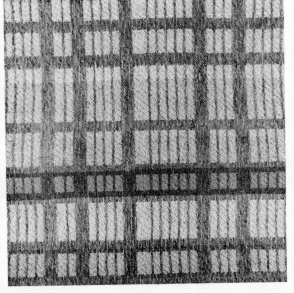
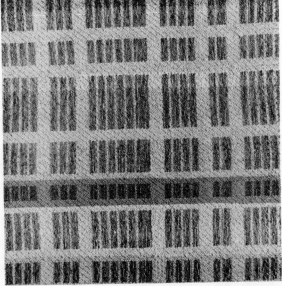

Threading draft, tie-up, and treadling order for ten-harness damask weave. Face and back of damask weave fabric.

Wall hanging in damask weave. ▲

"Shadows," wall hanging in damask weave. ▲
Collection of Oberlin College.

Wall hanging in damask weave, woven in one
piece. *Collection of Mr. and Mrs. R. V.
Steffel.*
◀

Weaves Beyond Classification

There are many weaves that fit no specific classification. They are combinations of different weaves in threading and treadling. They are just as valid as weaves that can be classified, and many have very interesting weave structure.

Try writing and weaving your own draft. I'm sure that in most instances you will be pleased with the results. Also, experiment to see what unconventional materials in warp and weft will produce.

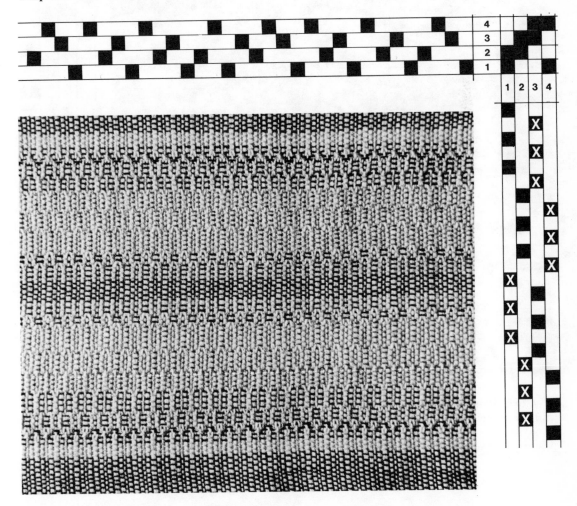

"Parquetry in Syncopation," a draft that fits no specific classification.

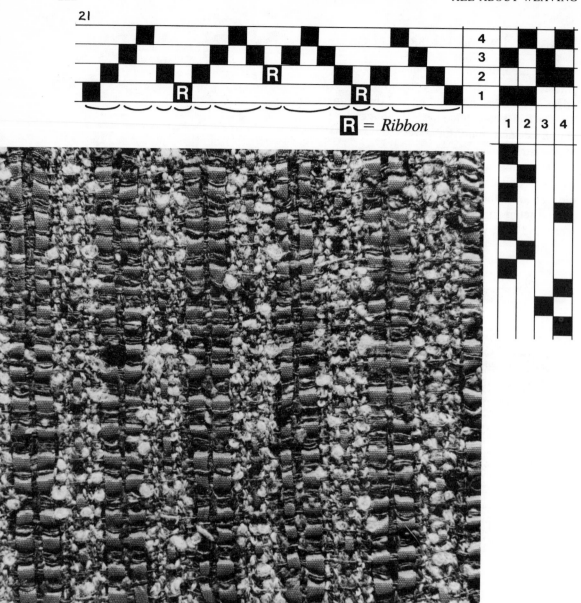

A twill draft using ribbon and various novelty yarns in the warp. Spacing in the reed helps keep the ribbon straight.

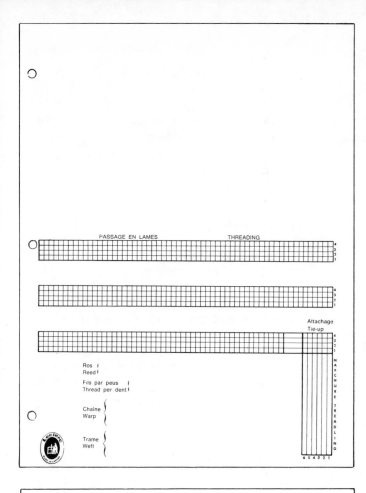

Use pattern draft sheets to record favorite weaves. Include information about warp and weft yarn, warp sett, and an actual sample of the woven piece. Printed sheets like this (or ones you can devise yourself) alternate the place for the woven sample, in order to have even distribution of samples when a number of sheets are put in a notebook. *Draft sheet courtesy Nilus Leclerc, Inc.*

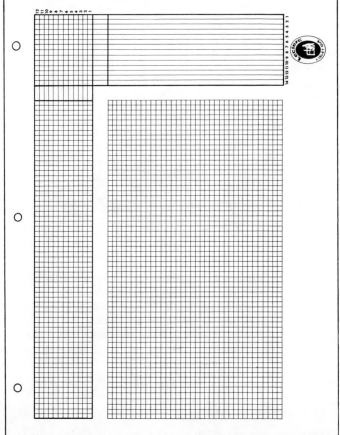

A pattern draft sheet for multiple-harness drafts. *Draft sheet courtesy Nilus Leclerc, Inc.*

Lace Weaving with Doups

A lace weave similar to finger-manipulated lace weaves can be woven by loom control with a special setup on the loom. A single twist can be made between two warp ends on a four-harness loom.

The loom setup requires that *doups,* or half-heddles, be used. The warp is threaded alternately through harnesses 3 and 4. The two front harnesses are used to make the twist. The heddles on harness 1 are the standards and the second harness carries the doups.

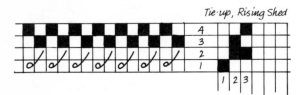

Threading draft and tie-up for weaving lace with doups. All warp ends are threaded on harnesses 3 and 4. To weave, use treadles 2 and 3 alternately for tabby. For the lace, use treadles 1 and 3 alternately. Treadle 3 must always precede and follow treadle 1.

A doup is a length of cord folded over and knotted. It is attached around the bottom heddle bar on harness 2. The doup should be long enough to just come through the eye of the heddle on harness 1.

Use strong cord that will not stretch to tie the doups. Put two nails in a board and tie the cord around them; in this way the

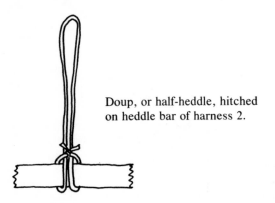

Doup, or half-heddle, hitched on heddle bar of harness 2.

doups will all be the same size. The number of doups required is half the number of warp ends.

Steps to follow in threading the loom for weaving lace with doups:

1. Thread all warp ends alternately on harnesses 3 and 4.
2. Attach the doups on the bottom heddle bar of harness 2.
3. Pull the loop of the first doup through the eye of the first heddle on harness 1.
4. Take the first warp end on harness 3 and lay it over the loop.
5. Put the first warp end on harness 4 through the loop.
6. Sley both warp ends through the same dent in the reed.
7. Continue threading the warp ends from harness 4 through the loops of the doups which are passed through the heddle eyes on harness 1, and the warp ends from harness 3 over the loops.

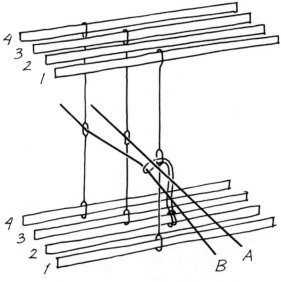

Method of threading warp for weaving lace with doups. All warp ends alternate on harnesses 3 and 4. All doups are on harness 2. The loop of the doup goes through the heddle eye on harness 1. Warp end on harness 3 (A) goes over doup; warp end on harness 4 (B) goes through the loop.

Sett the warp for a lace weave and use a wide-dent reed with two warp ends in each dent. Use yarn with some stretch and keep the warp tension taut. The lace shed is narrow, so use a stick shuttle for the weft. The warp ends sometimes stick together. To separate them, run the back of your index finger across the warp in front of the heddles. If doups become tangled while you are weaving tabby, raise harness 1.

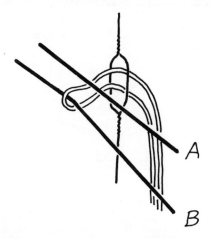

Close-up of warp end 3 (A) over loop of the doup and warp end 4 (B) through the loop.

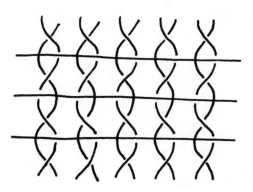

The lace weave made by using doups.

10

~~~~~~

Double Weave

Double weave produces two layers of weaving at one time. The layers can be completely separate from each other; they can be joined at one edge or at both edges; they can be mixed together during the weaving; or they can permeate each other, forming a design.

Two harnesses are needed for each layer of weaving, so that two layers can be woven on a four-harness loom, three layers on a six-harness loom, and so on. The weave is tabby when only two harnesses are used for each layer. On a six-harness loom you can also weave two layers: one a four-harness pattern and the other tabby. On eight harnesses, two layers of pattern weave can be woven.

The basic principle is to raise or lower the necessary harness frames to separate the warp ends in order to make the sheds for each layer.

On a four-harness loom, the two layers are woven at the same time. One weft shot is put in for the top layer, then one weft shot for the bottom one. You make one shed for the top layer, then raise all the warp ends for the top layer plus one shed of the bottom layer and put in a shot of weft for the bottom layer.

Thread the loom in a straight draw. Use double the number of warp ends that would be used for weaving one layer. All the warp ends for one layer will be on harnesses 1 and 3, and all the warp ends for the other on harnesses 2 and 4.

Use two shuttles, one for each layer.

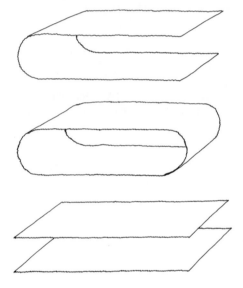

Double weave layers:
Top: Joined on one side to make a double width.
Middle: Joined on both sides to make a tube.
Bottom: Two layers, one woven on top of the other.

Weave each layer individually until the principle of double weave is understood.

To weave two layers: use treadle 1 and weave with one shuttle; use treadle 2 and weave with the other shuttle; use treadle 3, weave with the first shuttle; use treadle 4, weave with the second shuttle. Now two shots of weft have been woven on each layer. Continue in this manner for several inches.

If the two layers are joined on one edge,

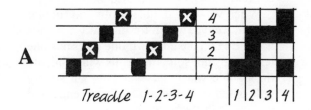

A

Treadle 1-2-3-4

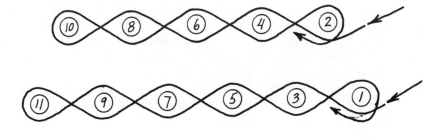

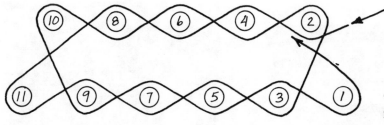

Threading order and tie-up for weaving double weave:

A. Draft for weaving two layers and tubular double weave. Schematic drawing shows direction of weft yarn around numbered warp ends for two layers *(top)* and tubular double weave *(bottom)*.

B. Draft and treadling order for weaving a double-width fabric. Schematic drawing shows direction of weft yarn around numbered warp ends.

B

Treadle 1-2-3-4

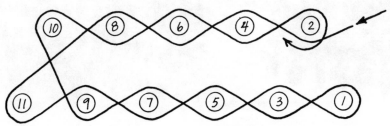

the weaving can be opened when completed and the piece will be double in width. EXAMPLE: A warp 20 inches (50 cm) wide will be 40 inches (100 cm) wide when opened. Follow the treadling order shown in the tie-up to weave a double-width piece. Use one shuttle. (Draft B)

If the two layers are joined on both sides, a tube is made. This is the ideal way to weave a pillow. Use one shuttle and follow the treadling order shown in the tie-up. (Draft A).

You can make each layer a different color by alternating color in the warp ends and using two shuttles. Interlock the weft yarns at the edges for a double width or a tube when using two shuttles.

This is just the beginning of many possibilities with double weave. If you exper-

iment, many more opportunities for creative expression will become evident.

When weaving double-width and tubular double weave, watch for double warp ends appearing on the edges. If one layer has one less warp end, sometimes this will eliminate the double warp ends—or you can simply pull out one of the double warp ends and not use it in the weaving.

The edges of a double-width piece must not pull in. When the piece is unfolded, there will be a marked line in the middle where the warp ends are closer if the edges pull in. A lot of practice, the right yarns, and the right sett of warp are the best ways to avoid a pulled-in edge.

Any project in double weave takes thoughtful planning. Use imagination and creative thinking.

Wall hanging in double weave, using two colors for both warp and weft. *Photo by Art Burt.*

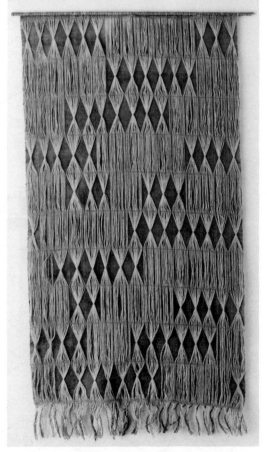

Window blind made using double weave: bottom layer woven solid, top layer woven intermittently and tied in groups in other areas. *Photo by Art Burt.*

How to make a four-harness pattern weave draft into an eight-harness double-weave draft:

A. Four-harness pattern weave draft.

B. The same draft on eight harnesses. This draft will weave two layers of pattern weave. Harnesses 1 through 4 will weave one layer, and 5 through 8 the other layer. The warp ends alternate in threading: one on top layer, second on bottom, third on top, fourth on bottom, etc. ▼

Wall hanging in double weave—hung ▲ sideways, the warp horizontal. *Collection of Multicon Corp.; photo by Charles Vorhees.*

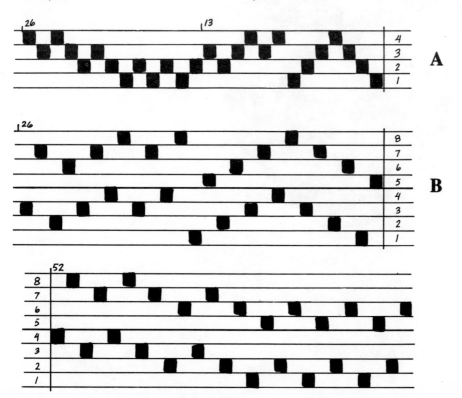

Wall hanging
with six layers
woven on a
twelve-harness
loom. *Collection
of Oberlin
College.*

Stitched Double Weave

This double weave produces a fabric with two distinct sides. One side will be tabby weave; the opposite, a twill weave. The two layers are joined or stitched together by half the warp ends, as they are used to weave both sides. This weave is most effective when woven on eight harnesses. You can weave each side in different colors for a reversible piece, or both sides the same. One side can be plaid, stripes, or checks, while the other is plain or textured. While weaving the top side, you can use tapestry techniques or tie Ghiordes knots (see Chapter 11) to create a pile on the surface. The weaving must, however, progress with one shot on the top and one on the bottom. One side cannot be built up more than the other and still have the two layers stitched, or joined by the warp ends, at regular intervals.

Stitched double weave is one of the most versatile weaves. Using the proper yarns, you can weave blankets, rugs, loom-shaped garments, wall hangings, and yardage for many different uses. The warp is sett the same as for any double weave; that is, use double the number of warp ends that you would need for a single layer.

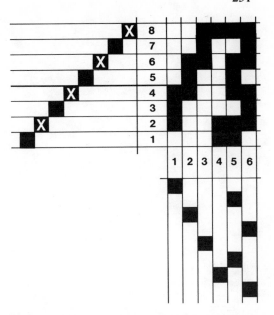

Draft, tie-up, and treadling order for stitched double weave. Warp yarn can be one color; with two colors in the warp, the fabric will be different on each side.

Two colors in both warp and weft on one side makes a checked pattern.

One-color weft makes a solid color on the other side of the piece.

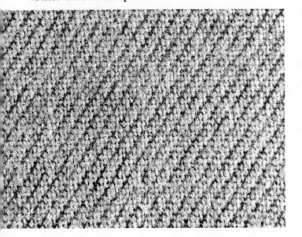

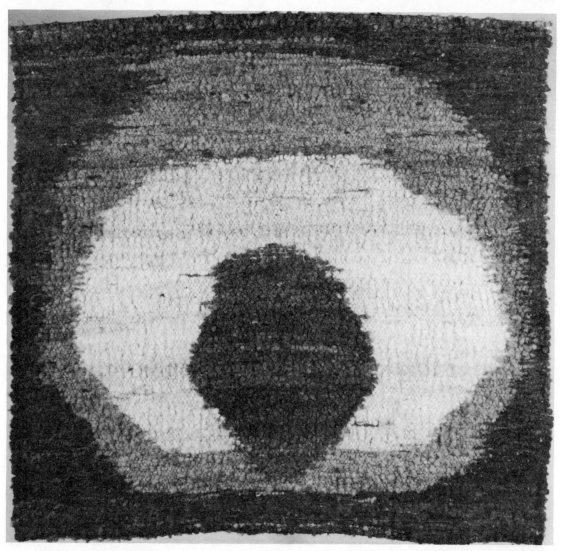

Wall hanging in stitched
double weave; detail of back,
in twill weave with heavy
yarn.

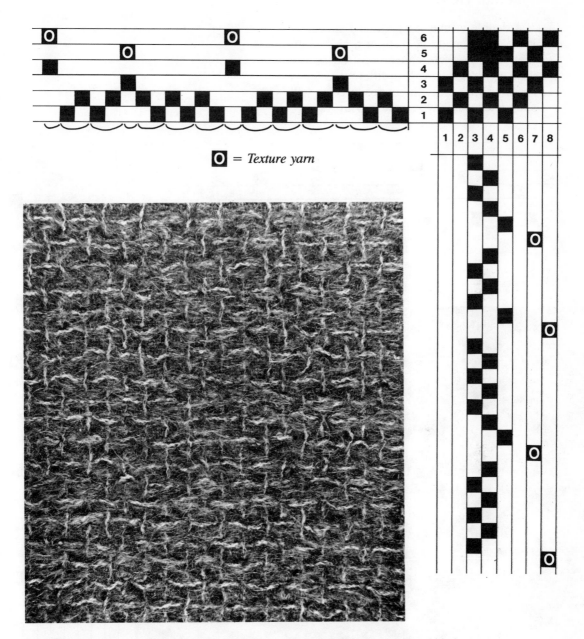

$\boxed{O}$ = *Texture yarn*

Threading draft, tie-up, and treadling order for a stitched double weave. One side has a loosely woven texture (shown in the photo) and the back is tabby.

Quilted Weave

A double weave can be joined at regular intervals to create pockets or a quilted effect. The pockets can be stuffed as the weaving progresses. If a different color is used for each side, the opposite color will show like a stitch where the two layers join.

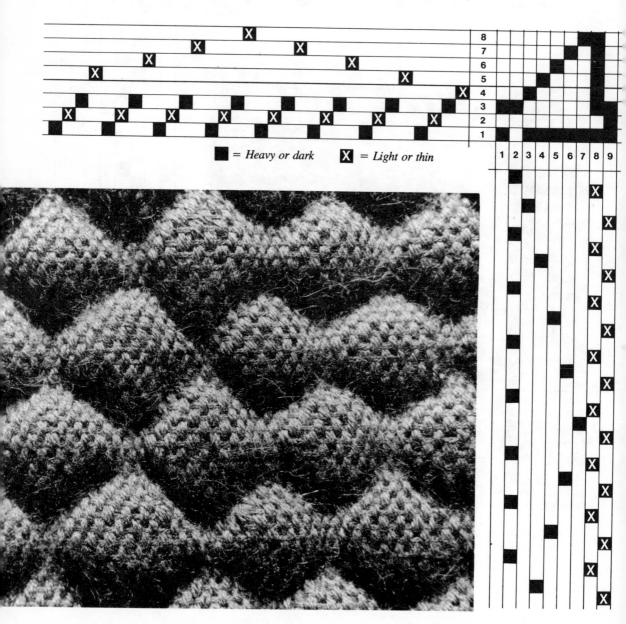

■ = *Heavy or dark*   X = *Light or thin*

Threading draft, tie-up, and treadling order for quilted weave. To stuff the pockets while weaving, open a shed by using treadle 1 just before treadle 2.

Pickup Double Weave

Sometimes called Finn Weave, this technique requires that each layer be a different color. The effect is that the color from one layer permeates the other layer, forming a design, and vice versa. If only one color is used for both sides, the effect could be like the quilting technique of trapunto.

To weave pickup double weave:

1. Plan a design on graph paper.
2. Prepare two shuttles, one for each color of the warp. One color of the warp should be on harnesses 1 and 3, the other on harnesses 2 and 4.
3. Weave the two layers for several inches. Join the sides or not, as you wish; this does not affect the design.
4. By treadling, raise all the warp ends of one color (treadle 1).
5. With a pickup stick, pick up the areas of the warp that will make that design. To pick up, the stick goes through the raised warp ends like a big basting needle. Push the stick close to the reed. Do not turn it on end.
6. Return all warp ends to a rest position, that is, with no sheds.

■ = Black

X = White

Treadle	1	2	3	4	Pickup/Weave instruction
1	X		X		1 and 3, Pick up White
2		■			2, Weave Black
3			■		2 and 4, Pick up Black
4	X				1 Weave White
5	X		X		1 and 3, Pick up White
6				■	4, Weave Black
7		■			2 and 4, Pick up Black
8			X		3 Weave White

Threading draft, tie-up, and treadling order for pickup double weave.
Lower left: Specific areas of the warp are picked up for the design.

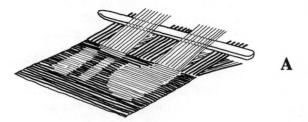

A

B

The pickup stick in the warp:
   A. The white areas are picked up and the black shed is woven.
   B. The black areas are picked up and the white shed is woven.

7. Raise the harness frame (treadle 2) to make a shed of the opposite color to the one just picked up.

8. Weave the color of the shed just made. The shed will be narrow and warp ends may stick together. The shuttle passes below the area where the warp ends are on the pickup stick.

9. Pull out the stick and beat the weft yarn into place.

10. Now raise all the warp ends of the color opposite the color that was picked up before. With the pickup stick, pick up the areas that are just the opposite of the areas picked up the first time. Push the stick near the reed.

11. Put all warp ends at rest. Raise a shed (treadle 1) of the opposite color to the one just picked up. Clear the shed and weave with that color of weft yarn. Pull out the stick and beat the weft into place.

12. Repeat these steps over and over until the design is completed. Be sure to weave with opposite sheds each time. There are four shots of weft in a complete repeat. The draft shows the treadling order for the repeat.

There are a few general rules to follow when weaving pickup double weave:

1. Pick up one color and weave the opposite color.

2. The pickup stick *must* be close to the reed when putting in the weft shot.

3. Weave opposite sheds for each color.

Design possibilities are endless. Straight, curved, and diagonal lines can be made and large or small areas can be picked up. The two layers are joined where the color changes.

Hanging in pickup double weave by Evelyn Nateman.

11

Pile Weaves

Pile is loops of yarn forming the surface of a weaving. There are many methods of making pile. Loops made of either weft or warp yarns can be left uncut or can be cut. Floats in warp or weft, when cut in the middle, will make pile. Some weft yarns will also make pile because of their very nature.

Most pile weaves are associated with rugs, but the same weaves can be used in any piece.

Pile can be made on a background tabby weave by manipulating the weft yarns on the surface. Individual weft yarns are used to tie knots around the warp.

The easiest method of making pile is by making loops with the weft yarn.

A Ghiordes knot rug woven by the author over a period of several years at her summer home. Growing children designed two color blocks, using geometric designs including their initials.

1. On a tabby threading weave a solid heading.
2. In the next shed, put a shot of yarn to be used to make the loops.
3. With a round rod, pick up loops at regular intervals from this weft shot. Make the loops in the area that will form the intended design.
4. Weave several more rows of tabby and beat solidly. Remove the stick that picked up the loops, which are now anchored in the weaving.

To make the most effective design, all yarn should be the same color. The weft yarn will best hold the loops if it has a soft twist. Loops can be made wherever desired in the weaving. If the design is charted to size on graph paper, it will be easy to follow.

Woven hanging with loops. *Collection of Mr. and Mrs. L. Paoletti; photo by Charles Vorhees.*

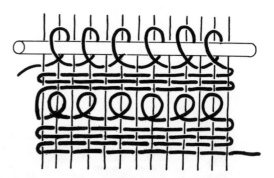

A woven piece using weft loops for the design. *Photo by Charles Vorhees.* ▼

Method of making loops with weft yarn. ▲

Chenille

When chenille yarn is woven in a tabby background, it will make a pile on the weaving. The piece woven of chenille yarn is called a *twice-woven fabric,* because chenille is itself a woven, not twisted, yarn.

On a tabby weave, use the chenille yarn as weft in either every shed, every other shed, or every third shed. The fiber and size of the chenille and the effect desired will determine how it is woven. Chenille is ideal for rugs, clothing, and decorative pieces. There are a variety of chenille yarns in various sizes and fibers available for weaving.

To make your own chenille yarn, put on the loom groups of warp ends, of fine yarn sett very close. The groups of warp ends should be at least 1 inch (2.5 cm) apart. The amount of space between the groups of warp ends determines the height of the pile of the chenille yarn: the greater the space, the longer the pile. The warp yarn can be as fine as sewing thread with each group sett no more than ¼ inch (6 mm) wide and up to six warp ends. The weft yarn can be soft, heavy yarn or fine yarn, depending on the chenille yarn to be made. Weave as usual, packing the weft in solidly. The weft yarn will interlace with the groups of warp yarns and will span the spaces between. After the weaving is removed from the loom, cut through the unwoven weft. The woven strips now look like fuzzy caterpillars—*chenille* is the French word for caterpillar.

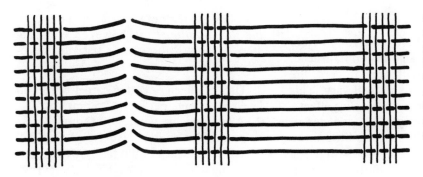

Chenille yarn is made by putting groups of warp (of fine yarn sett very close) on the loom. After weaving, the weft is cut; the strips are the chenille yarn.

Chenille yarn as it looks when woven. The ends make pile on both sides of the weaving. The number of shots of tabby between the chenille shots depends on the effect desired.

Ghiordes Knots

Pile can be made on a tabby ground by using weft yarn to tie Ghiordes knots on the warp. Design possibilities are endless, and with proper rug yarn and firm beating, excellent rugs can be made. The process is, however, very slow. This knot is also used for decorative purposes; it can be placed anywhere in a weaving, made any length, and used to create dense or sparse pile.

You can use this knot to create surface interest on many woven pieces, such as decorative borders on drapes, and the complete surface or specific areas of pillows, bags, and wall hangings. If you use fluffy yarn, the Ghiordes knot can simulate fur on clothing items. The Ghiordes knot is used in Norwegian rya rugs and very often in oriental rugs. When this knot is properly tied and secured with tabby shots, the pile will not pull out.

The knots are tied around a rod or ruler to make them all the same length. If, instead, you measure them with your fingers, the length of yarn in each knot will vary. This gives a more irregular and interesting effect.

The rod for measuring can be wooden or metal. The length should be a little more than the width of the piece of weaving. The height of the rod depends on the height of the pile desired. The rod should be narrow, with a groove through the middle of the top edge for cutting the loops. A wooden rod must be smooth and of hard wood such as maple. A metal rod can be of galvanized iron bent to size. The top edges must be even.

The knot is made on a wide-spaced warp. Make a butterfly of yarn for the knots. Weave a firm heading in tabby with a yarn that will cover the warp. With a closed shed, set the rod upright on the warp at the edge of the tabby heading. Do not make a knot on the two warp ends at the edge. Starting at the left, put the butterfly of yarn under the third warp end from right to left. The end of the yarn should be the length of the desired height of the knot. Put the yarn over the third and fourth warp ends, then around the fourth warp end to the same place you

started. Put the butterfly of yarn under the rod and pull the knot up tight. Carry the yarn over the rod and repeat the same process over the next two warp ends. Continue making the knots in this manner across the warp. Now weave a tabby shot. Use a tapestry fork to push this shot into place, giving it plenty of ease to work in between the knots. Put in several more rows of tabby, beating them in very firmly. Cut the knots by running a knife or razor blade in the groove along the top of the rod.

If you are not using a rod, tie the knots in the same manner but use your fingers as a measuring guide. After the tabby shots have been put in, cut the loops with scissors. The number of tabby shots between the rows of knots depends on how dense the pile is to be. A general rule is that the tabby binder should be two-thirds the height of the knot.

Follow these rules when making a rug using the Ghiordes knot; however, eliminate step 3 below if the knot is used for decorative purposes.

1. Use 10/5 linen or cotton carpet warp, sett 6 to 10 dents per inch (2.5 cm).
2. A good-quality wool is best for the knots and tabby binder. Use a size that will cover the warp in the tabby weave.
3. Using a butterfly at each selvage, weave a triangle by going over and under one, then two, then three warp ends, and reverse. Do this after each row of knots. This fills in the space on the two edge warp ends where the knot is not tied and makes the firm edge necessary for a well-constructed rug. Carry the butterflies along the edge as the weaving progresses; let them hang free when not in use.

Plan the design for the rug on graph paper—plot it to size. As you weave, lay a straight stick, such as a ruler or yardstick, across the design to mark the place you are working. This will clearly show when the design changes color in each horizontal row. One color area cannot be built up and then filled in, as in tapestry weaving.

Use color as desired, introducing a

new butterfly for a different color in any row of knots. You can start and end color at any time. Use one strand of heavy yarn or several strands of fine yarn in each butterfly—whatever is necessary to achieve the effect you want.

One of the more difficult aspects of planning a piece using Ghiordes knots is estimating the amount of yarn required for the project. A general rule is ¾ pound (340 g) per square foot (930 cm²) for close or high pile. When estimating yarn for any project, it is better to be generous.

Also, there is considerable warp take-up during the weaving of pile. Allow up to 1 inch (2.5 cm) for every woven foot (30 cm). Measure along the selvage, not on top of the pile.

Select an appropriate finish for any woven piece with pile. A facing can be woven with the piece, turned back, and hemmed; or any of the finishing techniques described for tapestries can be used. A five-strand braid is a satisfactory finish for a pile rug.

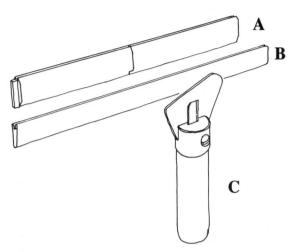

Tools used for Ghiordes knots:
  A. Wooden rod in sections, joined together to make the required length.
  B. Metal rod.
  C. Knife used to cut knots along rod.

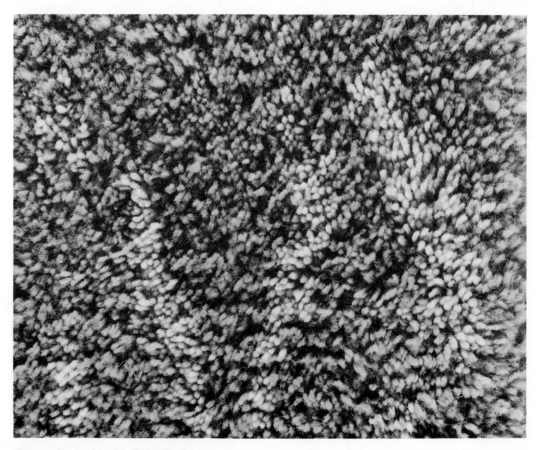

Dense pile made with Ghiordes knots.

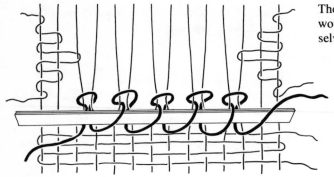

The Ghiordes knots tied around a rod and the woven triangle which makes a firm edge on selvages when weaving a rug.

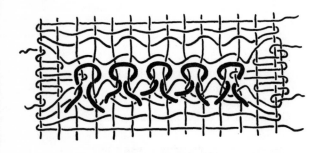

A completed row of Ghiordes knots, woven triangles on selvage, and tabby shots.

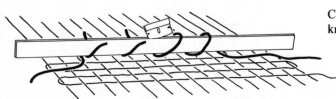

Cutting the yarn along the rod for a Ghiordes knot.

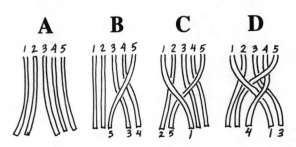

A five-strand braid for finishing the warp ends of a rug:

A. To begin, separate the warp ends in this manner.

B. Put strand 5 over 3 and 4.

C. Put strand 1 over 2 and 5.

D. Put strand 4 over 3 and 1.

Continue in this manner, putting the edge strands alternately over the adjoining two strands.

Corduroy

In corduroy weave, pile is made with rows of alternate floats on a tabby ground in a way similar to overshot weave. The floats are cut in the middle to form the pile. Many drafts can be used to make corduroy (see huckaback, in Chapter 9), but a draft that will make staggered floats will yield an overall pile. Yarn for the pile should be heavy and with a soft twist, whereas the warp must be strong and tightly twisted. The tabby binder must also have a soft twist so it will beat in solidly. Thick pile cannot be made in corduroy. If long pile is desired, the floats must be pulled up in a curve, making the float yarn longer. (See the sample in the color section of a rug woven in corduroy weave.)

Corduroy is known as the quick method of making pile because both pile shots and tabby binder shots are woven with a shuttle thrown across the warp. This limits design possibilities unless color is used in specific areas, but then this slows down the weaving process. A design of vertical color stripes can be made by alternating colors in the pile sheds. The basic characteristic of weaving, vertical and horizontal color lines (see page 156), is a distinct feature of the corduroy weave.

Try corduroy on any threading that makes floats and a tabby binder. Experimenting in this way will show the structure of the weave and the design possibilities. When the floats are left completely or partially uncut, the results are markedly different.

Corduroy weave can be used for many purposes, that is, in any piece where pile is desired. It can be used to produce pile on the total piece or used only in specific areas. In this instance, only the tabby shots are woven where no pile is needed. Always choose yarns appropriate for the project, such as heavy yarns for a rug and soft, pliable yarns for clothing.

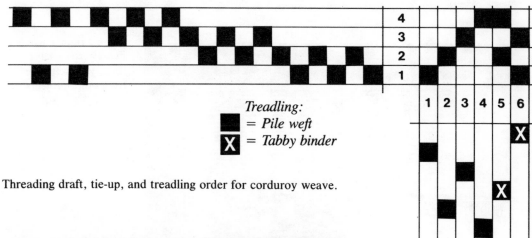

Treadling:
■ = Pile weft
X = Tabby binder

Threading draft, tie-up, and treadling order for corduroy weave.

"Cut Grass," woven in corduroy with cut and uncut pile. The green pile and red mower make a dramatic contrast. *Photo by Charles Vorhees.*

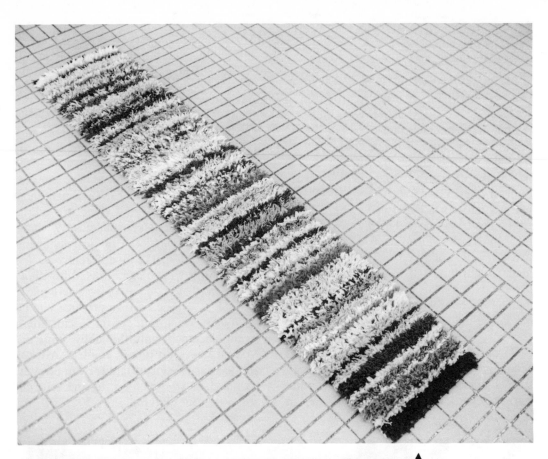

Striped runner woven
in corduroy weave
using yarn left over
from other projects.

◄
Wall hanging in
corduroy weave. Uncut
floats of many strands
of yarn make the
surface. *Collection of
Mr. and Mrs. Duncan
Creager; photo by
Charles Vorhees.*

Warp Pile

Warp pile can be made in the same manner as in corduroy by "turning" a draft (see the discussion of turned weaves on page 210). The floats making the pile will then be in the warp.

Another warp pile weave, called *Velvet Weave,* can be made by putting two warps on the loom, one for the pile and the other for the tabby ground. Each warp has its own warp beam so that the tension can be controlled separately. Thread the warp for the ground on harnesses 1 and 2 and the pile warp on harnesses 3 and 4. The pile warp must be about eight times longer than the ground warp.

To make the pile in Velvet Weave, you will need at least four rods. These are the same as the rod used for making Ghiordes knots (see page 240). If your loom is not equipped with a second warp beam, see page 250 for ways to make your own.

Follow these steps to make the warp pile in Velvet Weave:

1. Weave three shots of tabby ground, using all the warp ends.
2. Raise the pile harnesses and insert a rod through the shed, allowing the pile warp ends to go over the rod and make a loop.
3. Repeat steps 1 and 2 until four rods have been inserted. Beat the tabby ground very solidly. The rods are left in the warp so that the loops are not pulled out before they are securely anchored.

4. Using a razor blade, cut the loops on the first rod (see under Ghiordes knots, page 240). Insert this rod in the fifth pile shed; weave the tabby ground.

There will be four pile warp rods in the weaving at all times. Continue to cut the pile on the lowest rod, open the pile shed, and insert the rod and weave tabby ground.

When the piece is taken off the loom, the pile must be brushed in all directions and beaten with a flat piece of wood such as a stick shuttle. This process opens up the pile so it will cover the ground weave.

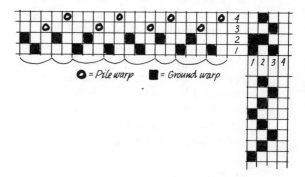

Threading draft, tie-up, and treadling order for warp pile weave.

Velvet Weave as it looks when woven. The loops have been cut and the rod removed.

12

~~~~~~

Unconventional Methods

There are methods of weaving on a loom that challenge the basic mechanical operations described earlier. Understanding them will enable you to comprehend the ways in which many of the hangings seen in museums were executed. These methods require complete familiarity on the part of the weaver of the operation of a handweaving loom. The weaves and techniques described in this book can be used.

Weaving Without Beaming

A basic method that can be used in conjunction with others is to tie the warp to the back lash rod (apron bar) without winding it on the warp beam. Simply knot it to the rod and leave the ends to hang loose until needed. The top bar of a wall hanging can

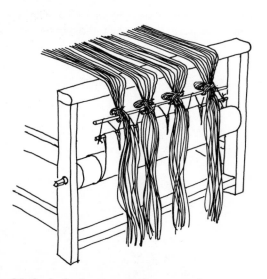

Method of tying warp ends to warp beam lash rod so tension can be easily adjusted.

be fastened to the cloth beam lash rod. The warp ends go around this rod and through the reed and heddles; then the tension is adjusted and the warp is tied to the lash rod of the warp beam. The extra warp hangs to the floor. As weaving progresses and the lash rod moves close to the harness frames, untie the knots, place the lash rod near the warp beam again, and retie the warp to the rod, adjusting the tension. When the piece of weaving is finished, untie it from the back lash rod and pull the ends through the heddles and reed. The end where the weaving was started needs no additional finishing. This method is not effective with a long warp.

No-Reed Method

Weaving without a reed offers the opportunity to weave an irregular shape.

Remove the reed and batten from the loom. Put the warp on by the method just described. While weaving, move the warp ends in or out (close together or spaced) as required by the particular shape you are weaving. (No rule says that all warp ends must be parallel!) Tying the warp to the warp beam lash rod means that the tension can be adjusted at any time, and it will have to be adjusted as the weaving moves from a broad to narrow width or the opposite. You can use any weave or technique; results are almost unpredictable, which adds to the enjoyment of trying this method. A tapestry fork must be used to put the weft yarn in place.

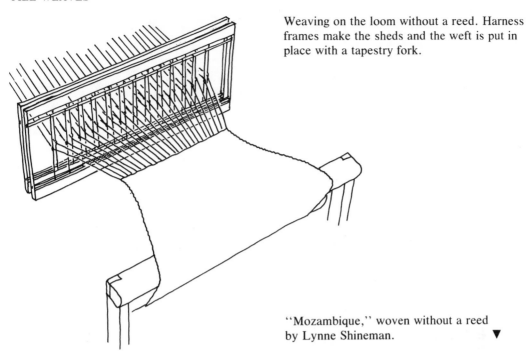

Weaving on the loom without a reed. Harness frames make the sheds and the weft is put in place with a tapestry fork.

"Mozambique," woven without a reed by Lynne Shineman. ▼

Rethreading the Warp

Put the warp on the loom as described under "Weaving Without Beaming," above. Weave strips using the tapestry slit technique. Then untie the warp ends of one strip and pull them out of the heddles and reed. This strip can be crossed over others, twisted, tied in a knot, or manipulated in any number of ways. The warp ends are then rethreaded and retied to the lash rod and weaving can continue. Being able to adjust the tension of the warp ends at the warp beam is essential when using this method of rethreading.

Fringe on Four Sides

Fringe on two sides of a piece of weaving is easy to achieve because under normal circumstances it just happens—the fringe is the beginning and end of the warp that can't be woven. To put fringe on the other two sides is also easy. If it is made during weaving, the fringe is better than if added later.

To weave fringe on sides:

1. Place a heavy cord at each edge of the weaving. Each cord should be parallel to

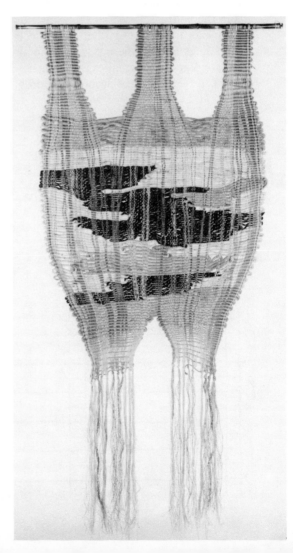

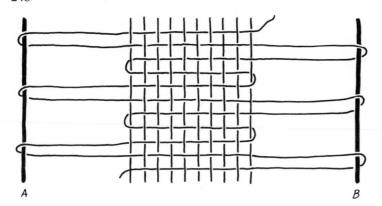

Method of making fringe on selvages. Heavy cords (A and B) are placed on each side of the warp. Alternate weft shots go around these cords.

the warp ends, and its distance from the edge is the desired length of the fringe. The cords (A and B) are put on the loom in the same manner as the warp. They are sleyed in the reed but not threaded through a heddle. Tension may have to be adjusted during weaving because there will be no take-up on these cords as there is in the warp.

2. Weave as usual. Every other pair of weft shots goes around the cords and the alternate pair of shots makes the usual selvages. If all shots went around the cords,

the edge warp ends would not stay in place but would unravel.

3. When the weaving is completed, the fringes can be cut or left in loops.

Spaced Warp

A warp does not have to be evenly spaced or sett in the reed. By grouping several warp ends together in one dent or skipping dents when sleying the reed, you can work out many different effects.

If you want spaces in the weaving, sett

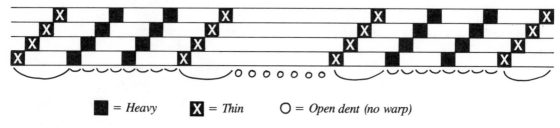

■ = Heavy   X = Thin   O = Open dent (no warp)

Threading draft showing sett in reed for a spaced warp. Fine warp ends prevent other warp ends from sliding into the spaces.

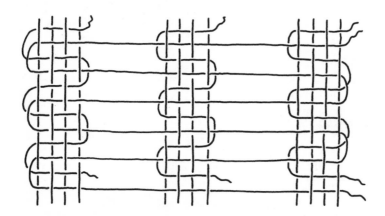

Method of weaving a tabby binder in each strip of a spaced warp.

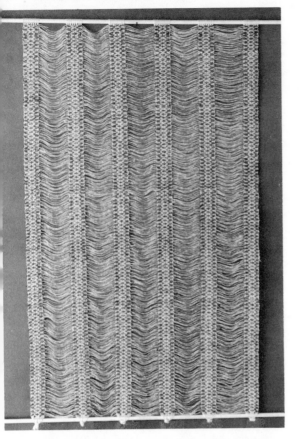

Window blind with a spaced warp. Strips are threaded in an overshot pattern; tabby binder is used in weaving the strips. *Photo by Charles Vorhees.*

the warp in the reed in strips. To prevent the warp ends from sliding in and closing the spaces when the piece is removed from the loom, thread a few fine yarns along the edges of the spaces. The fine yarns follow the threading order but are grouped in one dent of the reed.

Another method of preventing the warp ends from sliding into the spaces is to weave each strip with its own tabby binder. Every other weft shot goes right across the warp. These full-width weft shots hang pleasingly when the weaving is removed from the loom.

Double-Tension Warp

There are many times when certain warp ends should be under different tensions. Some looms can be equipped with two beams, and there are very satisfactory alternative methods that can be used in the place of two standard beams.

The reasons for wanting different tensions on warps are numerous. The most common reason is to hold yarns with different stretching qualities under different tensions within one warp. Stitched double weaves require a different tension for each layer if they are woven with different weights of yarn. The warp take-up on each layer will

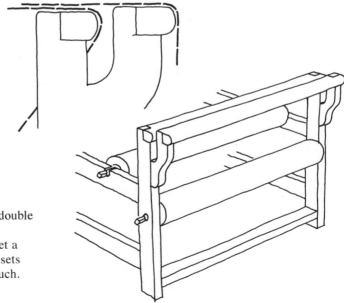

A loom equipped with double warp beams. Note the additional back beam set a little higher so the two sets of warp ends do not touch.

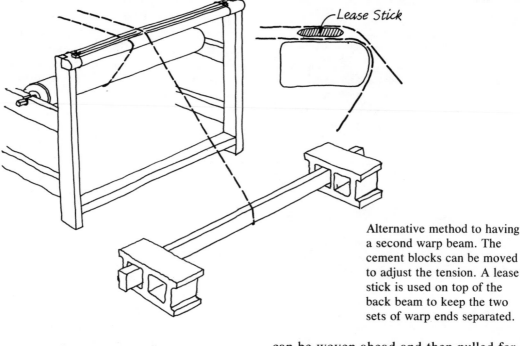

Alternative method to having a second warp beam. The cement blocks can be moved to adjust the tension. A lease stick is used on top of the back beam to keep the two sets of warp ends separated.

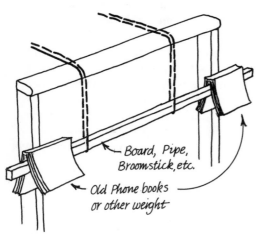

Another method of keeping tension on a second warp.

be different, and the double tension will alleviate this problem. There are also many instances when a double-tension warp is needed to create special effects. One warp can be woven ahead and then pulled forward, making a loop or pleat on the surface (see color section, the wall hanging entitled "Saharan I"). For making warp-loop pile it is essential that one warp be controlled under different tension.

Double tension warps can be a creative tool; on the other hand, they are a necessity for weaving some fibers and techniques.

An idea for any weaving can be successfully executed by thorough planning of all aspects of the project. You should have a good working knowledge of your loom and its operation and should use familiar yarns and weaves or techniques. Consider the result you wish to accomplish and plan each process of setting up the loom and weaving so that you may achieve it. Think creatively and try an unconventional method of weaving or setting up of the loom. Try something you haven't tried before—it may become a favorite way of working. Above all, be willing to attempt something even though you may not have previously seen it done.

13

Building Your Own Loom

Building your own loom is a great way to learn about looms, and the more you know about how and why they work, the better your weaving will be.

The loom design in this chapter is for the beginning weaver who has some knowledge of woodworking. It is not intended to be compared to the precision-engineered looms manufactured today, which are finely crafted pieces of professional equipment, rede-

A homemade loom: 36-inch weaving width, four-harness.

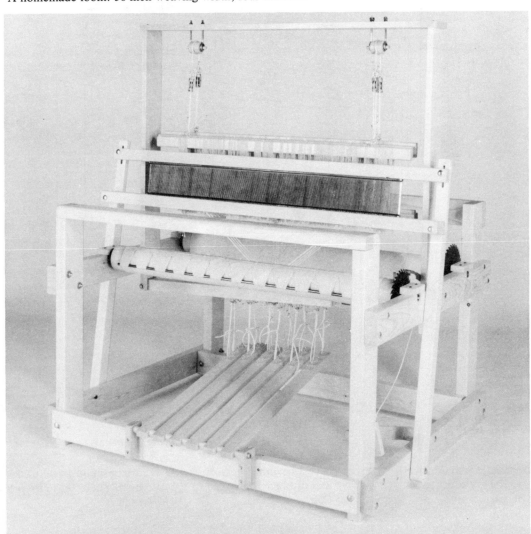

signed and refined over the years as new materials and factory methods become available.

The floor loom presented here was designed to be simply built with hand tools from easily obtained materials. Everything except the reed can be found in most large hardware and lumber stores. It is a small loom, but rugged enough to withstand years of use.

The plans are only a starting point for your own innovations. You may want to substitute store-bought heddle frames instead of string heddle bars, or to change the number of treadles or the weaving width. This loom can be built from scrap lumber or the finest

hardwood. Any sanding or finishing is done *before* the parts are assembled; see suggestions for finishing on page 263.

Before starting to construct the loom, check the plans carefully to be sure you understand every phase. Plan ahead to avoid errors. Remember the carpenter's adage "Measure twice, cut once," and always use caution when using any cutting tools. Cut all pieces to size, lay the parts on the floor or table in proper position, and check for errors before assembling.

Detailed diagrams for assembling each part of the loom are followed by step-by-step instructions for setting up your loom (see page 263).

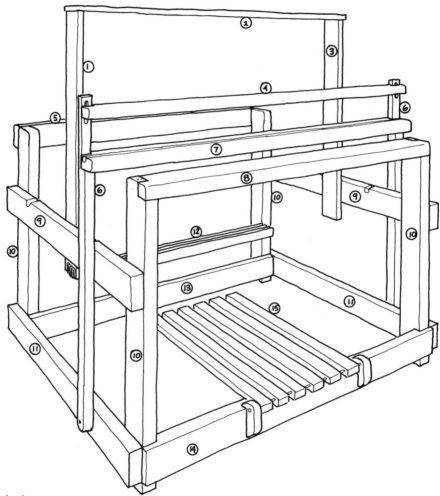

Parts of the loom:
1. Castle support (left).
2. Castle (top).
3. Castle support (right).
4. Handtree.
5. Back beam.

6. Sword.
7. Shuttle race and sley.
8. Breast beam.
9. Rail or brace (upper).
10. Corner post.

11. Rail or brace (lower).
12. Lams.
13. Cross beam or brace (back).
14. Cross beam or brace (front).
15. Treadles.

Materials

Use any wood you prefer, hard or soft, but *dry!* Most lumber yards stock 2×4s in pine, fir, hemlock, etc. Each wood has its advantages. A 2×4 today measures 1½×3½ inches. If you use old or used lumber it may not be this size, so change dimensions to fit. You can use the layout given or make your own. Note that a few parts require the wood to be straight and knot-free. Stack your wood where you will build the loom a few days before you start so it will become acclimated.

Modify the following lumber and hardware list to suit your needs and double-check sizes and lengths as you proceed. The lumber and hardware list is for the loom pictured.

2×4 Lumber (1½″ × 3½″)

Description	Number Required	Length
Side rails or braces	4	36″
Posts	4	29½″
Beams & braces	4	42″
Shuttle race	1	48¾″

2×2 Lumber

Swords	2	~35¾″
Handtree	1	48¾″

1×4 Lumber

Castle supports	2	35¼″
Castle top	1	42¾″
Lams & treadles and misc.		About 10 linear feet

Quantity	Description	Use
1 each	6″ and 7½″ combination circular saw blade	Brake and take-up
4	1″ awning pulleys	Harness
4	½″ pipe flanges	Beam axle
1	2″ spring (not too heavy)	Brake
8″	½″ iron pipe	Beam axle
81″	3″ PVC or comparable plastic pipe	Warp and cloth beams
15″	⅛″ × ¾″ or 1″ steel strap	Brake dogs
1 each	¾″ hardwood dowel, ⅜″ hardwood dowel	Treadle spacers
4	¼″ × 3½″ or 4″ eyebolts (eye must be ⅜″ or larger)	Harness
4	¼″ wing nuts with washers	Harness
70	Standard screw eyes (eye must be ¼″ or larger)	Lams, heddle bars, treadles
4	#10 × 2½″ flathead wood screws	Back beam
4	#10 × 2¼″ flathead wood screws	Treadle bracket
3	#10 × 1½″ flathead wood screws	Treadle bracket and brake release
4	#10 × 2″ roundhead wood screws	Castle
8	#7 × 1½″ roundhead wood screws	Beam hold-downs
3	#12 × ¾″ roundhead wood screws	Brake dogs and spring
2	¼″ × 2½″ lag screws	Sword
4	⁵⁄₁₆″ × 5½″ carriage bolts	Cross braces
1	⁵⁄₁₆″ × 4½″ carriage bolt	Brake release pedal
2	⁵⁄₁₆″ × 4″ carriage bolts	Shuttle race
16	⁵⁄₁₆″ × 3¼″ or 3½″ carriage bolts	Side rails
4	⁵⁄₁₆″ × 2½″ carriage bolts	Castle
2	⁵⁄₁₆″ × 2″ carriage bolts with wing nuts	Handtree
1	¼″ × 4″ hex head (cap) bolt	Lams
24	¼″ flat washers	
38	⁵⁄₁₆″ flat washers	
1	¼″ nut	
26	⁵⁄₁₆″ nuts	
1 spool	heavy string	Heddles
50′	nylon cord or venetian blind cord	Tie-up and harness
3 yards	36″-wide canvas, duck, or denim fabric	Aprons
4	⁴⁄₁₆″ × 37″ steel rod	Apron rods
24	#6 × ½″ pan-head sheet metal screws	Apron fasteners

LUMBER LAYOUT USING 2x4's, 10' LONG

| CROSS BRACE | CROSS BRACE | SWORD * |
| | | SWORD * |

| CORNER POST | CORNER POST | CORNER POST | CORNER POST |

| SIDE RAIL | SIDE RAIL | BREAST BEAM * |

| SIDE RAIL | SIDE RAIL | BACK BEAM * |

| SHUTTLE RACE * | SCRAP | SCRAP |
| | HANDTREE * | |

* STRAIGHT & KNOT-FREE

FRONT CROSS BRACE

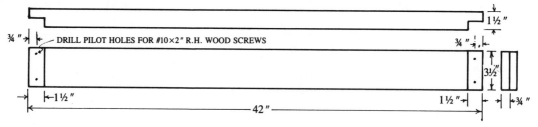

DRILL PILOT HOLES FOR #10×2" R.H. WOOD SCREWS

¾" · 1½" · 42" · 1½" · ¾" · 3½" · 3½"

BACK CROSS BRACE

1½" · ¾" · ¾" · 3½" · 42"

BREAST BEAM

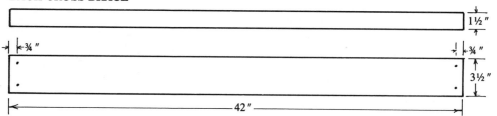

1½" · 1½" · 2" · 42"

ROUND EDGES

BACK BEAM

1½" · ROUND EDGES · 42" · 3½"

BACK CORNER POST *MAKE 2*

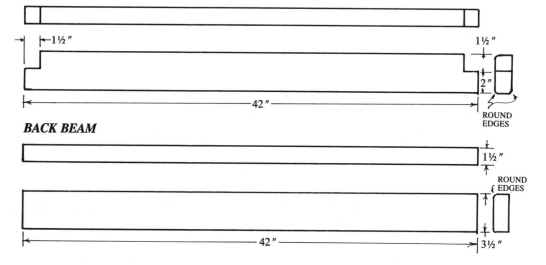

1½"

ROUND CORNER (ABOUT ½" R.)

3½"

29½"

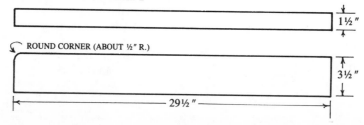

FRONT CORNER POST MAKE 2

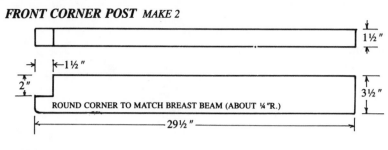

ROUND CORNER TO MATCH BREAST BEAM (ABOUT ¼"R.)

TOP SIDE RAIL MAKE 2

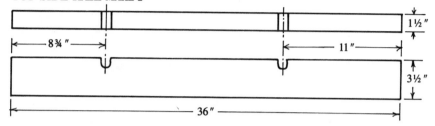

BOTTOM SIDE RAIL MAKE 2

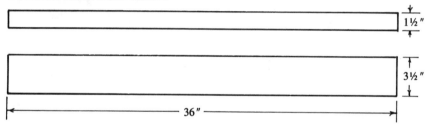

Loom Body Assembly

Clamp or tape each joint together, in turn, making sure it is square and in the right spot. Drill bolt holes and pilot holes, using a "backup" block to prevent splintering the drill hole. Check bolt and screw clearances carefully, especially where the bottom cross braces join the sides. *Do not use glue.* Proceed until the entire body is standing four-square on the floor.

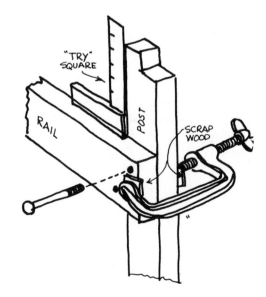

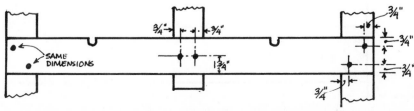

Brake and Take-up System

Saw blades of two different diameters are used and accomplish the same purpose as double dogs (or pawls) on a commercial loom. They allow finer adjustment of the tension. The dogs are made from strap iron and twisted 90 degrees with a wrench and vise. Depending on the angle of the dogs, adjustments in placement may be needed on your loom.

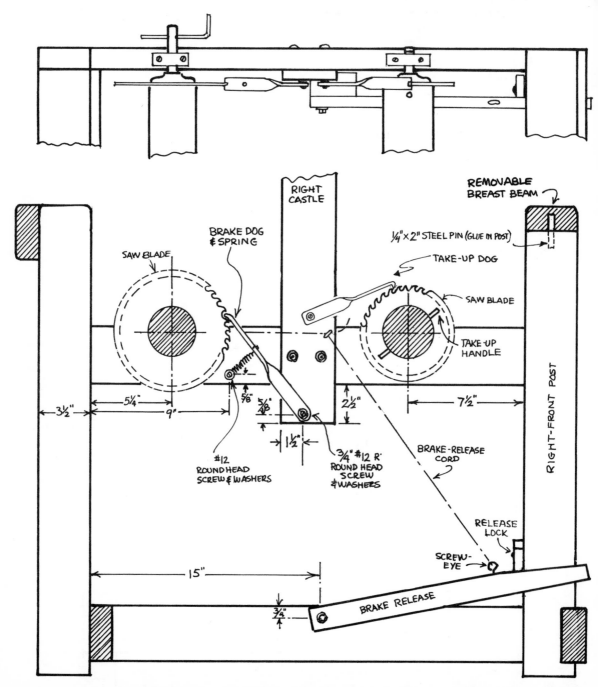

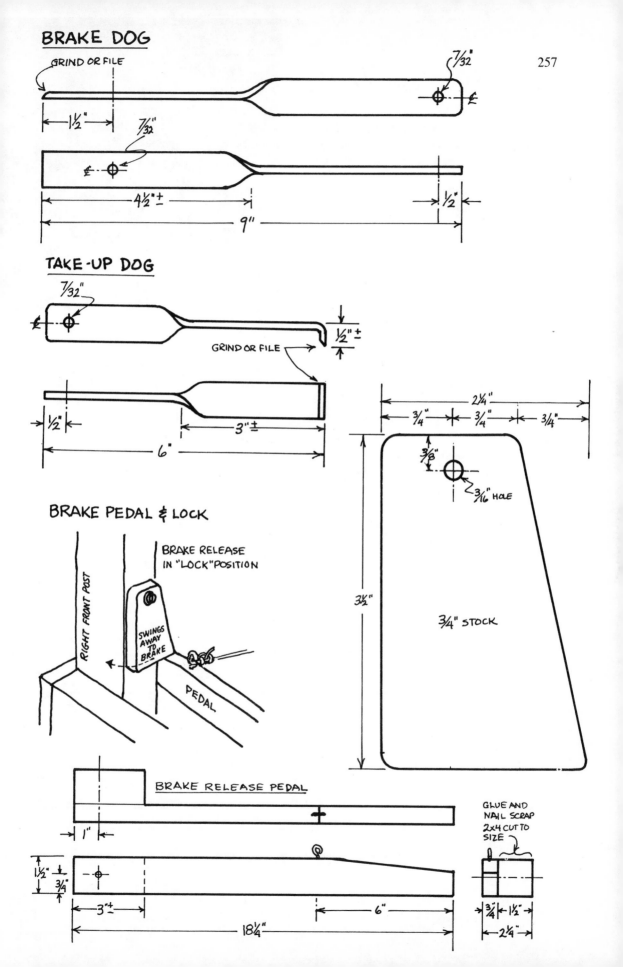

BRAKE DOG

GRIND OR FILE

7/32"

257

1½"

7/32"

4½"±

9"

½"

TAKE-UP DOG

7/32"

GRIND OR FILE

½"±

½"

3"±

6"

2¼"

¾"   ¾"   ¾"

3/8"

3/16" HOLE

3½"

¾" STOCK

BRAKE PEDAL & LOCK

BRAKE RELEASE
IN "LOCK" POSITION

RIGHT FRONT POST

SWINGS
AWAY
TO
BRAKE

PEDAL

BRAKE RELEASE PEDAL

GLUE AND
NAIL SCRAP
2x4 CUT TO
SIZE

1"

1½"
¾"

3"±

6"

18¼"

¾" 1½"

2¼"

Castle and Lam Assembly

The lams are made out of ⅜″-thick wood. Sometimes this may be hard to get. Some lumber dealers will stock standard moldings, such as "lattice" or "door stop," that are ⅜″ thick, or will plane your lumber to size. In an emergency, ⅜″ cabinet-grade plywood could be substituted.

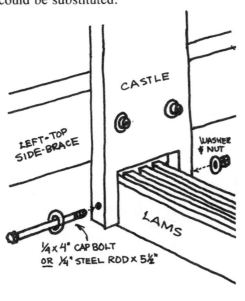

CASTLE

LEFT-TOP SIDE-BRACE

WASHER & NUT

LAMS

¼ x 4″ CAP BOLT OR ¼″ STEEL ROD x 5½″

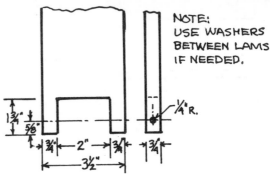

NOTE: USE WASHERS BETWEEN LAMS IF NEEDED.

1¾″   ⅝″   ¾″ ← 2″ → ¾″   ¾″
3½″

¼″ R.

CASTLE PARTS (¾″ LUMBER)

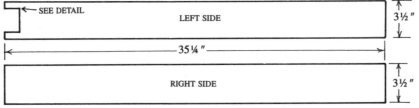

← SEE DETAIL

LEFT SIDE   3½″

35¼″

RIGHT SIDE   3½″

¾″   PILOT HOLES FOR #10×2″ R.H. WOOD SCREWS

CASTLE TOP   3½″

42¾″

LAMS (MAKE 4)

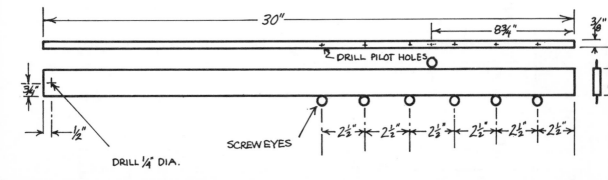

30″

8¾″

⅜″

DRILL PILOT HOLES

¾″

½″

SCREW EYES

2½″   2½″   2½″   2½″   2½″   2½″

DRILL ¼″ DIA.

Upper Harness Assembly

There seem to be as many ways of attaching the counterbalance harness as there are looms. This is just one method. Again, ⅜″ wood is used for the heddle bars. Substitutes could be made. For the roller, a substitute such as a tin can with a dowel through it would also work. Use your ingenuity.

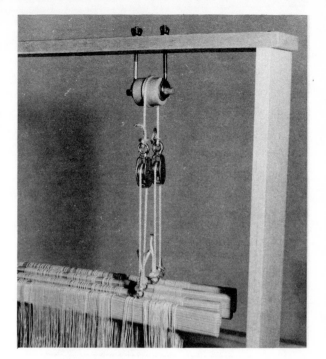

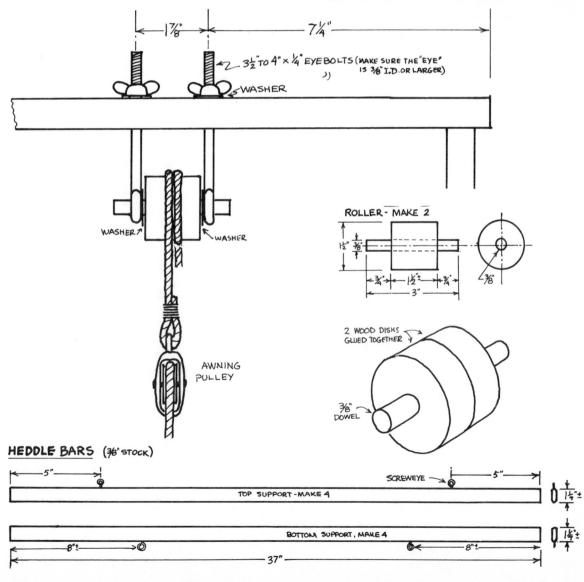

WASHER

2 3½″ TO 4″ × ¼″ EYEBOLTS (MAKE SURE THE "EYE" IS ⅜″ I.D. OR LARGER)

1⅞″   7¼″

WASHER   WASHER

AWNING PULLEY

ROLLER - MAKE 2

1½″   ⅜″

¾″   1½″±   ¾″

3″

⅜″

2 WOOD DISKS GLUED TOGETHER

⅜″ DOWEL

HEDDLE BARS (⅜″ STOCK)

5″   SCREWEYE   5″

TOP SUPPORT - MAKE 4   1½″±

BOTTOM SUPPORT, MAKE 4   1¼″±

8″±   8″±

37″

Treadles

The treadles take a lot of wear and should be made out of hardwood. Here is where you may want to customize your loom if you have wide feet (make sure the screw eyes on the lams are also moved), or plan to weave stocking-footed, as many weavers do.

The treadle spacers could be made from dowels, as shown, or of any number of substitutes, such as beads, blocks, spools, or springs.

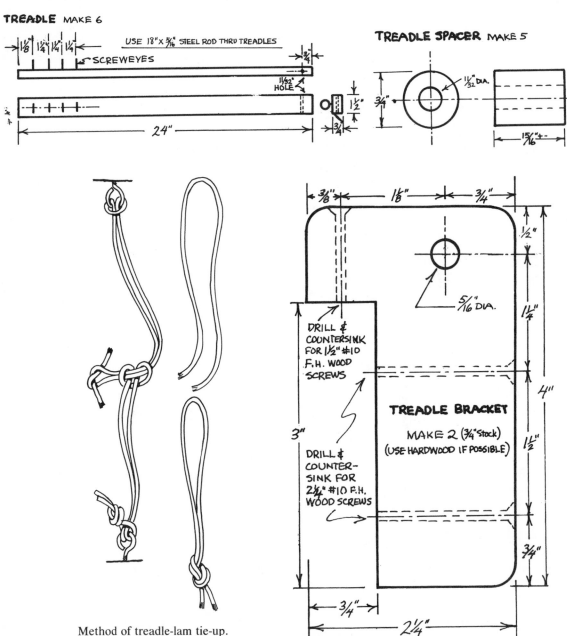

TREADLE MAKE 6

USE 18" x 5⁄16" STEEL ROD THRU TREADLES

SCREWEYES

11⁄32" HOLE

24"

TREADLE SPACER MAKE 5

11⁄32" DIA.

15⁄16"+

TREADLE BRACKET

MAKE 2 (3⁄4" Stock)
(USE HARDWOOD IF POSSIBLE)

DRILL & COUNTERSINK FOR 1½" #10 F.H. WOOD SCREWS

DRILL & COUNTERSINK FOR 2½" #10 F.H. WOOD SCREWS

5⁄16" DIA.

Method of treadle-lam tie-up.

Warp and Cloth Beams

Variety is the spice of loom construction. These beams are made from plastic pipe with a wood reinforcing core. The beams could also be made from solid wood 4×4s. I've even seen a 16″ sycamore log used as a warp beam. The brake and take-up dogs are old saw blades with the points filed down to make them blunt. Some sort of guard placed over these would be a good idea. If you use the new "throw-away" type of saw blade, it may be too hard to drill. If so, the steel will have to be annealed (softened). This can be done by heating the blade until it is a dull cherry-red and then allowing it to cool covered up in a bed of sawdust.

The warp beam crank may be removable or not. The loom in the photo has a removable crank. The take-up crank on the cloth beam is a steel or wood dowel inserted in a hole drilled through or into the beam and glued or pinned in place. Fasten the apron on the beams with sheet metal screws.

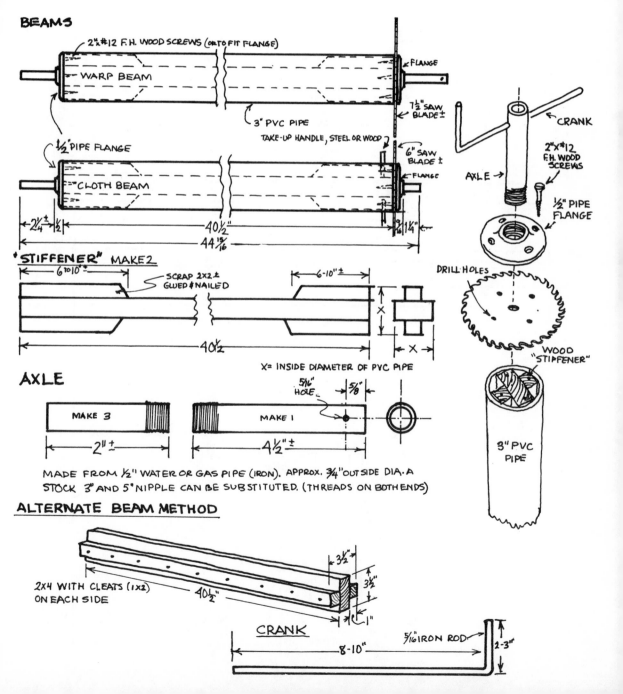

Batten Assembly

To make the slot in the sword, drill multiple holes and finish with a chisel and file. The reed notch should be about ½ inch wide and ½ inch deep. This can be done by mallet and chisel or by cutting a V groove with a table saw. Another way would be to screw or tack on strips of wood to form the reed notches (this was often done on very old rug looms). When the beater is installed on the loom body, the handtree and shuttle race *must be parallel* to the breast beam. Loosen and thumb-tighten the bolts in turn until they lie evenly against the posts and breast beam. Then tighten the bolts. In extreme cases, when the wood is warped, the lag screws at the pivot point may have to be moved forward or back.

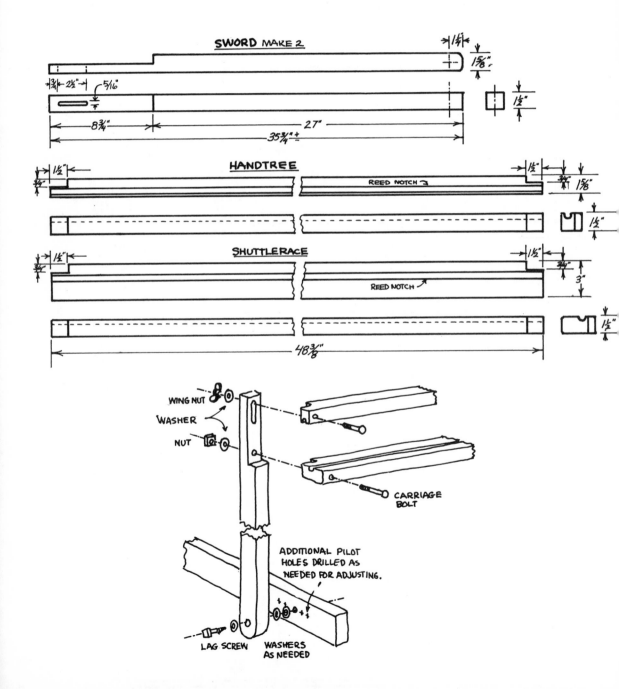

Finishing and Setting Up Your Homemade Loom

After you have cut and prepared all the pieces and parts to your satisfaction, and they all fit properly, you are ready to set up your new loom. If by some chance you have drilled a hole in the wrong place, you can leave it as it is or patch it with wood putty. It is not unusual to see homemade looms with a few extra holes or cuts in them, because frequently they were made with whatever lumber was at hand, and also the best loom builders make mistakes. You could say a mistake gives the loom character.

All finishing—sanding, varnishing, painting, or waxing—should be done by this time. The finish is up to you. It can be as simple as rubbing a coat of wax or tung oil into the raw wood, or you can stain and varnish the wood.

If you choose to paint your loom, why not use a bright color such as red, yellow, or blue? There's no reason for a loom to look drab. The early French Canadian spinning wheels were often painted bright colors. Be sure to prime the wood before painting and to pick a good-quality semigloss enamel, whether oil- or water-based. As with most painting, several light coats are much better than one thick coat. After the paint is thoroughly dry on the breast and back beams, wax them with a hard wax or varnish them so that the paint will not rub off on the warp. The metal parts of your loom can be painted or coated with a rust preventative.

String heddles should be made before you set up your loom. Make a frame for tying string heddles as pictured on page 109. You can purchase special heddle cord from a weaving supply dealer or substitute any good-quality 3/2 cotton warp yarn. The heddles don't have to be white; you could use cotton cord in one bright color or a variety of colors.

Use the illustration on page 252 as a guide while putting your loom together. Start by assembling the sides of the loom body: join both the upper and lower rails or braces to the corner posts. Tap the carriage bolts into place with a rubber or wooden mallet. Put on the washers and the nuts, and tighten until firm, but not so much as to cause the washer to bite into the wood. Your loom will breathe with the seasonal changes, and the bolts need a little breathing room. Now put on the castle supports (the one with the notch for the lams goes on the left side as you face the front of the loom). Next fasten the cross braces onto the sides. The loom should be able to stand on its own now. Fasten the back beam to the back corner posts with wood screws.

Place the castle board on top of the supports, and screw it into place. The brake dog and spring, take-up dog and spring, and brake release pedal and lock are now attached to the right-side frame (see pages 256–57). Tie the brake cord with a strong knot to the brake release pedal. (The pedal should be in a position so that the warp beam is locked and doesn't turn.) Use the illustration on page 256 as a guide.

Attach the lams in the notch on the left-side castle support (see page 258). The upper harness rollers are now installed, and the heddle bars with the heddles on them are hung from the roller cords (see page 259). Make sure that the cords are even and that the knots will not slip. Adjust the height of the heddle bars with the wing nuts on top of the castle. A yoke cord (harness yoke) is now attached to the screw eye on the bottom of each heddle bar with a slip-proof knot. Each yoke cord is threaded through the screw eye on the top of the lam and tied to the screw eye on the other side of the heddle bar, again with a slip-proof knot.

The treadles are now attached to the front cross brace (see page 260), and the lower tie-up cords are inserted through the screw eyes for the tie-up (see Chapter 7, "Drafting: The Language of Weaving"). The upper tie-up cord is put through the appropriate screw eye on the lam, and the upper and lower tie-up cords are tied together as shown on page 260.

The warp and cloth beams are put into place and secured (see page 261). The dogs and brake release cord are now adjusted. The aprons are attached by drilling pilot holes through the folded hem of the apron into the PVC pipe and are then fastened with sheet metal screws. Use masking tape to hold the apron square and parallel on the beam while working.

The batten (beater) is assembled and put on the loom according to the instructions on page 262. The reed and apron rods are put in place, and your loom is ready to be warped.

Your homemade loom should last for many years with minimal maintenance. If a part should break, make a new one right away—don't fight a broken part. The same is true of loose knots. Perhaps, after using your loom a few times, you'll want to modify or change something. Do it, experiment: every weaver has his or her own ideas of how a loom should work. After all, you built it and you can change it.

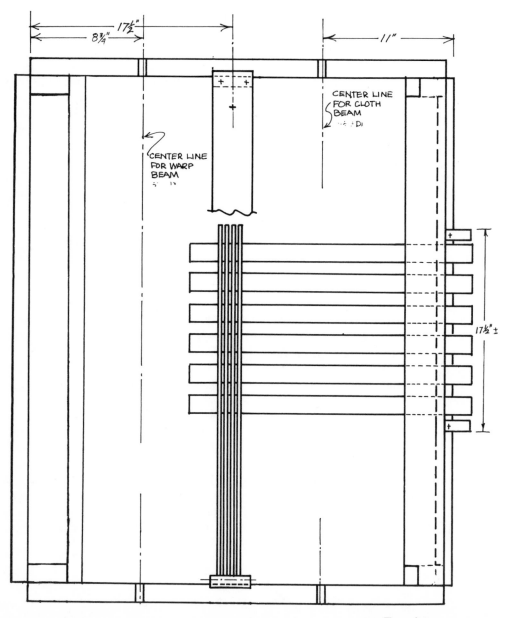

Top view.

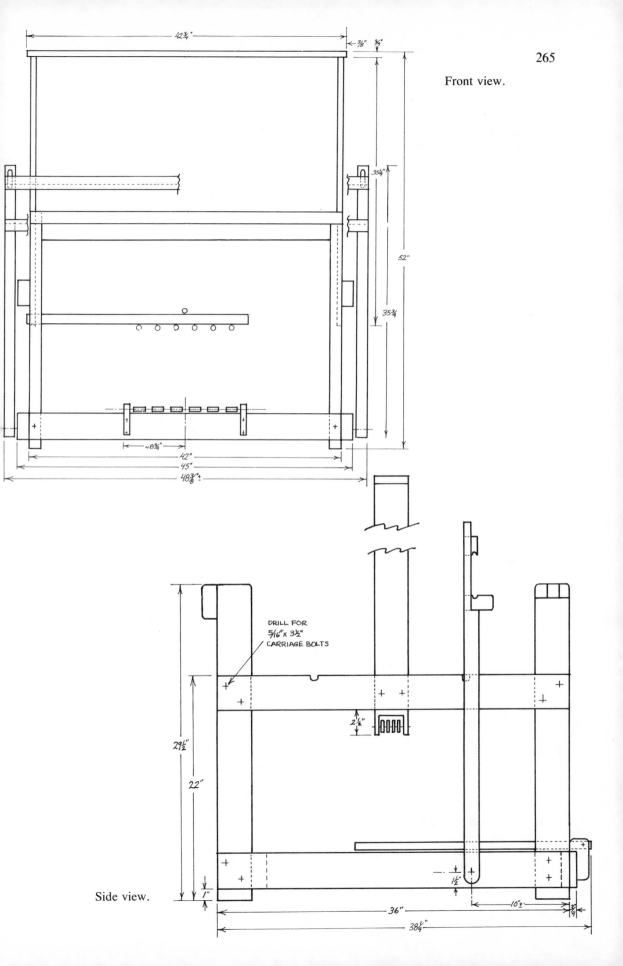

265

Front view.

Side view.

DRILL FOR
5/16" x 3½"
CARRIAGE BOLTS

Glossary

Weaving Terms

Apron: Fabric or cord that fastens the rod to cloth or warp beam.

Back Beam: Stationary beam over which the warp passes after leaving the warp beam.

Balanced Weave: Having warp and weft yarns of similar size and spacing.

Band Loom: Any loom for weaving narrow bands.

Bast: Fibers from the center portions of stalks of a dicotyledonous plant such as flax, hemp, jute, and ramie.

Batten: The part of the loom in which the reed is fastened and which serves to beat the weft into place. Also called beater.

Beam (noun): Horizontal members of the loom over which the warp or cloth passes or is wound.

Beam (verb): To wind the warp on the warp beam.

Beater: *See* Batten.

Belly Wool: Wool from the belly of the sheep.

Binding: A system in which warp ends and weft picks are bound or fixed in place while weaving.

Block: A group of warp and weft yarns arranged together to produce an element of the pattern. The number of blocks in a particular weave is determined by the number of harness frames.

Blotch: A place in the weaving where the shuttles missed warp ends.

Bobbin: Tube of wood or plastic on which the weft is wound for insertion in the shuttle. *See also* Quill.

Bouclé: Novelty yarn plied with different tension on each ply.

Bound Weave: A weft-faced weave.

Brake: The part of the loom that keeps the warp beam from turning.

Break: A thinning of the wool fibers in the staple that will break under tension.

Breaking: The process in which flax stalks are broken so the fiber can be separated from the stalk. *See also* Scutching.

Breast Beam: Beam over which the woven cloth passes before being wound on the cloth beam.

Brocade: A plain weave with a design superimposed using floating weft threads. Also describes most inlaid (or laid-in) weaves.

Broken Twill: Any twill in which the diagonal line is broken.

Bubbling: The process of putting ease in a weft shot to prevent drawing in.

Butterfly: Yarn wound around the hand in a figure-eight fashion and held together to function as a bobbin.

Canvas Stretcher: Frame used by an artist to stretch canvas.

Cape: (1) Top bar or cover of a raddle used to keep warp yarns in the raddle. (2) Part of loom that supports overhead beater.

Carding: Method of preparing wool for spinning.

Carpet Wool: Coarse, hairy wool.

Castle: The center part of a loom. It contains the harness frames.

Catch Cord: A warp end used on the selvage edge of the weaving to aid in making a good selvage. It is not put in a heddle, and the shuttle goes over or under the cord as needed.

Chain: To form a loop and pass another loop through it, and so on. A warp is put into a chain when it is taken from the warping board. Also, the weft can be chained or looped around warp ends for surface interest.

Chenille: A yarn with a woven core and cut weft that forms short tufts. The term also describes the fabric woven from such yarn.

Clasped Weft: *See* Locked Weft.

Cloth: A woven fabric.

Cloth Beam: Roller on which the cloth is wound as weaving progresses.

Comb: Small forked object used to beat the weft into place on the simplest looms. Also used for tapestry weaving on high- or low-warp looms.

Combing: A method of preparing fibers for

spinning in which they are placed parallel to one another. The spun yarn is smooth and even.

Contrast: Relationship between two very different colors or textures.

Cord: A fabric with a raised rib in warp or weft.

Corduroy: A weft-pile fabric.

Cotton: Vegetable fiber surrounding the seed pod of the cotton bush from which cotton yarn is spun.

Count: Measurement of size of yarn based on the relationship between length and weight.

Counterbalanced Loom: A treadle loom in which all harnesses are interdependent. The harness frames not pulled down by the treadles rise in counterbalance.

Countermarche Loom: A loom with two sets of lams, one for a rising and the other for a sinking shed.

Coverlet: A colonial bedcover in a pattern weave.

Crackle: A pattern weave derivative of diamond twill.

Crepe: Fabric made from highly twisted yarns.

Crimp: The waves in a wool staple.

Cross: A cross in the warp formed while warping to keep the proper order of warp ends. *See* Porrey Cross and Portee Cross.

Dead Wool: Wool from a dead sheep.

Degum: To boil silk in a strong soap solution to remove the gum sericin.

Denier: A unit expressing the size of silk and artificial fibers.

Dent: Space in the reed through which the warp ends pass.

Diagonal: A ridge in biased twills. Also the line in color or texture that runs across the fabric in pattern weaving when it is woven-as-drawn-in.

Direct Tie-up: A tie-up when one harness is tied to each treadle.

Distaff: A tool used to hold prepared flax fibers for spinning. It can be held on a stand, under the arm, or attached to the spinning wheel.

Dobby: A device used on a loom for automatic shedding.

Double-face Weave: A weave that produces a fabric with different color or texture on each side.

Double Weave: A weave that gives two distinct layers at one time.

Doubling Stand: A device used when two yarns are wound at once on a bobbin.

Doup: A half-heddle used in lace weaves.

Dovetail: A tapestry technique. Weft yarns warp-interlock in groups of two or more where color areas meet.

Draft: Diagram on paper for setting up loom and showing the order of weaving.

Drawdown: The part of the draft that shows the interlacement of warp and weft yarns.

Drawing In: The narrowing of the warp sett during weaving by pulling in the edges.

Drawloom: A loom preceding the Jacquard where one or more heddles are raised individually by cords.

Dressing: The process of putting the warp on the loom.

Embroidery Weave: A small pattern woven in a tapestry technique on a woven background.

End: An individual warp yarn.

Entering: The process of putting the warp ends through the heddles.

Eye: The loop in the center of the heddle through which each warp end passes.

Fabric: The finished web or cloth.

Face: The right side of a fabric. *See also* Warp-faced and Weft-faced.

Fell: The last beaten pick of weft.

Felt: A fabric made without weaving by using heat and moisture to press together wool and hair fibers.

Fiber: A natural or synthetic filament capable of being spun into yarn.

Filament Yarn: Yarn made of many long strands of fiber twisted together.

Flax: A vegetable fiber from which linen yarn is spun.

Float: An end or pick that crosses at least two yarns between two points of binding. *See also* Overshot Weave.

Flossa: A Scandinavian knotted pile rug.

Fly Shuttle: A simple mechanism that pushes the shuttle through the shed without its being touched by the weaver's hands.

Folding Loom: Any loom with a frame that can be collapsed, making it portable or easily stored.

Frame Loom: Any frame used to keep warp yarn under tension for weaving.

Fringe: Free ends of warp or weft on a finished fabric, forming a border.

Fur: An animal fiber characterized by being fine and thick.

Gating: Adjusting parts of the loom just before starting to weave.

Gauze: A lace-type weave.

Ghiordes Knot: Weft yarn tied on two warp ends and forming a pile, as in oriental rugs.

Ground: The background of the design.

Ground Weave: Usually a tabby weave. Used as a foundation for pattern.

Hackle: A tool for combing flax fiber before spinning.

Hair: An animal fiber characterized by being coarse and straight.

Handle: The feel of wool.

Handloom: Any loom that requires a human operator.

Handtree: The horizontal part of the batten that rests on top of the reed.

Harness: A frame with heddles hung on it.

Heading: The solid, usually tabby-weave, area at the beginning of a warp to check the threading, sleying, and warp tension.

Heddle: Vertical wire or string with a loop in the center through which the warp end passes.

Heddle Frame: The frame and bars between which the heddles are suspended. Also called harness.

Hemp: Vegetable fiber similar to but coarser than flax.

Herringbone Twill: A twill weave with the diagonal changing direction at regular intervals.

High Warp: Warp on a tapestry loom without a beater.

Horses: Small pieces of wood to which the harness frames are tied, and which are hung from the top castle of a counterbalanced loom.

Huckaback: A pattern weave with tabby ground and repeat designs formed by warp floats on one side and weft floats on the other.

Inkle Loom: A simple loom used for making narrow belts or tape.

Interlock: To loop together two wefts at the point where they meet and turn back, as in tapestry weaving.

Jacquard Loom: A loom equipped with a machine that uses punched cards to control the heddles. It is known for the intricate patterns it can produce. Named for inventor Joseph-Marie Jacquard.

Jute: Coarse vegetable fiber native to India.

Kemp: Short, hairy wool fibers.

Knee Beam: A beam on the loom frame between the breast and cloth beam. By passing over this beam the cloth is lifted, making room for the weaver's knees.

Knotted Pile: Weft yarns attached to the ground with simple knots.

Lamb's Wool: Wool from lambs up to six months old.

Lams or Lamms: The horizontal wooden bars on a floor loom to which the harnesses are tied and which in turn are tied to the heddles.

Lea: A measure of linen yarn indicating 300 yards (275 m). The count of linen yarn is determined by the number of leas in one pound (450 g).

Lease: *See* Cross.

Lease Sticks: Rods used to keep warp ends in order while putting the warp on the loom. They preserve the cross.

Leno: Term used for certain types of gauze weave.

Lever: Used to move the harnesses on a table loom. Same as the treadle on a floor loom.

Line: The long fibers of flax left after hackling.

Linen: Yarn or fabric made of flax fiber.

Linsey-Woolsey: A fabric woven in tabby with a wool weft on a linen or cotton warp.

Lock: A tuft of wool.

Locked Weft: Method of joining two colors in the weft. In each shed, two weft yarns of different color come from opposite directions. They weft-interlock, or clasp each other, and return in the same shed to the side from which they started. The point of interlock can change in each shed to create any desired design. Also called clasped weft.

Loom: Any device on which a warp may be arranged and sheds formed for the passage of a pick. The simplest loom may be two bars between which warp ends are stretched.

Looped Weft: Weft pulled up to form rows of loops.

Low Warp: The warp on a tapestry loom with a beater.

Mercerizing: A chemical treatment for cotton and linen yarns to make them silky and shiny.

Mixed Warp: Two or more different yarns used in one warp. Also termed multiple warp.

Mohair: Hair from the angora goat and the fabric made from this hair.

Monk's Belt: An overshot weave. *See* Overshot.

M's and O's Weave: Pattern weave with contrasting areas of tabby and of short weft floats.

Mordant: A chemical compound used in dyeing to fix colors.

Mother-of-all: The horizontal part of the spinning wheel that includes the spinning mechanism.

Mother's Helper: The part of the spinning wheel that supports the maidens.

Multiharness Loom: Generally used to refer to looms of more than four harnesses. Also called multiple-harness loom.

Multiple Warp: *See* Mixed Warp.

Nap: Raised fibers on the surface of a fabric.

Niddy Noddy: A simple tool for making skeins of yarn.

Nylon: First man-made fiber not made of natural materials.

Overhead Beater or Batten: A beater suspended from the capes of the loom.

Overshot Weave: A pattern produced by floats on a tabby ground.

Paddle: A small tool used in warping when a portee cross has more than four warp ends.

Pattern: The design in the weaving. A pattern may be done in different weaves. Each weave has its own set of patterns.

Pattern Weft: Weft from selvage to selvage forming a design in a fabric that has a ground weft.

Pedal: *See* Treadle.

Pick: One or more weft yarns carried by a single passage through the shed.

Pickup Stick: Flat, smooth wooden stick used in finger-manipulated techniques.

Pickup Weaving: Weaving where part of the warp ends are picked up by hand to make a shed.

Piece: The whole fabric as taken from the loom.

Piece Dyeing: The process of dyeing fabric a solid color after it is woven.

Pile: Yarns that project above the ground weave of a fabric.

Pile Warp: A supplement warp much longer than the ground warp, used to weave velvet.

Plain Weave: Any weave in which there is a regular binding of warp and weft. *See also* Tabby.

Plied Yarn: A yarn composed of two or more previously twisted or spun yarns that have been united by twisting.

Ply: To twist together two or more strands of yarn.

Porrey Cross: The cross made at the end of the warp with individual warp ends. It is used when threading the heddles.

Portee Cross: The cross made at the beginning of the warp, composed of groups of warp ends used for spacing the warp for beaming.

Profile: *See* Short Draft.

Quill: A paper or cardboard bobbin.

Quilt Weave: A double weave in which the layers are stitched together during weaving.

Race: *See* Shuttle Race.

Raddle: A flat stick with vertical pegs used during warping the loom to keep the warp evenly spread.

Ramie: A flaxlike fiber from an Asian plant.

Ratchet: A toothed wheel and pawl fastened to the cloth and warp beams to prevent the beams from turning, thus keeping the warp under tension.

Rayon: A man-made fiber made from cellulose.

Reed: Used to keep the warp ends evenly spaced and to beat up the weft. It is fastened in the batten.

Reed Hook: A flat steel hook for pulling the warp ends through the dents of the reed.

Reel: A frame used to make or unwind a skein of yarn.

Rep: A fabric with a horizontal or vertical rib.

Repeat: The number of ends or picks that forms one complete pattern in a threading or treadling draft.

Rep Weave: A close-sett warp with alternating coarse and fine yarn. It produces ridges parallel to the weft.

Retting: The process of soaking flax in water until it ferments, so that the fibers can be separated from the stalk.

Reverse: Wrong or back side of a fabric.

Rib: A line on the surface of a textile formed by the ends and picks.

Rigid Heddle: A frame with alternate holes and slits through which the warp ends are threaded. It is used on simple looms and makes two sheds.

Rising Shed: The upper part of the shed made by the harnesses attached to the working treadle.

Rolag: The fiber after it has been carded ready for spinning.

Roving: Fibers placed parallel ready for spinning.

Rya: Knotted pile, usually quite long.

Satin: A weave with long warp floats.

Scob: *See* Blotch.

Scutching: The process of breaking the straw away from the flax fiber.

Second Cuts: Short pieces of wool caused by poor shearing.

Selvage: The lengthwise edge of a fabric.

Sett: Refers to the warp: the number of ends per inch.

Shaft: *See* Harness.

Shed: The separation of the warp ends to permit the passage of the pick.

Shedding Device: Any means of separating warp ends to make a shed.

Short Draft: Refers to a draft written in a condensed form.

Shot: *See* Pick.

Shuttle: Device in which the pick is passed through the shed in the warp.

Shuttle Race: The part of the loom where the reed rests and where the shuttle moves through the warp.

Silk: The continuous filament secreted by the silkworm larva when constructing its cocoon.

Sisal: Coarse fibers of the sisal plant, native to Indonesia, East and West Africa, and Haiti.

Skein: Method of packaging yarn.

Skirting: Wool of lower grade removed from a fleece.

Slabstock: *See* Back Beam.

Sley: The part of the loom batten that supports the reed.

Sleying: Putting the warp ends through the reed.

Slipknot: A simple knot with a loop so that it can be easily untied.

Slit: A tapestry technique when two yarns meet but do not interlock.

Sorting: Breaking up of a fleece into different grades.

Soumak: A knotted tapestry technique or weft-wrap weave worked on a closed shed. The weft goes over a group of warp ends, then passes under and around part of the group.

Spin: To draw out and twist fibers together in a continuous yarn.

Spindle: Simple tool used for spinning yarn.

Spot Weave: A loom-controlled lace weave with warp and weft floats.

Spun Yarn: Yarn made of short lengths of staple fibers.

Staple: A small group of fibers considered according to length, texture, and degree of coarseness.

Stock Dyeing: Dyeing fibers before spinning.

Straight Draw: The basic threading order. The warp ends are threaded in order on the harness frames, that is, harnesses 1, 2, 3, 4, and repeat. Also referred to as twill threading.

Stretcher: A device used during weaving to keep the woven part from drawing in.

S Twist: The direction of the twist of yarn also called right-handed twist.

Suint: Dried sweat in a wool fleece.

Summer and Winter Weave: A pattern weave of geometric design.

Swift: Holder for a skein of yarn for unwinding.

Sword: (1) Flat stick used on frame looms to push the weft into place and to separate warp ends. (2) The upright supports of the loom batten to which the handtree and sley are attached.

Synthetic Yarns: Yarns made from fibers made by chemical synthesis from raw materials.

Tabby: A simple weave where the weft alternates over one and under one warp end; a type of plain weave.

Take-up: The difference in the length and width of the warp and the finished fabric.

Tapestry: A weave with one warp and a weft composed of yarns of different color, each woven with that part of the warp required by the design.

Temple: *See* Stretcher.

Tension Box: A device used in sectional warping to keep warp yarns under even tension.

Texture: The structure of the surface of a fabric.

Threading: The process of entering the warp through the heddle eyes.

Thrum: The end of a warp that is too short to weave.

Tie-up: The order of the connection between the harness frames and the treadles.

Top: Combed wool for spinning.

Treadle: The foot pedal of a floor loom used by the weaver to raise and lower the harness frames.

Treadling: (1) The order in which the treadles are used to open the shed. (2) The part of the draft that shows this order.

Tromp-as-Writ: Colloquial term meaning woven-as-drawn-in *(which see)*.

Twice-woven: Usually refers to rugs or other pieces woven of chenille yarn.

Twill: A weave in which warp and weft yarns pass over each other in units of two or more yarns.

Twill Threading: *See* Straight Draw.

Twist: The manner in which fibers are twisted together to make a yarn.

Velvet: A warp pile fabric.

Vertical Loom: A loom that holds the warp in a vertical position.

Warp: The lengthwise yarns of a fabric; the yarns that are arranged on the loom.

Warp Beam: The part of the loom on which the warp is rolled and stored before weaving.

Warp-faced: A fabric in which the warp predominates.

Warping: The process of preparing the warp.

Warping Board: A device used in the preparation of the warp. Other devices for this purpose are the warping frame, warping mill, and warping reel.

Weave (noun): The system of interlacing warp ends and weft picks according to a plan to produce a fabric.

Weave (verb): To make a fabric by interlacing warp and weft in a specific weave.

Web: The woven part of the warp.

Weft: The crosswise yarns of a fabric.

Weft-faced: A fabric in which the weft predominates.

Woof: *See* Weft.

Wool: Animal fiber used for making yarn; characterized by being fine and kinky.

Wool Card: A tool used in pairs to straighten wool fibers ready for spinning into yarn.

Woolen Yarn: Yarn made from carded wool fiber.

Worsted: Yarn spun of wool fibers that have been laid parallel by combing.

Woven-As-Drawn-In: An order of treadling that produces a squared pattern with a diagonal.

Yarn: Fibers spun into a continuous thread for weaving.

Yarn Count: The size of yarn based on the relation between length and weight.

Yield: The amount of clean fiber obtained from a fleece.

Yolk: A mixture of wax and sweat in a wool fleece.

Z Twist: The direction of the twist of yarn also called left-handed twist.

Knots

Hitch

Clove Hitch

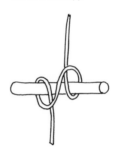

Square Knot

Binding Knot

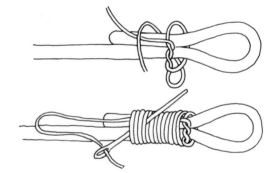

Weaver's Knot

Granny Knot

Wrapping or Binding

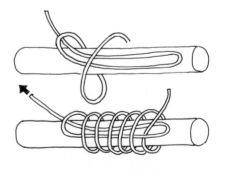

Overhand Knot

Slip Knot

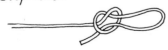

Overhand Knot (double strand)

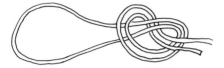

Half-Bowknot for Warp Ends

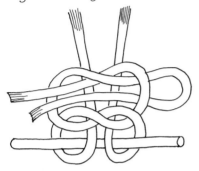

"Package" Knot

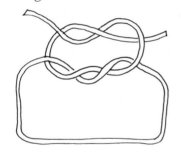

Bowline Knot

Bowknot

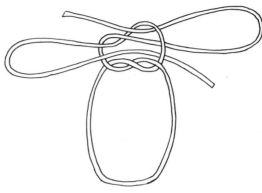

Butterfly Knot

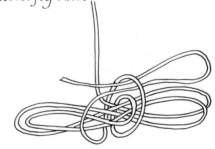

Half-Bowknot

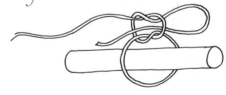

Lease Stick Tie

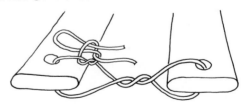

Appendix

Some Common Foreign Weaving Terms

Abbreviations:

G. – German
Fi. – Finnish
Fr. – French
Sw. – Swedish

Armure – weave. Fr.
Atlas – satin. G., Sw.
Attachage – tie-up. Fr.
Aufbäumen – beaming. G.
Banquine – breast beam. Fr.
Basse lisse – low warp. Fr.
Bâti – loom frame. Fr.
Battant – batten. Fr.
Baumwolle – cotton. G.
Bindung – weave. G.
Blatt – reed. G.
Blattstechen – sleying. G.
Bobine – bobbin. Fr.
Bomull – cotton. Sw.
Bonad – tapestry. Sw.
Bref – drawdown. Fr.
Bremse – brake. G.
Bride – float. Fr.
Brokat – brocade. G.
Bundväv – tabby weave. Sw.
Cannetage – weft bobbin winding. Fr.
Cannette – bobbin. Fr.
Cardage – carding. Fr.
Chaîne – warp. Fr.
Contremarche – lam. Fr.
Coton – cotton. Fr.
Croisé – twill. Fr.
Damas – damask. Fr.
Doppeltuch – double fabric. G.
Draht – twist. G.
Dräll – huckaback; two- to four-block weave. Sw.
Dreherbindung – gauze weave. G.
Duite – weft pick. Fr.
Écheveau – skein. Fr.
Einarbeiten – take-up. G.

Einfache Bindung – basic weave. G.
Einziehnadel – threading hook. G.
Einzug – threading. G.
Einzugrapport – repeat. G.
Enrouloire – breast beam. Fr.
Ensouple dérouleuse – warp beam. Fr.
Ensoupleau – cloth beam. Fr.
Envergeure – lease. Fr.
Étoffe – cloth. Fr.
Fach – shed. G.
Faden – thread. G.
Fadenkreuz – cross. G.
Faser – fiber. G.
Fil – yarn. Fr.
Filage – spinning. Fr.
Flachs – flax. G.
Flor – pile. G.
Flossa – short pile. Sw.
Fond – ground. Fr.
Frange – fringe. Fr.
Frappe – overshot. Fr.
Frein – brake. Fr.
Gang – portee. G.
Garn – yarn. G., Sw.
Gaufre or goffre – waffle weave, honeycomb. Fr.
Gaze – gauze. G.
Gelese – lease. G.
Genuakord – corduroy. G.
Gestell – (loom) frame. G.
Gewebe – cloth. G.
Grund – ground. G.
Hälkrus – honeycomb weave. Sw.
Harnais – harness. Fr.
Helfe – heddle. G.
Inlagd – inlay. Sw.

Inploc – pickup or inlay. Sw.
Inslag – weft. Sw.
Kaksinkertaiset Kankaat – double cloths. Fi.
Kam – reed. Sw.
Kamm – reed. G.
Kammeinzug – sleying. G.
Kangas – cloth. Fi.
Kangaspuut – handweaving loom. Fi.
Kankuri – weaver. Fi.
Karjalanraanu – shaggy coverlet. Fi.
Karvalanka – hair (fur) yarn. Fi.
Kattunbindung – tabby. G.
Kehrätä – to spin. Fi.
Kerta – repeat. Fi.
Keskusta – the center. Fi.
Kette – warp. G.
Kettendichte – sett of warp. G.
Kettenscheren – warping. G.
Kiintapujotuskankaat – tapestry weave. Fi.
Klot – satin. Sw.
Knut – knot. Sw.
Knyta – tie. Sw.
Konst – art. Sw.
Köperbindung – twill. G.
Kotikutoinen – homespun. Fi.
Köyhändrelli – "poor man's" damask. Fi.
Krok – hook. Sw.
Kude – weft. Fi.
Kuderipsi – weft-faced rep. Fi.
Kutoa – to weave. Fi.
Kutomamalli – weaving pattern. Fi.
Kypert – twill. Sw.
Lade – batten. G.
Laine – wool. Fr.
Lanka – yarn. Fi.
Lastakudos – stick weave (Finn Weave). Fi.
Lastalle – with a pickup stick. Fi.
Latta – lever. Sw.
Lattiaryijy – floor rug of rya technique. Fi.
Leinen – linen. G.
Leinwand – tabby. G.
Lin – flax. Fr., Sw.
Lisse – heddle. Fr.
Litze – heddle. G.
Loimi – warp. Fi.
Loimiripsi – warp-faced rep. Fi.
Lunnus – draft. Fi.
Luomaohje – warp plan. Fi.
Maille – heddle. Fr.
Maillon – heddle eye. Fr.
Mallikerta – pattern repeat. Fi.
Mangskaft – multiharness. Sw.
Marche – treadle. Fr.
Marchure – treadling. Fr.
Marmousset – jack, lever. Fr.
Matto – rug. Fi.

Métier – loom. Fr.
Métier pliant – folding loom. Fr.
Mönster – pattern. Sw.
Munkabälta – monk's belt. Sw.
Muster – pattern. G.
Navette – shuttle. Fr.
Niisi – heddle. Fi.
Niisintä – draft. Fi.
Noeud – knot. Fr.
Nukka – pile (rug). Fi.
Nystvinda – swift. Sw.
Oblekt – unbleached. Sw.
Ontelo – double weave. Fi.
Ourdir – to warp. Fr.
Palttina – plain, tabby weave. Fi.
Pas – shed. Fr.
Passage en lames – threading. Fr.
Passage en ros – sleying. Fr.
Patron – pattern draft. Fr.
Pedal – treadle. G.
Pellava – flax, linen. Fi.
Perussidokset – basic weaves. Fi.
Peus – dent. Fr.
Piquage en peigne – sleying. Fr.
Pirta – reed. Fi.
Plocka – to pick up. Sw.
Poil – pile, nap. Fr.
Poimi – pick. Fi.
Poljenta – the treadling. Fi.
Polkusia – treadles. Fi.
Pujotus – pickup weaves. Fi.
Puuvilla – cotton. Fi.
Raanu – shaggy coverlet. Fi.
Raccord – treadling draft. Fr.
Ram – frame. Sw.
Rapport – threading draft. Fr.
Redkam – reed, raddle. Sw.
Remettage – threading. Fr.
Remise – harness. Fr.
Ried – reed. G.
Rippe – rib. G.
Rips – rep. G.
Ripsi – rep weave. Fi.
Rör – dent. Sw.
Ros – reed. Fr.
Ruuki – spinning wheel. Fi.
Ruusakas – "rose path" threading. Fi.
Samt – velvet. G.
Säterilkanka – rayon yarn. Fi.
Schlitz – dent. G.
Schuss – weft. G.
Schütz(e) – shuttle. G.
Seide – silk. G.
Serge – twill. Fr.
Siden – silk. Sw.
Sidokset – weaving classifications. Fi.

Sidonta – tie-ups. Fi.
Silkki – silk. Fi.
Sitous – tie-up. Fi.
Skål – shed. Sw.
Sked – reed. Sw.
Skyttel – shuttle. Sw.
Slut – end. Sw.
Soie – silk. Fr.
Solv – heddle. Sw.
Spets – lace. Sw.
Spinnen – spinning. G.
Spinrad – spinning wheel. G.
Spole – bobbin. Sw.
Spule – bobbin. G.
Stad – selvage. Sw.
Stuhlgestell – loom frame. G.
Sukkula – shuttle. Fi.
Suomen – Finnish. Fi.
Tablier – apron. Fr.
Taffetas – tabby. Fr.
Taft – taffeta. Sw.
Tapis – rug. Fr.
Teppich – rug. G.
Tissage – weaving. Fr.
Tissé-à-la-main – handwoven. Fr.
Tisseur – weaver. Fr.
Toile – tabby. Fr.
Toimikas – twill. Fi.
Trame – weft. Fr.
Trasmatta – rag rug. Sw.
Treten – treadling. G.

Tritt – treadle. G.
Tuch – cloth. G.
Tuskaft – tabby, plain two-harness weave. Sw.
Tyg – cloth. Sw.
Ull – wool. Sw.
Uppknytning – tie-up. Sw.
Vaate – cloth. Fi.
Vadmal – homespun cloth. Sw.
Väft – weft. Sw.
Vakosidokset – rib weaves. Fi.
Varp – warp. Sw.
Varpning – warping. Sw.
Varsi – harness frame. Fi.
Väv – weave. Sw.
Vävning – weaving. Sw.
Vävnota – weaving draft. Sw.
Vävstol – loom. Sw.
Velours côtelé – corduroy. Fr.
Villa – wool. Fi.
Vipuset – levers. Fi.
Vivut – lams. Fi.
Vlies – fleece. G.
Vohveli – waffle weave. Fi.
Vuodematto – bed quilt. Fi.
Vyyhti – skein of yarn. Fi.
Weben – to weave, weaving. G.
Weber – weaver. G.
Webstuhl – loom. G.
Wolle – wool. G.
Yksinkertanen – plain, simple. Fi.
Ylle – woolen material. Sw.

Household Chemicals and Their Scientific Names

Alum, common	Potassium aluminum sulfate
Baking soda	Sodium bicarbonate
Bleaching powder	Calcium hypochlorite
Bluestone	Copper sulfate
Blue vitriol	Copper sulfate
Boracic acid	Boric acid
Borax	Sodium borate
Caustic soda	Sodium hydroxide
Copperas	Ferrous sulfate
Cream of tartar	Potassium bitartrate
Glauber's salt	Sodium sulfate
Green vitriol	Ferrous sulfate
Lye	Sodium or potassium hydroxide
Oil of vitriol	Sulfuric acid
Potash alum	Potassium aluminum sulfate
Sal soda	Sodium carbonate
Salt (table)	Sodium chloride
Soda ash	Sodium carbonate
Vinegar	Solution of acetic acid
Washing soda	Sodium carbonate
White vitriol	Zinc sulfate

It is recommended that health and safety precautions be observed when using these chemical substances.

Metric Conversion Table

To convert from	To	Multiply by*
Centimeters	Inches	.39
CCs (Cubic centimeters)	Ounces (U.S. fluid)	.034
Cups	Ounces (U.S. fluid)	8
Feet	Meters	.305
Grams	Ounces (avdp)	.035
Inches	Centimeters	2.54
Kilograms	Pounds	2.205
Liters	Quarts (U.S. liquid)	1.057
Meters	Feet	3.281
Meters	Yards	1.094
Millimeters	Inches	.039
Ounces (avdp)	Grams	28.35
Ounces (avdp)	Pounds	.063
Ounces (British fluid)	Ounces (U.S. fluid)	.96
Ounces (U.S. fluid)	CCs	29.57
Ounces (U.S. fluid)	Liters	.029
Ounces (U.S. fluid)	Milliliters	29.5
Ounces (U.S. fluid)	Quarts	.03
Pounds	Grams	453.59
Pounds	Kilograms	.45
Pounds	Ounces (avdp)	16
Quarts (U.S. liquid)	Liters	.95
Quarts (U.S. liquid)	Ounces (U.S. fluid)	32
Tablespoons	Ounces	.5
Teaspoons	Ounces	.17
Yards	Centimeters	91.44
Yards	Meters	.91

*Rounded off.

Suppliers Directory

B. Blumenthal & Co., Inc.
P.O. Box 798
Shawnee Mission, Kans. 66201
Cotton yarn

Braid-Aid Fabrics
466 Washington Street
Pembroke, Mass. 02359
Looms, fabric strips

Caswell-Massey Co. Ltd.
575 Lexington Avenue
New York, N.Y. 10022
Essences and oils for natural mothproofing

Clemes & Clemes, Inc.
650 San Pablo Avenue
Pinole, Calif. 94564
Spinning wheels, equipment, fibers

Wm. Condon & Sons Ltd.
P.O. Box 129
203 Fitzroy Street
Charlottetown, Prince Edward Island
Canada CIA 7K3
Yarn

Creager Tools for the Crafts
40 West College Avenue
Westerville, Ohio 43081
Looms, spinning wheels, books

Curtis Fricke
8702 State Road 92
Granite Falls, Wash. 98252
Bench and hand carders

Fibre Crafts
38 Center Street
Clinton, N.J. 08809
Looms, yarn

Frederick J. Fawcett, Inc.
320 Derby Street
Salem, Mass. 01970
Linen yarn, equipment

Fort Crailo Yarn Co.
2 Green Street
Rensselaer, N.Y. 12144
Yarn

Harry M. Fraser Co.
192 Hartford Road
Manchester, Conn. 06040
Cloth cutting machines, books

Gilmakra Looms 'n Yarns, Inc.
19285 Detroit Road
P.O. Box 16157
Rocky River, Ohio 44116
Looms, yarn

Martha Hall
46 Main Street
Yarmouth, Maine 04096
Looms, yarn

Harrisville Designs, Inc.
P.O. Box 281
2 Central Square
Harrisville, N.H. 03450
Looms, yarn

Heritage Woodcraft, Inc.
2470 Dixie Highway
Pontiac, Mich. 48055
Looms

The Robert Joseph Co., Inc.
2533 Gilbert Avenue
Cincinnati, Ohio 45206
Yarn

Leclerc Corp.
Box 491
Plattsburg, N.Y. 12901
Looms, spinning wheels, books, yarn

The Mannings
RFD 2
East Berlin, Pa. 17316
Yarn, looms, books

Mid-States Wool Growers
3900 Groves Road
Columbus, Ohio 43227
Raw wool, top

Museum Books, Inc.
6 West 37th Street
New York, N.Y. 10018
Craft books

Old Mill Yarn
P.O. Box 8
Eaton Rapids, Mich. 48827
Yarn

The Oriental Rug Co.
214 South Central Avenue
P.O. Box 917
Lima, Ohio 45802
Looms, cotton rug warp

The Pendleton Shop
465 Jordan Road
P.O. Box 233
Sedona, Ariz. 86336
Looms, yarn

Robin & Russ Handweavers
533 North Adams Street
McMinnville, Oreg. 97128
Looms, yarn, books

Schacht Spindle Co. Inc.
P.O. Box 2157
2536 49th Street
Boulder, Colo. 80302
Looms

School Products Co., Inc.
1201 Broadway
New York, N.Y. 10001
Looms, yarn, books

Textile Artists' Supply
3006 San Pablo Avenue
Berkeley, Calif. 94702
Fibers, dyes, yarn, spinning wheels,
mordants

The Unicorn
Box 645
Rockville, Md. 20851
Craft books

Weavers Web
24 Elm Street
Montpelier, Vt. 05602
Looms, yarn

Bibliography

Books

Albers, Anni. *On Designing*. Middletown, Conn.: Wesleyan University Press, 1961.

_____. *On Weaving*. Middletown, Conn.: Wesleyan University Press, 1965.

Atwater, Mary Meigs. *Byways in Handweaving*. New York: Macmillan Company, 1954.

_____. *Shuttle-Craft Book of American Handweaving*. New York: Macmillan Company, 1951.

Baines, Patricia. *Spinning Wheels, Spinners and Spinning*. New York: Charles Scribner's Sons, 1977.

Beriau, Oscar. *Home Weaving*. Quebec: Arts & Crafts of Gardenvale, 1939.

Black, Mary E. *The Key to Weaving*. 2nd ed. New York: Macmillan Publishing Company, 1980.

Burnham, Dorothy K. *Warp and Weft: A Textile Terminology*. Toronto: Royal Ontario Museum, 1980.

Burnham, Harold B., and Dorothy K. Burnham. *Keep Me Warm One Night*. Toronto: University of Toronto Press, 1972.

Collingwood, Peter. *The Techniques of Rug Weaving*. New York: Watson-Guptill Publications, 1968.

Creager, Clara. *Weaving: A Creative Approach for Beginners*. Garden City, N.Y.: Doubleday & Company, 1974.

Cyrus, Ulla. *Manual of Swedish Handweaving*. Newton Centre, Mass.: Charles T. Branford Co., 1956.

Davenport, Elsie. *Your Handspinning*. London: Sylvan Press, 1964.

_____. *Your Yarn Dyeing*. Pacific Grove, Calif.: Craft & Hobby Book Service, 1970.

Davison, Marguerite P. *A Handweaver's Pattern Book*. Swarthmore, Pa.: M. P. Davison, 1963.

Emery, Irene. *Primary Structures of Fabrics*. Washington, D.C.: The Textile Museum, 1966.

Forbes, Robert J. *Studies in Ancient Technology*. Vol. 4, "Textiles." New York: W. S. Heinman, 1964.

Frey, Berta. *Design and Drafting for Handweavers*. New York: Macmillan Company, 1958.

Gallinger, Osma. *Joy of Weaving*. Scranton, Pa.: International Textbook Company, 1950.

Hochberg, Bette. *Handspinner's Handbook*. Santa Cruz, Calif.: Bette Hochberg, 1976.

Hooper, Luther. *Handloom Weaving*. London: Sir Isaac Pitman & Sons, 1934. Paperback reissue 1979.

Kaufmann, Ruth. *The New American Tapestry*. New York: Reinhold, 1968.

Kluger, Marilyn. *The Joy of Spinning*. New York: Simon & Schuster, 1971.

Larsen, Jack Lenor, and Mildred Constantine. *Beyond Craft: The Art Fabric*. New York: Van Nostrand Reinhold, 1973.

Lesch, Alma. *Vegetable Dyeing*. New York: Watson-Guptill Publications, 1970.

Moorman, Theo. *Weaving As an Art Form*. New York: Van Nostrand Reinhold, 1975.

Neher, Evelyn. *Four-Harness Huck*. New Canaan, Conn.: Evelyn Neher, 1953.

Rainey, Sarita. *Weaving Without a Loom*. Worcester, Mass.: Davis Publications, 1966.

Regensteiner, Else. *The Art of Weaving*. New York: Van Nostrand Reinhold, 1970.

Robertson, Seonaid M. *Dyes from Plants*. New York: Van Nostrand Reinhold, 1973.

Selander, Malin. *Swedish Handweaving*. Göteborg, Sweden: Wezäta Förlag, 1959.

Straub, Marianne. *Hand Weaving and Cloth Design*. New York: Viking Press, 1977.

Teal, Peter. *Hand Woolcombing and Spinning*. Poole, England: Blandford Press, 1976.

Thorpe, Azalea Stuart, and Jack Lenor Larsen. *Elements of Weaving*. Garden City, N.Y.: Doubleday & Company, 1967; rev. ed. 1978.

Thorpe, Heather G. *A Handweaver's Workbook.* New York: Macmillan Company, 1966.

Thurston, Violetta. *Use of Vegetable Dyes.* Leicester, England: Dryad Press, 1943.

Tod, Osma Gallinger, and Josephine Couch Del Deo. *Rug Weaving for Everyone.* New York: Bramhall House, 1957.

Tovey, John. *The Technique of Weaving.* New York: Van Nostrand Reinhold, 1965.

Wingate, Dr. Isabel, ed. *Fairchild's Dictionary of Textiles.* New York: Fairchild Publications, Inc., 1975.

Worst, Edward. *Weaving with Foot-Power Looms.* New York: Dover Publications, 1974 reissue of 1924 classic.

Zielinski, Stanislaw A. *Encyclopedia of Hand-Weaving.* New York: Funk & Wagnalls Company, 1959.

Periodicals

American Craft
  401 Park Avenue South
  New York, N.Y. 10016

Crafts Magazine
  Crafts Council
  8 Waterloo Place
  London SW1Y 4AT
  England

Fiberarts
  50 College Street
  Asheville, N.C. 28801

Handwoven
Spin Off
  Interweave Press
  306 North Washington Avenue
  Loveland, Colo. 80537

Shuttle, Spindle & Dyepot
  Published by Handweavers Guild of America
  65 LaSalle Road
  West Hartford, Conn. 06107

The Textile Booklist
  R. L. Shep
  Box C-82
  Lopez Island, Wa. 98261

The Weavers Journal
  Association of Guilds of Weavers, Spinners
    and Dyers
  BCM 963
  London WC1 3XX
  England

The Weaver's Journal
  P.O. Box 2049
  Boulder, Colo. 80306

The Web
  c/o Business Manager
  P.O. Box 233
  Greymouth
  New Zealand

Index